Law

Ian Yule & Peter Darwent

Philip Allan Updates, an imprint of Hodder Education, an Hachette UK company, Market Place, Deddington, Oxfordshire OX15 0SE

Orders

Bookpoint Ltd, 130 Milton Park, Abingdon, Oxfordshire OX14 4SB
tel: 01235 827827
fax: 01235 400401
e-mail: education@bookpoint.co.uk

Lines are open 9.00 a.m.–5.00 p.m., Monday to Saturday, with a 24-hour message answering service. You can also order through the Philip Allan Updates website: www.philipallan.co.uk

© Philip Allan Updates 2008

ISBN 978-1-84489-424-6

First printed 2008
Impression number   6 5 4
Year   2015   2014   2013   2012   2011

This textbook has been written specifically to support students studying AQA AS Law. The content has been neither approved nor endorsed by AQA and remains the sole responsibility of the authors.

Table 4.1 and the subsequent paragraph on p. 50 and the evaluation section on pp. 192–95 are reproduced by kind permission of Routledge-Cavendish from *AS Law* (2nd edition, 2007) by Andrew Mitchell.

All efforts have been made to trace copyright on items used.

Design by Neil Fozzard

Printed in Dubai

Hachette UK's policy is to use papers that are natural, renewable and recyclable products and made from wood grown in sustainable forests. The logging and manufacturing processes are expected to conform to the environmental regulations of the country of origin.

P01898

Contents

Unit 2: The concept of liability

key points, issues and cases. This will enable you to acquire better understanding of that topic from the lesson, and encourage you to ask questions to clarify more difficult issues or to develop and improve examination technique.

This learning method also strengthens your knowledge of basic facts about a topic and provides a summary that can form the basis of revision notes.

Assessment

At AS, the assessment methods recognise candidates' ability to recall selected relevant material in a given context and to make limited evaluation or application of the material. To gain the highest marks available, candidates have to provide not only a detailed, accurate explanation of relevant law, but also thoughtful evaluation and precise application to short scenarios.

Assessment objectives

Assessment objectives (AOs) are common to the AS and A2 units and are intended to assess candidates' ability to:

❖ recall, select, deploy and develop knowledge and understanding of legal principles accurately and by means of examples

❖ analyse legal material, issues and situations, and evaluate and apply the appropriate legal rules and principles

❖ present a logical and coherent argument and communicate relevant material in a clear and effective manner, using correct legal terminology

Command words

The key to maximising marks in both Unit 1 and 2 examinations is to understand and obey the **command words** in the questions. Words such as 'describe' and 'explain' require candidates to provide relevant and accurate facts within the context of the question. 'Outline' requires a less detailed account, but key facts and authorities are still needed.

Words such as 'discuss', 'comment on', 'assess', 'evaluate' or 'analyse' require candidates to provide a reasoned opinion on the relevant topic. Quite often in Unit 1 this focuses specifically on advantages and disadvantages.

Mark scheme descriptors

You should be familiar with the following mark scheme descriptors which your teacher should be using to annotate homework and examination answers. Relevant chapters contain sample answers to illustrate these marking descriptors.

'Fragment'

The answer contains one or two relevant facts only, and there are no case or statutory authorities, or examples.

'Limited'

The answer contains some relevant facts only with no additional explanation. It is not supported by relevant authorities and/or examples. The candidate is unable to demonstrate any understanding of the potential content beyond the few given facts.

'Some'

The answer shows some accuracy and relevance to the potential content. It may occasionally be supported by generally relevant authority and/or examples. The answer deals with some of the potential content in a manner required by the question. Few of the concepts of the potential content are established as there are errors, omissions and/or confusion which undermine the essential features of the potential content.

'Clear'

The answer is broadly accurate and relevant to the potential content. It is supported by some use of relevant authority and/or examples. The underlying concepts of the potential content are present, although there may be some errors, omissions and/or confusion which prevent the answer from being fully rounded or developed.

'Sound'

The answer is generally accurate and contains relevant material to the potential content. It is supported by generally relevant authority and/or examples. It deals with the potential content in a manner required by the question. The essential features of the potential content are dealt with competently and coherently.

Keeping up to date

Useful websites include the following:

❖ Department for Constitutional Affairs (www.dca.gov.uk) — offers materials about the judiciary and courts.

❖ Incorporated Council of Law Reporting (www.lawreports.co.uk/WLRD/AboutWRLD.htm) — provides headnotes and summaries of recent cases.

❖ St Brendan's Sixth Form College (www.stbrn.ac.uk/other/depts/law) — includes detailed notes covering the whole A-level specification, together with numerous case reports and updates. It also has links to many other websites.

- Bournemouth and Poole Sixth Form College (www.sixthformlaw.info) — as well as including teaching and learning materials, it also has a blog.
- Statute Law Database (www.statutelaw.gov.uk) — the government has made available online and free of charge an almost complete set of Acts of Parliament.
- Judiciary (www.judiciary.gov.uk) — the judiciary now has its own website with a range of statistical information about judges.
- Delia Venables (www.venables.co.uk) — this site is one of the best legal gateways, providing links to a large number of legal websites.
- British and Irish Legal Information Institute (www.bailii.org) — a comprehensive source of free legal information.

Planning your revision

At this level of study, it is essential that you understand the need to learn basic factual information thoroughly. Do this as each unit is being taught. Do not leave it to the revision stage, otherwise you will find that there is simply too much detailed knowledge to absorb.

The word 'revise' is defined in the *Concise Oxford Dictionary* as to 'read again to improve one's knowledge'. Skimming over some notes is *not* revision if you have not already learned the material. The first stage of revision requires organisation of all your work. Ensure that:
- your class notes are up to date
- you have used the material in this book effectively
- you have made accurate notes on any wider reading, especially of case studies

Use past exam papers

Look at past exam papers online and attempt to answer the problem-solving questions. Use the IDEA scheme to formulate an effective answer plan (see page xiii).

Summarise

The final stage is to **summarise** all the material, organised under the headings and subheadings, within each unit specification. The revision period is the time to go over all your notes and reduce them to manageable proportions. This is, in itself, an effective learning exercise. Summarising makes it easier to recall the material and should reduce the chance of forgetting parts of it in the examination. Most exam marks are lost not through a failure to understand the material, but simply through omitting fuller explanations and, in Unit 2 particularly, by not using relevant cases.

Examination advice

Plan your answers effectively

Make sure you read the question carefully and that you understand what it is asking. Then make a short plan — it could be in the form of a spider diagram or just a series of headings and subheadings. After this, read the question again to check that your plan is both relevant and accurate.

Use the IDEA mnemonic

This provides a basic plan you can follow in answering problem-solving questions:

❖ **I**dentify the appropriate offence, referring to the actual injury suffered by the victim, and the Joint Charging Standard for guidance. Identify any issues such as causation or transferred malice that can be part of these problem-solving questions.
❖ **D**efine the *actus reus* and *mens rea* of the offence you have chosen.
❖ **E**xplain these in greater detail.
❖ **A**pply the legal rules of both *actus reus* and *mens rea* to the particular facts of the scenario, and ensure that **A**uthorities (cases) are used effectively.

Following this structure should ensure a clear answer.

Use cases correctly

It is rarely necessary or desirable to describe the facts of the cases cited — the important part of a case is the **legal rule** it created or demonstrates. For instance, poor examination technique would cite the case of *Donoghue* v *Stevenson* and would simply retell the sad story of Mary Donoghue and the snail in the bottle. This is a waste of time. What the examiner wants is a *short and accurate explanation* of the 'neighbour principle', with brief reference to the facts, such as mentioning that this is the 'snail in the bottle case'.

The only occasion when a more detailed description of the facts is required is when the facts of the question scenario match them closely. A good example of this occurred in the June 2002 examination, when the tort scenario question was clearly based on the case of *Smith* v *Leech Brain*.

Match cases to the correct legal rule

Many candidates appear to believe that, as long as some cases are mentioned, it does not matter too much whether they are the right ones. When revising, make a point of learning the correct case for each offence in terms of *actus reus* and *mens rea*, and for the separate rules in tort law.

Quality of written communication (QWC) marks

There are 5 marks for each AS paper for the quality of written communication (and 10 marks for each A2 paper). The easiest way to lose marks is to misspell basic legal words such as *grievous, defendant, deterrence, assault* and *sentence.* Check your spelling, use paragraphs correctly and make your handwriting as clear as possible.

Plan your time well

Contrary to popular belief, few students have a problem with lack of time in the examination. By doing homework essays and timed or practice examination essays you will learn whether you are a quick or a slow writer, and whether you are likely to experience time difficulties. If you feel there is likely to be a time problem, then planning is even more vital. There is no point in wasting time on material which is inaccurate or irrelevant.

If you finish early, you should first check your answers to ensure that key legal rules and appropriate cases have been included. Next, you should look at your plans to ensure you have covered all the points. If at the end of this process there is still time left, you should consider what additional material can be added, such as an additional case or some extra details on a type of sentence. By adding such material, it may be possible to improve your overall result by one grade (which can be as little as 1 or 2 marks).

The Unit 2 exam

The Unit 2 exam can give rise to a number of problems for candidates, many of whom find Unit 1 much more straightforward. Here we outline the key reasons why you may find Unit 2 more difficult, and then give advice on how to tackle a question in Section A.

The problems

Omissions

This is the greatest single source of lost marks. Try to remember a series of facts or rules — for example, the three tests for duty of care and the different questions used to establish the 'reasonable man' test in breach of duty of care.

Lack of relevant and accurate detail

In Unit 1, most students are able to include *some* mark-worthy material in their answers. In Unit 2, however, there are times when answers receive no marks whatsoever if they lack the necessary details, especially in the problem-solving questions — both in criminal and tort law.

Poor knowledge of case law

This factor is much more important here than in the other units. You may have a good grasp of relevant legal rules and appropriate cases, but you must *apply* these rules and cases in order to 'solve' the problem set.

Case references

The cases you are taught do not just illustrate that rule of law; in many instances, they *are* the law. Without appropriate case references, it is impossible to demonstrate a sound understanding of relevant law. The mark scheme often prevents examiners from awarding marks if there are no references to case or statutory authorities. As a result, a case-free answer rarely obtains more than a D or E grade. There have been occasions when, although the content of an answer in terms of explanation could have merited a high mark band, the absence of cases has meant that up to 2 marks have been lost for a 10-mark question.

Tackling a question

Let us consider the make-up of the typical Unit 2 exam by looking at Section A, which deals with criminal law. The first question you are asked is likely to be theoretical. The topics include *actus reus*, *mens rea*, causation, crimes of omission and strict liability offences. These are best answered *without any reference being made to the scenario itself*. The next criminal law question requires you to consider what criminal liability arises from the scenario. This in turn requires appropriate offences to be examined.

Use appropriate offences

The scenario will have included some form of attack, which has caused a level of injury that can be related to battery or actual bodily harm, or wounding or grievous bodily harm. Sometimes, two or more offences are possible. You must learn the definition of each offence in terms of *actus reus*, *mens rea* and relevant cases.

Although not included in the specification, when answering the questions in the criminal law element, the Joint Charging Standard (agreed between the police and the Crown Prosecution Service) helps to identify the appropriate offence in terms of the level of injury sustained. For example, a black eye would be charged as battery (but this could also be s.47 ABH); a minor cut requiring stitches would be charged under s.47 (but could also be wounding under s.20).

Apply the facts to the rules

Once you have identified the appropriate offence(s) and explained the *actus reus* and *mens rea*, you then need to *apply the facts* from the scenario to these rules — both factual and legal — and ask whether the defendant intended to carry out the act or cause the consequences or was subjectively reckless.

If the final question in Section A is on sentencing, you should generally include the following:

❖ A brief summary of the aims of sentencing.
❖ A fuller explanation of the types of sentence.
❖ Some examples of mitigating and aggravating factors.

You should suggest a suitable sentence (probably a community or custodial sentence) only if you are asked to do so.

Online resources

The online resources (www.hodderplus.co.uk/philipallan) contain sample student answers to exam-style questions. The answers are accompanied by examiner comments, which highlight the elements for which marks can be awarded and explain what examiners are looking for.

Unit 1
Law making and the legal system

Chapter 1

The meaning of law and our legal system

All societies must develop rules to govern their members. In his book *The Concept of Law*, first published in 1961, Professor H. L. A. Hart argued that the reason we need rules lies in our knowledge of certain obvious truths: we know we are vulnerable to attack by others, we all have a limited concern for others and limited willpower.

We also know that we live in a world of finite resources. Given this knowledge and the natural will to survive, we realise that we must have rules in order to impose a measure of self-restraint. Without these, we could be prepared to attack others and take their property. This would in turn result in the break-up of society and leave us to face the hostile world alone. It is this realisation that leads human beings in all societies to create and accept rules of self-restraint that protect the person and the property of others. It also causes most of us to accept that the observance of such rules must be guaranteed by the provision of penalties directed against the rule-breaker.

As societies continue to develop and grow in size, more rules are required and we move from a system of largely criminal laws that prohibit murder and theft to rules that have been described as 'power-conferring' — those that enable certain activities to be carried out with some form of legal backing. The best example of this is the law of contract, which lays down rules whereby a valid contract may be created. Another example is family law, which sets down laws regarding marriage, divorce, adoption and the settlement of wills.

In today's complex society, legal rules cover most activities. Indeed, it is no longer true that the law governs us merely from the cradle to the grave — it is involved even before birth in respect of fertilisation, embryology and abortion, as recent cases have illustrated. Through laws of succession, it operates after death to deal with the distribution of a person's estate.

To give a graphic example of the all-embracing relevance of laws today, you need do no more than look at any newspaper. Of course, there will be articles dealing with major crimes, but you will also see features on business activities covering company takeovers, the issuing of new shares, and news on sport — English football clubs being taken over by rich Americans or Russians, female tennis players demanding equal prize money, or a Formula One motor-racing team being fined by the sport's governing body. Other stories may deal with a celebrity divorce action, where the wife or husband is demanding many millions of pounds in a divorce settlement, or a breach of contract action brought by a pop star against a record company. Still more articles will deal with politics and politicians. All of these are in effect 'law' stories. Even the weather forecast and television programme pages are covered by law — in this case the law of copyright (which covers everything in the newspaper).

Sir Paul McCartney and Heather Mills-McCartney underwent high-profile divorce proceedings at the High Court

Different types of law

When thinking about laws, we probably consider criminal laws first — those prohibiting murder, robbery, rape, assault and so on. However, the laws that regulate our lives most are civil, not criminal, laws. **Civil** (or **private**) **law** refers to those rules that regulate activities between individuals or businesses. For instance, **contract law** sets rules where one person is selling something to another. **Employment law** lays down rules that an employer must follow (such as no discrimination on the grounds

Chapter 2

Parliamentary law making

In order to learn about the law, you need to understand how the UK is governed and how the political system works. It is important first of all to appreciate the difference between Parliament and government.

Parliament is the law-making body (**legislature**) and consists of the House of Commons (elected), the House of Lords (unelected) and the **monarch** (who plays no part in the Parliament's decisions). The **House of Commons** is made up of Members of Parliament (MPs) elected by the local people to represent their individual constituencies. The political party that has the majority of seats forms the government. The **House of Lords** currently consists of hereditary peers (limited to 92), life peers appointed by the monarch on the advice of the government, Law Lords and senior bishops.

Many of our most important legal rules are made by Parliament

The **government** is the **executive**. It runs the country through departments, each headed by a minister. The government is formed by the party with the most MPs in the House of Commons. Because the government has more MPs than the other parties, it is usually able to get Parliament to agree to what it wants.

Historical background

In the past, the king or queen was the effective decision maker and in the days of Henry VIII or Elizabeth I the monarch really was sovereign. This means that the monarch was the supreme law maker and that royal decisions were final, as shown by the fate of those who tried to challenge Henry VIII's authority. The power of the monarch gradually reduced and in the 1640s the English Civil War was fought between King Charles I and Parliament, in part over the issue of the king making decisions without consulting Parliament. The outcome of this conflict was the defeat of the king and his eventual execution. Although the monarchy was restored in 1660, the ability of the monarch to control events gradually diminished. The last monarch to refuse to agree to an Act of Parliament was Queen Anne in 1707.

The monarch always needed a group of advisers and ministers to help run the country and during the eighteenth and nineteenth centuries the principle became established that these ministers should be answerable to Parliament as well as the monarch. By the mid-nineteenth century, it had become almost impossible for the monarch to choose a government that Parliament did not support. Nevertheless, the monarch retains a role in the way both government and Parliament work. Even today the government can exercise prerogative powers that come directly from the queen rather than Parliament.

In the nineteenth century, the House of Commons was also becoming more important as the franchise (the right to vote) was gradually extended. Until 1918, women were not allowed to vote in elections and it was not until 1928 that they gained the same voting rights as men. In 1969, the voting age was lowered from 21 to 18.

The extension of the franchise increased the significance of general elections so that governments had to leave office if they lost an election. A clear pattern had emerged by the end of the nineteenth century — that the government had to have a majority in the House of Commons if it was to stay in office.

However, the House of Lords remained important and many government ministers were peers rather than MPs. The last prime minister to be in the Lords rather than the Commons was Lord Salisbury, who left office in 1902. The influence of the House of Lords was reduced by Parliament Acts in 1911 and 1949, but although unelected it plays a significant role in the parliamentary process.

In summary, at the beginning of the twenty-first century the United Kingdom of Great Britain and Northern Ireland is a democracy, which means, in theory, that ultimately the people determine who is in Parliament, who forms the government and what laws are passed. Yet at the same time, there has never been a revolution to sweep away the institutions such as the monarchy and the House of Lords, which are undemocratic in origin, and they remain important even though they are unelected.

Questions

1 What does Parliament consist of?

2 What is the government?

3 What is the main difference between the House of Commons and the House of Lords?

4 When was the vote first given to everyone over 18?

5 What is a democracy?

Acts of Parliament

UK legislation comprises Acts of Parliament, which are also known as **statutes**. These are the result of a process involving the House of Commons, the House of Lords and the monarch (the queen). Statutes are referred to as **primary legislation**. Most legislation is drawn up (drafted) by the government.

How Acts are created

Types of bill

All Acts of Parliament begin life as bills. The great majority are **public bills**, which are subdivided into **government bills** and **private members' bills**.

Government bills are introduced and piloted through the parliamentary process by a government minister. Some are controversial and reflect the views of the political party in power (e.g. the privatisation of public utilities under the Conservative governments of Margaret Thatcher and John Major), while others are concerned simply with the smooth running of the country (e.g. Access to Justice Act 1999). There are some 40–50 government bills each year, most of which become law. In 2006, 52 government bills were enacted, but in 2007 only 27 reached the Statute Book. The bill is drawn up by **Parliamentary Counsel**, a group of specialised lawyers experienced in the drafting of bills and who act on the instructions of the relevant government department. They aim to ensure that the proposed law is written exactly as the minister intends and that it is clear and unambiguous.

Green and White Papers

Before a bill is drawn up, the government department involved in the proposed changes to the law may issue a consultative document known as a **Green Paper** or a **White Paper**.

Green Papers were brought in by the Labour government in 1967, but White Papers have been in use for much longer. The distinction is that White Papers announce firm government policy for implementation. Green Papers announce tentative proposals for discussion. Harold Wilson, who was prime minister when Green Papers were introduced, wrote:

A White Paper is essentially a statement of government policy in such terms that withdrawal or major amendment, following consultation or public debate, tends to be regarded as a humiliating withdrawal. A Green Paper represents the best that the government can propose on the given issue, but, remaining uncommitted, it is able without loss of face to leave its final decision open until it has been able to consider the public reaction to it.

A Green Paper often contains several alternative policy options. Following this consultation, the government usually publishes firmer recommendations in a White Paper, but a White or Green Paper does not need to be pubished before a bill is introduced into Parliament.

Green and White Papers were published on the future of the legal profession before the bill was introduced that became the Courts and Legal Services Act 1990. The Act was preceded by three Green Papers published in January 1989 and a White Paper (*Legal Services: A Framework for the Future*) published in July 1989, which set out the government's proposals in relation to legal services generally. The Civil Partnership Act 2004 was also preceded by a White Paper (*Civil Partnership: A Framework for the Legal Recognition of Same-Sex Couples*). Another example is the White Paper *Secure Borders, Safe Haven: Integration with Diversity in Modern Britain*. This set out the government's strategy towards the control and management of immigration, most of which was enacted in the Nationality, Immigration and Asylum Act 2002.

Green Papers and White Papers are likely to be published if the government is uncertain about how to proceed or if it knows that proposed legislation will be controversial. For example, in 1999, the White Paper *Modernising Parliament: Reforming the House of Lords* was published before a bill to abolish hereditary peers was introduced.

Private members' bills are introduced by backbench MPs whose names have been selected by ballot. This allows about 20 MPs each year to present a bill and gives them priority in the time specifically allocated to private members' bills. The top six in the draw are guaranteed a full debate on the **second reading** of their bills. Backbench MPs can also introduce bills under the **Ten Minute Rule**, which allows an MP to make a 10-minute speech in favour of a new piece of legislation. It is rare for Acts to emerge by this process, but the Bail (Amendment) Act 1993 is a successful example.

About 10% of Commons time is spent on private members' bills. The choice of subject is their own but, as time for debate on these bills is limited, only about ten of the 100 or so put forward each year become law. Success rates vary considerably

Royal assent

Once a bill has successfully passed through all the stages in both Houses, it has to receive the **royal assent**. The formal consent of the monarch is required for legislation to become law. Some Acts of Parliament come into force when the royal assent is given, but most start on a specific date that may be stated in the Act. Sometimes different parts of the Act may come into effect at different times, which can cause uncertainty, as it can be difficult to find out which sections are in force. The Disability Discrimination Act 1995 is a good example of an Act that has come into force in stages. The parts dealing with employment rights came into effect in 1996, but parts dealing with access to goods and services did not become law until 2004 and provisions dealing with access to transport have yet to be implemented.

The Easter Act 1928, which provides for Easter to have a fixed date each year, has never come into force because the various churches involved have not been able to agree on a date.

The informal process

As each bill progresses through Parliament, there is also an **informal process**: opportunity is provided for interested groups or individuals outside Parliament to make their views known. Often, there is a period of consultation before a bill is introduced and perhaps a Green or White Paper. Once a bill is introduced, there are still opportunities for external bodies to suggest changes. They do this in a variety of ways. Pressure groups, professional associations, trade unions and other large organisations prepare briefing papers to give to MPs and peers on bills they are interested in. Some organisations, particularly trade unions, may sponsor MPs or employ professional lobbyists. During the passage of the Hunting Bill through Parliament, the Countryside Alliance organised demonstrations outside Parliament and a mass lobbying of MPs and peers, but often the most effective lobbying is that which takes place quietly behind the scenes.

Role of the House of Commons

Because the House of Commons is the elected body, it has the most important role in the law-making process. All important legislation begins in the House of Commons and all finance bills must start there.

By using the Parliament Acts, the Commons can defeat any attempt by the Lords to oppose a measure that the Commons has passed. In practice, this power is rarely used and the Commons often has to compromise in order to get legislation through. In addition, because the Lords can delay a bill for a year, it has considerably more influence over the Commons during the last year of a Parliament's life.

Interior of the House of Commons, Westminster

Remember that in practice any bill that the Commons passes will be either a government bill or a private members' bill that the government supports. Therefore, the House of Commons is not a truly independent body. In most cases, it does what the government tells it to do because the majority of MPs will be members of the governing party and will be pressurised by the whips into supporting government bills.

Role of the House of Lords

Bills can start their life in the House of Lords, though most begin in the Commons. Usually, it is legislation that is not politically controversial or that has a legal subject matter that starts in the Lords — for example the Access to Justice Act 1999. The benefit of this system for the government is that it can enlarge its legislative output and take some pressure off the House of Commons.

Occasionally, more controversial legislation can start in the House of Lords. This happened with the Human Rights Act 1998 (see Box 2.2), which was introduced for the government by the Lord Chancellor, who was a peer rather than an MP.

However, the House of Lords is primarily a revising and debating chamber and it allows further detailed scrutiny of bills that have already passed through the House of Commons. The House of Lords is considered to act as a check on the executive's powers, a safeguard against the abuse of power. At times, the Lords has made the government rethink its proposals. For example, in March 2005, they forced the government to amend its plans in the Terrorism Bill for control orders to deal with terrorist suspects.

The unelected House of Lords used to be able to prevent legislation put forward by the elected House of Commons, as the agreement of both Houses was necessary. This power is now restricted by the Parliament Acts 1911 and 1949 (see Box 2.3). If the House of Lords rejects a bill, provided it is re-introduced to the House of Commons in the next parliamentary session and passes all the stages again, it can become law. In addition, the Lords are not allowed to delay finance bills. This power to force the Lords to pass a bill has been used only five times — for example, to push through the War Crimes Act 1991 and the Hunting Act 2004.

Usually, a government threat to use the Parliament Acts is enough. Initially, the Lords rejected the lowering of the homosexual age of consent from 18 to 16 when it was introduced as part of the Crime and Disorder Bill 1998, but in 2000 a new bill was introduced and after the government made it clear that it would invoke the Parliament Acts, the House of Lords gave in.

> ### Box 2.3 The Parliament Acts 1911 and 1949
>
> Until the early years of the twentieth century, the House of Lords had the power to prevent legislation, as bills had to be passed by both Houses of Parliament. David Lloyd George's so-called 'people's budget' of 1909 brought this arrangement under strain, when the House of Lords refused to pass it. Eventually, the budget was passed after a general election in 1910; a second election was then fought on the issue of reform of the House of Lords.
>
> The result was the Parliament Act 1911, which removed from the House of Lords the power to veto a bill, except one to prolong the lifetime of a parliament. Under s.2, peers would only be able to delay a bill for 2 years. Bills certified by the Speaker of the House of Commons as finance bills could only be delayed for 1 month. The Act also reduced the maximum lifespan of a parliament from 7 to 5 years.
>
> One interesting point is that the Act only applies to legislation introduced in the House of Commons, so that if a bill is introduced first into the House of Lords and the Lords refuses to accept amendments made in the Commons, the Act cannot be used to force through the Commons version of the Act. This situation is unlikely to arise because it is usually uncontroversial legislation that begins its life in the Lords, though it could have arisen during the passage of the potentially controversial Human Rights Act 1998, which started in the Lords.
>
> The Parliament Act 1949 stemmed from the Lords' rejection of the Labour government's plans to nationalise the steel industry. It further reduced the Lords' delaying powers to 1 year, over two parliamentary sessions.
>
> Since 1949, four Acts have been passed into law without the consent of the House of Lords:
> * War Crimes Act 1991
> * European Parliamentary Elections Act 1999
> * Sexual Offences (Amendment) Act 2000
> * Hunting Act 2004
>
> However, the Labour government had to use the 1911 Act to in order to get the Parliament Act 1949 onto the Statute Book and constitutional lawyers have debated whether the 1949 Act — and therefore any law introduced as a result of using it — is valid.
>
> In R (Jackson and others) v Attorney General (2005) the validity of the Parliament Act 1949 was challenged in the Lords by the Countryside Alliance after it was used to pass the Hunting Act 2004. Nine Law Lords unanimously rejected this challenge. In the leading judgement, Lord Bingham concluded that:
>
> *…there was nothing in the 1911 Act to preclude use of the procedure laid down by the Act to amend the Act. The language of the Act was wide enough to permit the amendment made by the 1949 Act, and also (in my opinion) to make much more far-reaching changes. For the past half century it has been generally, even if not universally, believed that the 1949 Act had been validly enacted, as evidenced by the use made of it by governments of different political persuasions. In my opinion that belief was well-founded…The 1949 Act and the 2004 Act are Acts of Parliament of full legal effect.*

Role of the Crown

The Crown plays a purely formal role and any attempt by a monarch to thwart the will of the Commons and Lords would not be tolerated. Since Queen Anne refused to pass the Scotch Militia Bill 1707, no monarch has declined to assent to a bill. The royal assent is needed for a bill to become an Act of Parliament. Nevertheless, the monarch is not simply a figurehead and is also involved in the law-making process through the **Queen's speech** at the State Opening of Parliament, which sets out the government's legislative programme for the parliamentary session.

Questions

1 List the stages through which every bill has to pass.
2 Briefly explain what happens at each stage (one sentence for each stage).
3 What sometimes happens at the committee stage to bills of constitutional importance?
4 When was the last time the royal assent was refused?
5 When do Acts come into force?

House of Lords reform

Before 1958, membership of the House of Lords consisted of:

* **Hereditary peers.** Over the centuries, people had been given peerages by the monarch (since the mid-nineteenth century on the advice of the prime minister), and these peerages remained for ever with the title and the right to sit in the House of Lords, passing by inheritance from father to eldest surviving son.
* **Law Lords.** Judges appointed to the position of Lords of Appeal in Ordinary to hear appeals on legal cases in the House of Lords were automatically members of the House of Lords as a Chamber of Parliament.
* **Senior bishops.** The two archbishops and the 24 most senior bishops of the Anglican church were also automatically members of the House of Lords.

In 1958, the Life Peerages Act was passed. This meant that future peers could be given peerages that lasted only for their lifetime. Most peerages created since then have been life peerages, though former prime minister Baroness Thatcher was made a hereditary peer.

When the Labour government came to power in 1997, it made clear its intention to reform the House of Lords. In January 1999 a White Paper was published, followed by a House of Lords bill designed to abolish hereditary peers altogether. This was amended as it passed through Parliament and in the House of Lords Act 1999, 92 hereditary peers were allowed to remain.

❖ It can be argued that Parliament does take note of public opinion. While a bill is going through Parliament, there are opportunities for people to lobby and express their views. A good example of this is the decision of the House of Commons in February 2006 to vote for a complete ban on smoking in public places. The government had originally favoured a compromise that would have allowed some exceptions, but MPs took note of the views being expressed by medical experts and by the public as expressed in opinion polls and rejected the government's proposal.

❖ The House of Lords is not elected and is made up of a wide variety of people from a range of backgrounds. Therefore, it is less concerned with staying popular with voters. It can often represent minority views — for instance, in March 2005 it opposed anti-terrorism legislation and forced the government to agree to amendments. The House of Lords is therefore a useful check on a government that has a big majority in the Commons. The Labour manifesto for the 2005 election included a proposal to reduce the power of the Lords to scrutinise legislation to a maximum of 60 days, prompting Mark Garnett and Philip Lynch in *AS UK Government & Politics* (2nd edn, 2006) to comment that this betrayed the government's main concern in all the discussions about reforming the House of Lords, 'which was to prevent the Lords from becoming a more powerful check on the executive'.

❖ There are many people in the Lords who have specialist expertise (e.g. lawyers, doctors, scientists) or who have been successful in running companies or charities. For instance, Lord Winston is a doctor and a specialist on fertility treatments, while Lord Rix ran a mental health charity and has campaigned on behalf of people with disabilities. They can therefore bring practical knowledge and experience to their examination of bills.

❖ The legislative process is thorough, with detailed committee examination of bills in both Houses as well as general debates.

❖ Delegated legislation means that much of the detail can be left to government departments to draw up through **statutory instruments** — regulations made by government departments to implement the provisions made in Acts. This is helpful because it prevents Parliament from having to spend time on technical detail and it also means that bills are shorter and less complex than they otherwise would be. Given the enormous volume of delegated legislation and the fact that over 3,000 statutory instruments are introduced each year, it is hard to see how Parliament could cope if delegated legislation were not used.

❖ The legislative process usually takes several months to complete, especially if the proposals are controversial. Sometimes, however, if all the parties agree that a new law is needed urgently, an Act may be passed quickly. For example, the Criminal Justice (Terrorism and Conspiracy) Act 1998 went through all its stages in 2 days and the Northern Ireland Bill 1972 was passed in just 24 hours.

2

Disadvantages of the UK law-making system

❖ There is not enough time to pass all the legislation that is needed and, in particular, reform bills (e.g. to modernise the law on non-fatal offences) are often left out of the government's legislative programme. It usually takes several months for a bill to go through all its stages. The House of Commons sits for an average of 163 days a year, which allows only some 10 hours to be spent on each bill.

❖ Because the government usually has a comfortable majority in the Commons (e.g. the governments of Margaret Thatcher and Tony Blair), it is difficult for Parliament to influence or change what the government wants. Several aspects of the Criminal Justice and Public Order Act 1994 were criticised and yet no changes were made during its passage through Parliament. In addition, it is almost impossible for ordinary MPs to get a private members' bill passed unless the government supports it — for example, the Abortion Act 1967 was passed only because of government support. This means that it is the government that determines which legislation is passed.

❖ There is inadequate scrutiny of legislation. The government controls the parliamentary timetable and through processes such as the **guillotine**, it can restrict discussion on a bill. If the government imposes a guillotine on a bill it means that a time limit is placed on discussion of each clause. When the time elapses, discussion is cut off even if there are more amendments to consider. For example, the Dangerous Dogs Act 1991 was guillotined twice during its passage through the Commons. Sixty pages of Lords' amendments to the Political Parties and Referendums Bill 2000 — an important constitutional bill — were never discussed properly because of a guillotine when the bill returned to the Commons. Furthermore, because the government has a majority on all the standing committees, it is able to defeat any amendments put forward in committee. As, even in committee, MPs tend to vote on party lines, so governments are inclined to view all amendments proposed by members of other parties as politically motivated, and this can mean that sensible

TopFoto

The Dangerous Dogs Act 1991 was guillotined twice during its passage through the Commons

❖ It follows therefore that Acts of Parliament passed using the proper procedures cannot be challenged and must be applied by the courts.

❖ They override any judicial precedent, delegated legislation or previous Act of Parliament covering that area of law.

❖ Parliament also has the power to make any law it wishes and **rescind** (unmake) any law it has passed.

❖ No parliament can bind its successors (i.e. no parliament can make laws that will restrict law making in future parliaments).

❖ Acts of Parliament can also apply retrospectively (i.e. to past events) and extra-territorially (i.e. to events outside the UK). An Act combining both these elements was the War Crimes Act 1991, which allowed prosecution for crimes committed in Europe during the Second World War.

Limitations on parliamentary supremacy

There have always been practical limits to what Parliament can do. All politicians are sensitive to public opinion and plans for law making are likely to reflect this. In addition, there are entrenched laws that deal with fundamental constitutional issues and that would be difficult for any future Parliament to change — for example, legislation extending voting rights to women and lowering the voting age to 18. Another example is the more recent granting of legislative powers to a Scottish parliament. On the other hand, it should be noted that s.28(7) of the Scotland Act 1998 expressly states that the devolution legislation 'does not affect the power of the Parliament of the United Kingdom to make laws for Scotland'. The example of Northern Ireland demonstrates that the UK Parliament can devolve powers and then take them back again.

In *R v Secretary of State for Transport ex parte Factortame Ltd* (1990), the European Court of Justice ruled that part of the Merchant Shipping Act 1988 was contrary to European Community law

Some limitations on Parliament's supremacy have resulted from the UK joining the European Community (now the European Union) in 1973. Under the Treaty of Rome 1957, European Community law, enacted by the powers set out in the treaties, takes priority over conflicting laws in member states. The European Communities Act 1972 incorporates this principle into UK law. Even if Parliament passes an Act that conflicts with EU law, EU law must prevail, as shown in the case of *R v Secretary of State for Transport ex parte Factortame Ltd* (1990). In this case, the European Court of Justice ruled that part of the Merchant Shipping Act 1988 was contrary to European Community law because it sought to discriminate against other EU nationals. The offending provisions restricted ownership of fishing boats registered in Britain to British nationals. This was challenged successfully by Spanish boat owners, who had registered in the UK so that they would have access to the British fishing quotas under the Common Fisheries policy. In *Equal Opportunities Commission* v *Secretary of State for Employment* (1994), the House of Lords, acting on the principle established in the *Factortame* case, ruled that part of the Employment Protection (Consolidation) Act 1978 was in breach of European Community law and the Act was subsequently amended by Parliament.

This is a clear restriction of parliamentary sovereignty and although, in theory, it is open to a future parliament to repeal the European Communities Act and withdraw from the European Union, in practice this would be difficult to accomplish. However, there are many areas of law not covered by the EU, and here parliamentary supremacy is unaffected.

The Human Rights Act 1998, which came into force in October 2000, incorporates the European Convention on Human Rights into English law. Under the Act, the Convention does not have superiority over English law and Parliament can still make laws that conflict with it. However, under s.19 of the Act, all bills require a statement from a government minister before the second reading in each House, saying that the provisions of the bill are compatible with the Convention, or if they are not compatible, that the government intends the bill to proceed (e.g. for reasons of national security). Under s.3 of the Act, the courts are required as far as possible to interpret Acts so that they comply with the Convention. If an Act cannot be reconciled with the Convention, a judge can make a declaration of incompatibility, but the minister is not obliged to change the law. By 2006, there had been 20 declarations of incompatibility, six of which were overturned on appeal. As Philip Lynch points out in 'Is Parliament still sovereign?' (*Politics Review,* Vol. 17, No. 2, pp. 30–33), although in theory Parliament could choose not to amend the law, in reality it 'finds its hands tied, because a law deemed contrary to human rights will lack moral authority and will be subject to further legal challenge'.

It could be argued that because Parliament can refuse to respond to a declaration by a judge that an Act is incompatible with the Convention, the doctrine of parliamentary sovereignty is unaffected. However, it is clearly significant that judges can now challenge the validity of Acts of Parliament, and in practice it is likely that a government will accept that the legislation has to change.

Questions

1 What does the doctrine of parliamentary supremacy mean?

2 What the five elements of parliamentary supremacy?

3 What are the four main limitations on parliamentary sovereignty?

Suggested reading

Darbyshire, P. (2002) *Eddey & Darbyshire on the English Legal System*, chapter 2, Sweet & Maxwell.

Dugdale, T. et al. (2002) *'A' Level Law*, chapter 7, Butterworth.

Ingman, T. (2006) *The English Legal Process*, chapter 8, Oxford University Press.

Norton, P. (2006) 'Reforming the Lords', *Politics Review*, Vol. 15, No. 4, pp. 14–16.

Russell, M. (2007) 'The House of Lords', *Politics Review*, Vol. 17, No. 1, pp. 2–5.

Russell, S. (2006) 'Legislation. What do I need to know?', *A-Level Law Review*, Vol. 1, No. 3, p. 24.

Zander, M. (2004) *The Law-Making Process*, chapter 2, Cambridge University Press.

Chapter 3

Influences on Parliament

In order to be effective, the law must be able to adapt to changes in society. As Parliament is involved in the law-making process, there are many influences on it. These include political considerations such as the party manifesto, law reform agencies, the media and other pressure or interest groups.

Exam questions may ask you to describe some of the influences on Parliament. Sometimes they specify the number (e.g. three). You will be required to give examples of their influence. You may also be asked to comment on advantages and disadvantages of this influence.

Political influences

Most of the law makers in Parliament are members of political parties. To a large extent, therefore, the legislation they pass is likely to be influenced by political considerations.

Government

The most important political influence on Parliament is the government. In order to form a government, a political party usually has a majority of MPs in the House of Commons, and this gives it the power to force through most of its political programme. It also controls the parliamentary timetable and so largely determines what laws are passed, and most bills originate from government departments. Most of the time, however, the government is concerned with political measures, rather than with 'pure law' reform.

When a general election is to be held, each political party presents a **party manifesto**, setting out its proposals if elected into government. Examples include the right to buy council houses, included in the Conservative Party's 1979 manifesto and implemented through the Housing Act 1980, and the Human Rights Act 1998, which implemented the Labour Party's manifesto commitment to incorporate the European Convention on Human Rights into English law. The House of Lords Act 1999, which greatly reduced the number of hereditary peers, was also the result of a manifesto commitment.

However, Professor Michael Zander claims that:

> *The belief that most government bills derive from its manifesto commitments is mistaken. Research established, for instance, that only 8 per cent of the Conservative government's bills in the period from 1970 to 1974 came from election commitments and that in the 1974–79 Labour Government the proportion was only a little higher at 13 per cent.*

The Law-Making Process (2004)

Response to events

Some bills are responses to particular and unexpected events, such as the Prevention of Terrorism (Temporary Provisions) Act 1974 in response to the Birmingham IRA bombings, or the Drought Act 1976, which was introduced to deal with a serious drought in the summer of 1976. The Dangerous Dogs Act 1991 was rushed through Parliament following a number of attacks on people by pit bull terriers. The events of 11 September 2001 led Parliament to pass the Anti-terrorism, Crime and Security Act 2001.

Europe

Membership of the EU is another political influence and under the European Communities Act 1972 the UK is obliged to follow European Community law. In particular, Parliament may be required to pass legislation in order to implement a European directive. For example, the Consumer Protection Act 1987 was passed to give effect to the Product Liability Directive, which imposes strict liability on producers for damage caused by their products.

Individual MPs

Individual MPs or members of the House of Lords can also influence the legislation that Parliament passes — though on their own they are clearly restricted in what they can achieve. If they want to initiate legislation, they need to persuade others to support them and their success depends on the view of the governing party. The reality of Parliament is that political parties expect loyalty from their elected members and this is enforced by party officials (**whips**). An individual MP is unlikely to persuade other MPs to support a measure that is opposed by the party whips, and if the governing party is opposed, the chances of success are limited.

Individual MPs can introduce bills into Parliament (see pages 11–12), but only about 10% of these measures ever become law. The ones that succeed do so because the government is prepared to make time for them in the parliamentary timetable.

Advantages of political influences

❖ Governments are elected and they usually respond to what the public wants. They wish to be re-elected, so it is unlikely they will pass unpopular Acts. Public concerns about rising crime levels have led the Labour government to bring in several pieces of legislation since it came to office in 1997. The anti-terrorism legislation introduced since 2001 has also, in part, been a response to public anxiety, but a readiness to respond to public opinion can distract Parliament from more routine concerns.

❖ It is also helpful that when there is an emergency, the government can respond quickly and use its influence over Parliament to pass appropriate emergency measures — for example, the Anti-terrorism, Crime and Security Act 2001.

❖ Parliament is also flexible enough to respond to other political influences. Individual MPs have been responsible for valuable reforms, such as the abolition of the death penalty and the regulation of minicabs in London.

❖ Ideas for legislation will be thought out and planned with the help of expert civil servants. They will have to implement the new laws, so it is likely that they will have considered any problems. The majority of legislative proposals come from government departments, where civil servants may have spent many months preparing them.

The government responded quickly to the 9/11 terrorist attacks, using its influence over Parliament to pass the Anti-terrorism, Crime and Security Act 2001

Some pressure groups only exist for a short time, as they are set up to deal with a specific issue (e.g. a campaign about a proposed by-pass). The group disbands once the issue is resolved. For example, the National Campaign for the Abolition of Capital Punishment was set up in 1955 and disbanded in 1969, when the death penalty was permanently suspended.

Sometimes a pressure group is set up as a result of a tragic event, such as the Dunblane massacre in 1996. The Snowdrop Petition, organised after the killing of 16 children and their teacher at a school in Scotland, campaigned for a total ban on handguns and after an inquiry into the massacre, the Conservative government introduced the **Firearms (Amendment) Act 1997**, banning the private ownership of most types of handguns. In November 1997, the new Labour government introduced legislation that banned all handguns. The Snowdrop campaign ended and the group disbanded.

Following the murder of Jane Longhurst in 2003 by a man said to be obsessed with internet sites portraying violent pornography, her family lobbied the Home Secretary to introduce a law to ban such websites. In September 2005, the government published proposals to make the possession of violent and extreme pornography an offence, punishable by up to 3 years' imprisonment. This provision is included in the Criminal Justice and Immigration Bill currently before Parliament. This is another example of a small but determined group campaigning on an issue commanding widespread popular support and provoking a sympathetic response from legislators.

The Snowdrop Campaign, established following the Dunblane massacre, led to a ban on handguns

Sectional groups

Sectional or **interest groups** further the ends of their own particular section of society. Examples are trade unions, the National Farmers' Union (NFU), the Confederation of British Industry (CBI) and professional associations such as the British Medical Association and the Law Society.

The degree of influence exercised by such groups varies. Trade unions traditionally have more influence under Labour governments and they declined sharply during the Conservative governments from 1979 to 1997. The Labour governments since 1997 have not restored the close relationship of the 1970s and although the trade unions welcomed the recognition of trade union rights to workers at GCHQ (Government Communications Headquarters) and the introduction of the minimum wage, they have not had a significant influence on other areas of legislation.

Groups such as the CBI and the NFU would expect to be consulted by governments of all political persuasion, though traditionally they have more influence under a Conservative government. Under the Agriculture Act 1947, it was a legal requirement for the NFU to be consulted before decisions were taken that affected farming. During the foot-and-mouth epidemic in 2001, the NFU played a part in the decision not to adopt mass vaccination as a means of combating the disease. The fuel protest in 2000 was organised by farmers who felt that their concerns over rising diesel prices were being ignored by the government.

It is perhaps inevitable that groups considered vital to the economy exercise considerable influence. Environmental campaigners have claimed that airlines and oil companies have been able to restrict the introduction of green taxes on air travel or gas-guzzling cars. Campaigners wanting tougher rules on the sale and advertisement of alcohol have long suspected that the influence of brewers and supermarkets has operated on both government and individual MPs to frustrate change.

Professional associations representing groups such as lawyers or doctors, made up of well-educated, articulate and often wealthy individuals, are influential. Governments of all parties tend to consult these groups before introducing a bill affecting their interests. For example, the Law Society, which represents solicitors, has a Parliamentary Unit that actively lobbies MPs and peers from all parties for changes in the law. The Unit works on a large number of public bills every session and briefings are usually produced for second readings, as well as more detailed briefings and amendments for parliamentarians to table at committee and report stages. In July 2007, for instance, it prepared a briefing expressing concern about several aspects of the Criminal Justice and Immigration Bill, at the time receiving its second reading in the Commons. The Unit also lobbies Parliament on more general campaigns for changes in the law. Its website claims that the Unit's Parliamentary work continues to draw positive feedback from MPs and peers across the political spectrum.

Advantages of pressure groups

❖ Pressure groups give the public, and particularly minorities, a voice. People feel that they are participating in law making. Pressure groups can act as a safety valve for frustrations (e.g. pro-hunting and anti-Iraq war protests). Far more people are involved in pressure groups than with political parties and they represent a huge variety of views.

❖ They help MPs keep in touch with what people think. Much parliamentary time is spent debating the government's political agenda, and pressure groups are useful in raising other issues that sections of the public regard as important. Pressure from environmental groups, for example, might have persuaded the government to change car tax regulations to favour smaller, more fuel-efficient cars.

❖ They bring attention to issues that affect their interest or cause. For example, Fathers 4 Justice, through a variety of stunts, has been successful in raising awareness of the plight of many fathers denied access to their children after a divorce. The Countryside Alliance was successful in drawing attention to the case in favour of hunting, though ultimately it was unsuccessful in persuading Parliament (see Box 3.2). Groups such as Shelter and Greenpeace have used more conventional methods to keep their issues in the public eye.

> ## Box 3.2 *An unsuccessful pressure group*
>
> ### *The Countryside Alliance and the hunting ban*
>
> The Countryside Alliance was set up in 1998 to try to defeat any attempt by the new Labour government to implement its manifesto pledge to ban fox hunting. Although primarily a group representing those involved in hunting, it appealed for support from all those anxious to preserve the countryside or from those concerned about the general erosion of freedom. It adopted a range of tactics, including mass demonstrations and lobbies of Parliament in 1999 and 2002, threats that its members would defy the law and make it unworkable and even a legal challenge to the validity of the Hunting Act 2004 itself. Ultimately, despite all the publicity and claims of widespread public support, the Countryside Alliance failed in its objective to prevent the ban on hunting. Ironically, as they became increasingly desperate, they adopted more militant tactics, not dissimilar to those used in the past by the opponents of hunting. However, MPs were more convinced by the reasoned arguments of respected animal welfare groups such as the RSPCA.

❖ Members of pressure groups often have considerable expertise and can therefore suggest detailed and well-thought-out law changes. Many groups have draft bills ready for backbench MPs to introduce. Sometimes, individual experts can have a significant influence over government policy. A good example is Jamie Oliver, whose views on healthy eating have helped to change attitudes on the type of school meals that should be provided.

Disadvantages of pressure groups

❖ Some large pressure groups who represent powerful organisations are extremely influential and it is difficult for smaller pressure groups to match their influence. Trade unions used to be powerful, but the reforms of the Thatcher years and the changing industrial landscape (e.g. decline in mining) have made the unions much less influential. On the other hand, large multinationals such as oil companies, supermarkets and brewers appear to be powerful groups. Environmental groups claim that the strength of the road lobby and the airline industry mean that new roads or airport extensions are difficult to fight.

❖ The methods of some pressure groups can be a problem — for example, strikes and protests can cause disruption, such as the blockading of oil depots. The direct action tactics of Fathers 4 Justice have been criticised. Members of the Countryside Alliance, as part of its campaign in favour of fox hunting, broke into the House of Commons. Many of these activities gain publicity but blur the line between acceptable and unacceptable protest. Extremist groups, such as animal-rights activists, may even break the law by attacking scientific laboratories and the homes and property of drug company employees. Ultimately, the legislative process needs to be driven by reason and argument, though supporters of groups that engage in direct action would claim that they are forced to use such tactics because their views are repeatedly ignored by Parliament.

Questions

1 Explain what cause groups are and give three examples.

2 Comment briefly on the methods that cause groups use.

3 Give two examples of legislation introduced following campaigns by cause groups.

4 Explain what sectional groups are and give three examples.

5 Comment briefly on the influence of sectional groups.

6 List the advantages and disadvantages of pressure groups. Write just a few words for each so that you can learn and remember them easily.

Research activity

Choose a pressure group and look on its website to find examples of issues it is concerned about. Identify a specific piece of legislation that the group has tried to influence or a bill currently before Parliament that the group has views on. What methods does the group use to try to influence Parliament? How successful has it been in bringing about changes in the law?

The media

The **media** include television, radio, newspapers and journals, and they can be used to highlight issues of public concern. Newspapers in particular promote specific issues or causes. For example, the *Daily Mail* has often run headlines on immigration or asylum issues in order to try to achieve tighter controls. The *Sun* has consistently campaigned against what it sees as the growing influence of the EU on British life. For instance, it strongly opposed the adoption of the new EU constitution and helped

the setting up of the Crown Prosecution Service. The Criminal Appeal Act 1995 and the Criminal Procedure and Investigation Act 1996 both resulted from the Runciman Royal Commission on Criminal Justice.

The Law Commission

The Law Commission was established by the Law Commission Act 1965 with the specific task of keeping the law under review and promoting law reform. Section 3 of the Act details the objectives of the Commission. These include:

* systematic development and reform of the law
* codification of certain areas of law (i.e. putting all the existing legal rules that may come from cases as well as Acts into a series of statutory rules)
* consolidation (i.e. replacing several Acts with one Act to cover a whole area of law)
* the repeal of obsolete laws and the general simplification and modernisation of the law

It is a full-time body with five law commissioners. The chairman is a High Court judge and the other four are from the legal professions and academic lawyers. Their staff are all legally trained.

The Commission may have topics referred to it by the Lord Chancellor and government departments, or may select a topic of its own. After researching a selected area of law, the Commission produces a consultative paper that details the present law, setting out the problems and options for change. The views of interested parties are sought, after which a final report is published, setting out its recommendations and, if legislation is proposed, a draft bill, which needs to go through the full parliamentary process if it is to become law. Examples of recent Law Commission reports include one published in August 2004 on partial defences to murder and another in December 2005 on the reform of the law on murder itself.

Legislation that has resulted from this process includes:

* Law Reform (Year and a Day Rule) Act 1996
* Contracts (Rights of Third Parties) Act 1999
* Sale and Supply of Goods Act 1994
* Computer Misuse Act 1990
* Family Law Act 1996
* Land Registration Act 1997

The success of the Law Commission in achieving law reform has varied. Initially, there was a high success rate in getting its proposals accepted and enacted (in the first 10 years, 85% of its proposals were enacted by Parliament), but this has not been maintained. During the following 10 years, only 50% became law and in 1990, not one of its proposals was adopted. In 1994–95, improvements were brought about by

the introduction of new parliamentary procedures. For example, the Jellicoe procedure is designed to speed up the legislative process and applies to non-controversial bills. Under this procedure, after the second reading in the House of Lords, a bill can go to a special public bill committee, which can hear written and oral evidence. This allows technical bills, such as those produced by the Commission, to be given expert scrutiny without taking up time on the floor. A second change in procedure allows a public bill to be automatically referred to a second reading committee if the bill is to give effect to a Law Commission report.

In recent years, the backlog of proposals has increased again. In 2003–04, the Law Commission reported that seven proposals had been made law, but a further 17 were awaiting parliamentary time and 13 were waiting for a government decision. A specific example is the Report and Draft Bill produced by the Law Commission in 1993 on reform of the law on non-fatal offences. It was widely welcomed as a long-overdue reform measure and the government indicated its intention to implement the proposals. In February 1998, the Home Office produced a consultation document containing a draft Offences Against the Person Bill, modelled on the Law Commission bill. However, despite the initial commitment from the government, the measure has never been presented to Parliament.

Another of the Law Commission's aims is to codify the law in certain areas, but this has not been achieved. The draft Criminal Code was published in 1985 but has never become law. The arguments in favour of codification are that it would make the law accessible and understandable, and provide consistency and certainty. People would be able to find out what the law is, as it is contained in one place. The arguments against codification are that a detailed code would make the law too rigid, but if it was insufficiently detailed it would need to be interpreted by the courts, thus creating uncertainty. Therefore, the Commission has selected areas of law such as family law and clarified them, hoping to codify them at a later date, if possible.

The Law Commission also aims to achieve consolidation of the law in particular areas. This involves drawing together all the provisions, which are set out in a number of statutes, so that they are all in one Act. About five consolidation bills are produced each year. Examples of consolidation Acts resulting from the work of the Commission include the Merchant Shipping Act 1995, the Employment Rights Act 1996, the Industrial Tribunals Act 1996 and the Justices of the Peace Act 1997.

The Law Commission also has the task of identifying obsolete legislation still on the Statute Book and proposing that it be repealed. These proposals are usually implemented quickly because they are treated as consolidation bills and can be enacted without the need for debate in either House. The Statute Law (Repeals) Act 1998 repealed over 150 complete Acts and parts of nearly 250 others, including the Slave Trade Act 1824, an Act of 1737 authorising the rebuilding of a church in Worcester, and an Act of Attainder passed by Henry VIII in 1533.

Advantages of the Law Commission

❖ The Law Commission is made up of lawyers with much expertise, headed by a High Court judge. The Commissioners change every 5 years, so a different range of views are brought into the law-reform process.

❖ It is a permanent, full-time body and can investigate any areas of law that it thinks need to be reformed.

❖ It produces draft bills ready for Parliament to introduce, which significantly reduces the workload for ministers.

❖ It has been responsible for many sensible changes to the law (e.g. the Unfair Contract Terms Act 1977) and the abolition of the 'year and a day' rule.

❖ It can undertake extensive research and engage in wide consultation, so its recommendations for law reform are well informed and this helps to avoid future problems in the application of the law.

Disadvantages of the Law Commission

❖ Parliament has often ignored the Commission's proposals. Up to 1999, only two-thirds of its proposals had been implemented.

❖ Sometimes, because its recommendations are usually balanced and measured, they may not suit the political agenda of the government of the day.

❖ More often governments simply cannot find time in the legislative programme for non-urgent law reform. The present Labour government accepted the proposals for reform to the law on non-fatal offences and the Home Office even produced a draft bill in 1998, but this has proceeded no further. Another example is the Law Commission proposals on the reform of the law on involuntary manslaughter. These were first published in 1996 and the government accepted the majority of the recommendations, but they are still not implemented.

❖ The Law Commission investigates as many as 20–30 areas at the same time. This may mean that each investigation is not as thorough as one carried out by a Royal Commission or a Commission of Inquiry.

Questions

1 When was the Law Commission set up?

2 What are its objectives?

3 Identify four areas of law that it has investigated.

4 Name two Acts that were based on Law Commission reports.

5 What was the position regarding the implementation of reports in 2003?

6 List the advantages and disadvantages of the Law Commission. Write just a few words for each so that you can learn and remember them easily.

Extension exercise

The following remarks made by Mr Justice Carnwath, Chairman of the Commission from 1999 to 2002, are adapted from an article in *The Times* in 1999.

The Commission's work has huge variety and depth. There are some 20 completed reports awaiting implementation. Each focuses on an area of law chosen in consultation with the government and seen to be in need of reform. The missing link, as my predecessors regularly complained, is a systematic procedure to put that work to practical effect. Although historically 70% of reports have led eventually to legislation, the timing has been unpredictable and the process haphazard.

Senior judges condemn the cost, injustice and delay caused by uncertainty in the criminal law. A political commitment to codification of the criminal law, with a programme to achieve it over this and the next Parliament, would be the ultimate prize of my term of office.

The problem at its starkest is illustrated by our proposals to reform the Offences Against the Person Act 1861. This 'outmoded and unclear Victorian legislation' (the Home Secretary's words) is one of the workhorses of the criminal law, responsible for 80,000 cases a year. It is a tired and confused old workhorse, and our proposals to replace it (published in 1993) were widely welcomed. Six years and half a million cases later, they remain unimplemented. The principles were accepted by the government early last year, but there is still no final decision, let alone a firm commitment to legislate.

Such problems are not confined to the criminal law. One of our most important projects is the review with the Land Registry of the law of land registration. This was the subject of a consultation paper last year. A draft bill will be published later this year, but again the timing of any legislation is unknown.

Given pressures on Parliament's time there are no easy solutions. There has been a reasonable flow of legislation to implement the more limited reform measures, but big projects have fared badly. Our proposals for desperately needed reform of the law on mental incapacity, for instance, were published in 1995, but still await a government decision.

The government's legislative programme is subject to intense competition and departmental bids put political priorities at the forefront, but if the government means what it says about law reform, a place must be found in its programme for law reform measures. Without this, progress towards modernisation of the law is a pipedream.

Questions

1 How many unimplemented reports were there in 1999? Which three does the writer refer to specifically?

2 What is meant by 'codification'? From the article, assess how likely it is that it will be achieved.

3 From what is written in the article, explain why many of the Law Commission's proposals have not been implemented.

4 What solution does Mr Justice Carnwath suggest?

Research activity

Go to the Law Commission website (www.lawcom.gov.uk):

1 Find out the names of the current Commissioners.

2 Identify two recent Law Commission reports and explain which areas of law they cover.

3 Mention one specific reform proposal that each report contains.

Exam hints

You are likely to be asked to write about a specific number of influences on Parliament, usually three. Choose those that you can write most about. You must be able to refer to examples that relate to how effective the influence is. When talking about pressure groups, for example, a good answer will have examples of pieces of legislation that pressure groups played a part in persuading Parliament to pass.

The evaluative part of the question may ask you to comment on advantages or disadvantages. You may be asked to write about just one advantage or disadvantage for each. To get high marks, you will need to develop your comments.

Sample exam questions

1 Outline three influences on the parliamentary law-making process. (15 marks)

Tasks

1 Choose as one of these influences the Law Commission and write briefly about it under the following headings:
   ❖ its main task
   ❖ personnel
   ❖ how it decides what to investigate
   ❖ how it operates
   ❖ examples of successes
   ❖ problems with getting proposals adopted
   ❖ codification of the law
   ❖ consolidation of the law
   ❖ abolition of obsolete laws

2 The following is part of a sample answer to question 1, which deals with pressure groups. How adequate is it as a response? Rewrite it as a 'sound' answer.

   Pressure groups consist of people who share a common interest in getting the government to change the law in certain areas. They may represent a cause such

as Shelter on homelessness or Friends of the Earth on environmental matters, or interest groups such as the Confederation of British Industries, trade unions or professional organisations such as the Law Society. They target politicians by lobbying MPs, organising petitions and gaining as much publicity for their cause as possible. At times, groups may link together to support a common cause. Some pressure groups have many members but some are only small. Sometimes a pressure group may only come into existence for a limited period of time, until the issue in question is resolved.

3 The following is part of the same answer that deals with the media. Would you assess it as 'limited', 'some' or 'clear'? Rewrite it as a 'sound' answer.

The media, newspapers, television and radio, plays a part in influencing Parliament by bringing issues to the attention of the government. They do this by giving an issue plenty of coverage in the newspapers, on television and radio so that it can be brought to the notice of the public.

2 Identify and discuss one advantage and one disadvantage of each of the three influences.   (15 marks)

Task

The following answer would be rated as 'some'. How could it be improved to make it 'clear' or 'sound'? Rewrite it as a 'sound' answer.

An advantage of the media is that they bring issues to the attention of Parliament and provide a focus for public concerns. A disadvantage is that the media can whip up public opinion and create hysteria so that the situation is made worse.

An advantage of pressure groups is that they are often able to make informed comment on an issue, because they take an interest in it and may well have experts working for them. A disadvantage is that some of them may use violent or anti-democratic methods

An advantage of the Law Commission is that it is full time and made up of experienced lawyers, so that it is able to produce thorough and well-researched reports. A disadvantage is that the government can ignore its proposals and many of its ideas, like reform of the non-fatal offences that have not been implemented

Hints

A 'sound' answer would have examples or other evidence to back it up. Look back to the examples given in the chapter and not just those in the section on advantages or disadvantages. Add any examples of your own.

You also need to include discussion — i.e. you should comment on the advantages or disadvantages and consider questions such as:

❖ How significant is the advantage or disadvantage?

❖ Is there a solution (if a disadvantage)?

❖ Are there any problems (if an advantage)?

❖ Is the situation getting worse or better?

❖ Does everyone agree?

Suggested reading

Elliott, C. and Quinn, F. (2002) *AS Law*, chapter 6, Pearson Education.

Harris, P. (2006) *An Introduction to Law*, chapter 7, Cambridge University Press.

Chapter 4

Delegated legislation

Delegated legislation (also known as secondary legislation) is law that is not made by Parliament but which has its authority. Parliament does not have the time or resources to make all the law needed in society and there are often circumstances in which it is more convenient for Parliament to delegate the responsibility to others. For example, laws may be needed for a specialised purpose or in a specific geographical location.

Authority (permission) is usually given in a 'parent' Act of Parliament known as an **enabling Act**. This Act creates the framework of the law and then delegates the power to others to make more detailed law in the area. The Act specifies the limits within which the delegated power can operate and also any procedures that must be followed. For example, there is often the requirement that consultation should take place before delegated law is introduced.

Examples of enabling Acts

* The Local Government Act 1972 allows local authorities such as district and county councils to make bylaws.
* The Road Traffic Act 1988 gives the Secretary of State for Transport the authority to make detailed regulations, for example in s.17 to specify the types of crash helmet to be worn by motorcyclists.
* The Access To Justice Act 1999 gives the Lord Chancellor wide powers to alter aspects of the system of state funding for legal cases.

The Disability Discrimination Act 1995 gives ministers power to make regulations on issues such as access by disabled people to transport

Brian Haw's anti-war demonstration in Parliament Square, London

Unreasonableness

The courts will also declare invalid delegated legislation that is unreasonable, under the principle established in *Associated Provincial Picture Houses* v *Wednesbury Corporation* (1948). This may be because the rules are unjust, made in bad faith or are so perverse that no reasonable person would have made them. An example is *Strickland* v *Hayes* (1896), in which a bylaw was passed prohibiting the singing or reciting of any obscene song or ballad, and the use of obscene language generally. This was held to be unreasonable and therefore void because it was drawn too widely and not restricted, for example, to public places and to acts that caused annoyance to the public.

In *R (on the application of Smeaton)* v *Secretary of State for Health* (2002), the validity of the Prescription Only Medicines (Human Use) Amendment (No. 3) Order 2000 was challenged. The order, created by the secretary of state for health, allowed pharmacists to dispense the 'morning-after pill' (or emergency contraceptive) directly to women without the need for a prescription. The challenge was on behalf of an anti-abortion pressure group, who argued that such a pill in effect procured a miscarriage, and that the supply of it thus amounted to a criminal offence under s.59 of the Offences Against the Person Act 1861. This challenge was unsuccessful: the court did not accept that contraception of this nature gave rise to a 'miscarriage' within the current understanding of that word. Thus, the order remains in effect as a valid piece of delegated legislation.

Human Rights Act

In addition, since October 2002, the Human Rights Act 1998 can be used as a ground for a challenge to an administrative decision made by a public authority. Section 6(1) provides that it 'is unlawful for a public authority to act in a way which is incompatible with a Convention right'.

4

Effectiveness of the controls on delegated legislation

There are drawbacks to control by Parliament. The use of the affirmative procedure usually draws Parliament's attention to the delegated legislation, but only on rare occasions is it possible to stop the legislation from being passed. The Scrutiny Committee is more important and has managed to have changes made to some pieces of delegated legislation. Its powers are limited, however, as it can only consider whether the delegated powers have been used correctly, and not the merits of the legislation. In addition, its reports are not binding.

Control by the courts has been successful in many cases but even this has problems. The delegated legislation may have been in force for years before someone affected by it is prepared to challenge it. In addition, the courts cannot amend it, but simply declare that it is 'void'. Another problem is that the discretionary powers conferred on the minister by the enabling Act may be extremely wide, which can result in difficulties in establishing that he or she has acted *ultra vires*.

Advantages of delegated legislation

There are a number of reasons why delegated legislation is needed.

* It saves parliamentary time. For example, the Local Government Pension Scheme Regulations 1995 are extremely detailed and take up 185 pages. Nothing would be gained from debating these in Parliament: the time taken for 650 MPs and 300 or so peers even to read the draft regulations would be better spent on other things.

* There is not enough time for Parliament to consider every detail of every regulation or rule. More than 3,000 SIs are passed every year, so delegated legislation allows Parliament to concentrate on broad issues of policy rather than masses of detail. The Road Traffic Act 1972 included a general requirement for motorcyclists to wear protective helmets, but left the secretary of state to draw up detailed regulations as to the type of helmet required. The Motor Cycles (Protective Helmets) Regulations 1980 contain further detail about the requirements.

* Parliament does not have the knowledge or technical expertise necessary in certain areas (e.g. building regulations or health and safety regulations at work). Delegated legislation allows the use of experts in the relevant areas to make the rules and often follows consultation with a wider body of expert opinion. It allows technical matters to be determined by those competent to do so, and can make use of expert knowledge. The Air Navigation Order 1995

The Secretary of State was left to draw up detailed regulations as to the type of helmet required by motorcyclists

contains 140 pages of highly technical rules (including tables and maps) governing the flying of civil aircraft around the UK; it is doubtful whether any MP (including the minister) would have the technical expertise even to comment on these rules, let alone draft them.

* Local people understand local needs: it is likely that only local people will know what parking restrictions are appropriate for their area. Local authority bylaws, as a result, are more appropriate than broad and general national legislation.

* It allows rapid action to be taken in times of emergency. The Food Protection (Emergency Provisions) Order 1986 was made and laid before Parliament and came into effect less than 2 hours later, prohibiting the movement or slaughter for food of sheep in certain areas thought to have been affected by radioactive fallout from the incident at the Chernobyl power station.

* Delegated legislation is easily revoked if it causes problems. In contrast, an Act of Parliament would require another statute to amend or revoke it, which takes much longer.

* It is impossible for Parliament to foresee all problems that might arise when passing a statute. When problems do arise, delegated legislation to rectify this can be put into place quickly.

Disadvantages of delegated legislation

* The main argument against delegated legislation is that it is undemocratic, as it is made by unelected people rather than Parliament. This is not a problem with bylaws, as local authorities are elected bodies and accountable to the voters in their area, but other bodies such as London Underground are unelected and therefore not accountable to the electorate.

* In addition, much legislation is sub-delegated and made by civil servants in the relevant government departments and then 'rubber stamped' by the minister. This removes the decision still further from elected people.

* The large amount of delegated legislation makes it difficult to keep track of the current law. More than 3,000 SIs are published each year and many of these are lengthy and detailed. Employers frequently complain about the mass of detailed regulations that they have to keep up with.

* There is little publicity compared to Acts of Parliament, so people may be unaware that a particular ruling exists. Although SIs are published and available on the Parliament website, they receive much less attention than statutes. There is nothing in the parent Act to show how many SIs have been made under it. Local authority bylaws receive even less publicity. These are not available even in major public libraries, and local authority websites often make no reference to them. As a result, there is no easy way of knowing what bylaws have been made within a given area.

❖ Control by Parliament is not always effective. For example, very few SIs have affirmative resolution and MPs are too busy to look at the others. Scrutiny Committee recommendations are often ignored.

❖ There is a lack of scrutiny. It has been argued that delegated legislation can be used by governments to make quite significant changes to the law and avoid the inconvenience of submitting them to the scrutiny of the parliamentary process. This is particularly the case with 'Henry VIII clauses', which allow delegated legislation to be used to amend or repeal Acts of Parliament.

Questions

1 List the various ways in which Parliament might be able to control delegated legislation.

2 Suggest one reason why this control might not be effective.

3 Explain what is meant by *ultra vires*.

4 What is substantive *ultra vires*? Give an example.

5 What is procedural *ultra vires*? Give an example.

Extension exercises

1 Henry VIII clauses

A clause is sometimes added to a bill to enable the government to repeal or amend the bill after it has become an Act of Parliament. Such provisions are known as 'Henry VIII clauses'.

The House of Lords Select Committee on the Scrutiny of Delegated Powers, in its first report of 1992–93, defined a Henry VIII clause as 'a provision in a bill which enables primary legislation to be amended or repealed by subordinate legislation, with or without further parliamentary scrutiny'.

The clauses were so named from the Statute of Proclamations 1539, which gave King Henry VIII power to legislate by proclamation. They have become increasingly common since the 1950s. For example, the Hallmarking Act 1973 gave ministers the power to vary, supplement or replace parts of the Act, an extraordinarily wide power.

Arguably, a more legitimate use is in allowing ministers to alter legislation that is incompatible with European Union law. This is provided for in the European Communities Act 1972, and similarly the Human Rights Act 1998 gives powers to amend legislation to ensure compliance with the European Convention on Human Rights.

However, the clauses remain controversial because they allow delegated legislation to be used to amend Acts of Parliament, and critics have argued that they are an attempt to extend the power of the government to bypass Parliament.

In 2006 there was widespread concern about clause 2 of the Legislative and Regulatory Reform Bill, which gave ministers power to 'make provision amending, repealing or replacing any legislation' in order to reform legislation or implement Law Commission proposals. In an

6 Is there any evidence in the article to suggest that the system is working quite well?

7 What does the writer mean when he says that 'there is simply no mechanism for airing the collective choices that are made every day on our behalf'? Does the writer regard this as a serious criticism?

Exam hints

Most questions will ask you to identify and describe the different types of delegated legislation. Sometimes the question will ask you to choose two or three. To get high marks, you will need to include examples. Read the question carefully — some questions ask you to comment on advantages and disadvantages, but not all. Avoid including information the question doesn't ask for. You won't lose marks for including unnecessary material, but you will use up time you need for the things that are relevant.

Sample exam questions

1 Describe three types of delegated legislation, giving examples.

(15 marks)

Task

Look at the following answer. For each part decide whether the answer should be graded as 'limited', 'some', 'clear' or 'sound'. Rewrite the whole answer as a 'sound' response.

Orders in Council are used mainly in emergency situations when Parliament is not sitting. These legislative processes are made by the monarch and the Privy Council and are rarely used.

Statutory instruments — ministers and government departments can be given the power, in the enabling Act, to make statutory instruments relating to the jurisdiction of their ministry. These take the form of rules, regulations and orders. They apply to the whole country in their effect. They cover areas such as road traffic signs, town and country planning general development orders.

The last form of delegated legislation is bylaws. These are made by local authorities such as county or district councils. They are local in effect, only applying in the area of the council concerned, and are involved with such things as parking restrictions, and activities which can or cannot be carried out in certain public places. Some public bodies such as British Rail can make bylaws to enforce rules covering behaviour in public places, e.g. the ban on smoking in the London Underground.

2 Discuss the advantages and disadvantages of delegated legislation as a source of law. (15 marks)

Some questions will ask for a specific number of advantages or disadvantages. When answering a general question like this you can mention several, but you should try to write about three in some detail.

Task

Write an answer to this question using the following approach:

* ❖ Choose three advantages. For each advantage, write one sentence explaining what it is. Add a sentence giving an example or a piece of evidence. In a third sentence, make some kind of comment about the advantage.
* ❖ Choose three disadvantages. Write three sentences, following the outline above.

How would you adapt this answer if you were only asked to write about advantages?

3 Identify and discuss the means by which delegated legislation is controlled by both the courts and Parliament. (15 marks)

Table 4.2 summarises the parliamentary and judicial controls over delegated legislation. You may find it helpful to summarise your own notes in this way.

Table 4.2 Parliamentary and judicial controls over delegated legislation

Controls by Parliament	Controls by the courts
1 Enabling Act defines nature and scope of the powers.	1 Delegated legislation may be challenged under the judicial review procedure, on the basis of *ultra vires*.
2 Negative resolution procedure — 40 days, passes unless objections.	2 There are two main grounds for judicial review:
3 Affirmative resolution procedure (approval required by both Houses of Parliament).	❖ Procedural *ultra vires*, e.g. that a minister has failed to follow the correct procedures for making delegated legislation: *Aylesbury Mushroom* case (1972).
4 House of Commons Standing Committee on Delegated Legislation. Delegated legislation is examined by Joint Committee on Statutory Instruments, also referred to as the Scrutiny Committee.	❖ Substantive *ultra vires* — challenge on the basis of alleged abuses of delegated law-making power, e.g. that the use of delegated power exceeds that permitted: *Attorney General* v *Fulham Corporation* (1921); *R (on the application of Smeaton)* v *Secretary of State for Health* (2002).
5 The Delegated Powers Scrutiny Committee in the House of Lords can decide whether the provisions in a bill to delegate legislative power are inappropriate.	
6 House of Lords Select Committee on the Merits of Statutory Instruments.	

Task

Use Table 4.2 as a starting point for writing an answer to the question, but remember that in the exam you are expected to write your answer as continuous prose rather than in table form. What do you think it needs to make it a better answer? Write a 'sound' answer to this question.

Suggested reading

Ingman, T. (2006) *The English Legal Process,* chapter 8, Oxford University Press.

Mitchell, A. (2008) *AS Law*, Routledge-Cavendish.

Mitchell, A. (2007) 'Delegated legislation matters!', *A-Level Law Review*, Vol. 2, No. 2, pp. 6–9.

Zander, M. (2004) *The Law-Making Process*, chapter 2, Cambridge University Press.

Chapter 5

Statutory interpretation

Acts of Parliament (also known as **statutes**) have a unique and important status as sources of law. Parliament is the sovereign law-making body in English law and this means that Parliament can alter the law in whatever ways it chooses. Acts of Parliament cannot be challenged by other institutions and only Parliament itself can alter what a statute says.

Judges' constitutional role is that they must apply Acts of Parliament *as they are written*. They are not at liberty to give their own interpretation or to modify the meaning that Parliament intends.

As a result, care is taken to try to ensure that the meaning of Acts of Parliament is clear. Unfortunately, it is inevitable that from time to time disputes will arise over what particular sections mean or how they should be applied. These disputes come before the courts and it is for judges to determine how such disputes are resolved. **Statutory interpretation** is the name given to the process by which judges decide what particular words in statutes mean.

Why do statutes need to be interpreted?

* There may be a mistake in the drafting so that the words used do not mean what was intended. This happened in *Fisher* v *Bell* (1961) where the Act referred to an 'offer for sale', which in contract law had a technical meaning that differed from the everyday meaning. The result was that something could be displayed in a shop window and yet was not being offered for sale.
* Words can change in their meaning. For example, in *Cheeseman* v *DPP* (1990), the court decided that the word 'passenger' had a different meaning today to that in use in 1847 when the Act in question had been drafted.

In *London and North Eastern Railway Co.* v *Berriman* (1946), Mrs Berriman was unable to obtain any compensation when her husband was killed while carrying out maintenance work (oiling points on the railway line). The relevant statute said that a look-out should be provided to warn the rail workers of approaching trains when relaying or repairing the track. Berriman was maintaining the track, not relaying or repairing it. The words 'relaying' and 'repairing' were given their literal meaning, so the company did not have to have a look-out and Berriman's widow was not entitled to compensation.

Despite Lord Denning's observation in *Nothman* v *London Borough of Barnet* (1978) that 'the literal method is now completely out of date', the literal rule is still used by judges. It was used, for instance, in *Cutter* v *Eagle Star Insurance Co.* (1998), in which the House of Lords decided that the word 'road' in the Road Traffic Act 1988 could not include a car park. The issue was significant because the insurance company would have to pay compensation only if a car was parked on a road.

In *The Governor of HMP Wandsworth* v *Kinderis* (2007), the defendant was wanted in Lithuania and the UK for alleged sexual offences, but a dilemma arose as to whether he should face trial in the UK or, as the Extradition Act 2003 suggested, he could choose his own extradition and thus avoid trial in the UK. The High Court stated that the 2003 Act was flawed on this issue and rendered domestic law 'subordinate...regardless of the relative seriousness of the charges in this country or abroad'. Lord Justice Laws acknowledged that Parliament may have intended domestic law to take priority, but on literal interpretation it did not. Asked to interpret this section (presumably by using the purposive approach) he stated: 'We cannot correct the mistakes of the legislation by adopting impermissible modes of interpretation.'

Advantages of the literal rule

❖ The main argument used to justify the rule is that it respects the sovereignty of Parliament and prevents unelected judges making law. Viscount Simmonds in *Magor and St Mellons RDC* v *Newport Corporation* (1952) argued that it was not open to judges to fill in gaps, as Lord Denning wanted, or otherwise alter statutes. If a gap was disclosed then 'the remedy lies in an Amending Act'.

❖ The literal rule encourages certainty and, because there is less scope for interpretation, there is likely to be less litigation. People know where they stand because the wording will not change. This argument was expressed well by Lord Simon in *Stock* v *Frank Jones (Tipton) Ltd* (1978), when he claimed that leaving Parliament to make changes was 'far preferable to judicial contortion of the law to meet apparently hard cases with the result that ordinary citizens and their advisers hardly know where they stand'.

❖ It will often lead to quick decisions because the answer can be found by referring to dictionaries, though this will only be the case when the words are clear and unambiguous.

5

Disadvantages of the literal rule

❖ Its use can lead to unfair or unjust decisions, as for example in *London and North Eastern Railway Co.* v *Berriman* (1946).

❖ It can also lead to absurd decisions that were clearly not what Parliament intended. Examples of this would be *Fisher* v *Bell* (1961) and *Whitely* v *Chappell* (1868).

❖ Words may have more than one meaning, making it difficult to apply a dictionary definition.

❖ It is not always possible to word an Act so as to cover every situation. Circumstances that were not anticipated by Parliament may occur.

❖ The Law Commission has been critical of the literal rule. In a 1969 report, it said that 'to place undue emphasis on the literal meaning of words is to assume an unattainable perfection in draftsmanship'.

❖ The literal rule gives judges little discretion to adapt the law to changing times.

❖ The literal rule is likely to become less relevant because of the growing importance of European law. When applying EU law and the **Human Rights Act**, judges are required to use the purposive approach.

Questions

1 Give a one-sentence definition of the literal rule.

2 Explain the facts of two cases that illustrate it.

3 Identify what you think are the two strongest arguments in favour of the literal rule and the two strongest against.

The golden rule

The golden rule is a modification of the literal rule and says that judges should use the literal rule unless it would produce an absurd result. Lord Blackburn explained it in *River Wear Commissioners* v *Adamson* (1877) as 'giving the words their ordinary signification, unless when so applied they produce an absurdity or inconvenience so great' as to convince the court that it could not have been Parliament's intention to give the words their ordinary meaning.

There are two views on how far the rule should be used: the **narrow application** and the **wider application**.

Narrow application of the golden rule

Under the narrow application, proposed by Lord Reid in *Jones* v *DPP* (1962), if a word is ambiguous the judge may choose between possible meanings of the word in order to avoid an absurd outcome. He argued that if a word had more than one meaning 'then you can choose between those meanings, but beyond this you cannot go'.

For example, in *R* v *Allen* (1872), the issue was that s.57 of the Offences Against the Person Act 1861 made it an offence to marry if you were already married. The court decided that 'marry' could have two meanings: to become legally married or to go through a ceremony of marriage. The court decided that 'marry' was ambiguous. This was relevant because Allen argued that since he was already married, his second marriage could not be valid, so he could not be guilty of bigamy. It would clearly be absurd to apply the first meaning because no one could then be convicted of the offence.

Wider application of the golden rule

The wider application is where there is only one meaning, but this would lead to an absurd or repugnant situation, which for policy reasons would be unacceptable. Note that normally if there is only one meaning and it is absurd or there are several equally absurd meanings, the literal rule should be applied. For the wider application of the golden rule to be used, the court would have to be persuaded of the policy issues in allowing what in effect would be a rewriting of the Act.

A clear example is *Re Sigsworth* (1935). Under the Administration of Estates Act 1925, the property of a person who died without making a will would pass to his or her next of kin. In this case, Sigsworth had murdered his mother. It was clearly repugnant that a person who had murdered his mother could then under the provisions of a statute inherit her property. In the case of *Adler* v *George* (1964), s.3 of the Official Secrets Act 1920 made it an offence to be found 'in the vicinity of a prohibited place'. The accused was arrested *inside* the prohibited place; therefore, he argued that he could not be convicted. It was clearly both repugnant and absurd that the offence could be committed by causing an obstruction in the vicinity of a prohibited place but not within the place itself.

In *R* v *Registrar General ex parte Smith* (1991), the applicant was detained in a secure mental hospital after killing two people, including someone he killed while under the delusion that he was killing his adoptive mother. He was now applying under s.5 of the Adoption Act 1976 for a copy of his birth certificate. The court held that, despite the absolute nature of the duty in s.5 to supply the information requested, public policy allowed the request to be refused, because there was a significant risk that his natural mother's life would be in danger if he discovered her identity.

Advantages of the golden rule

❖ The courts can alter the wording and make sense of absurd or repugnant wording.
❖ It respects the authority of Parliament because in all other circumstances the literal rule should be used.

5

Disadvantages of the golden rule

❖ Michael Zander describes it as 'a feeble parachute', because it allows judges to change the wording only when it is absurd or repugnant. It can therefore only be used in limited circumstances.

❖ He also notes that it is 'an unpredictable safety valve', because there are no real guidelines on when it should be used. What seems to be absurd to one judge may not be absurd to another.

❖ The Law Commission (1969) argued that the rule was of limited value and noted that the rule provided no clear means to test the existence of the characteristics of absurdity, inconsistency or inconvenience, or to measure their quality or extent. As it seemed that 'absurdity' was in practice judged by reference to whether a particular interpretation was irreconcilable with the general policy of the legislature, 'the golden rule turns out to be a less explicit form of the mischief rule'.

Questions

1 Explain the narrow application of the golden rule.
2 Name a case and explain how it fits the definition.
3 Explain the wider application of the golden rule.
4 Name a case and explain how it fits the definition.
5 Identify two advantages of the golden rule.
6 Why does Michael Zander describe the golden rule as 'a feeble parachute'?

The mischief rule

This is the oldest rule and was first used in *Heydon's Case* in 1584. In this case it was held that the court should consider four things:

❖ What the common law was before the Act was passed.
❖ What the mischief was that the Act was designed to remedy.
❖ The remedy proposed in the Act.
❖ The reason for the remedy.

The judge should therefore look for the mischief that the Act was designed to remedy, and interpret it to ensure that this purpose is achieved. This may mean disregarding the literal meaning and adding words. Lord Denning later spoke of filling the gaps that Parliament had left inadvertently, but his view was too radical for most judges to follow.

In *Jones* v *Wrotham Park Settled Estates* (1980), Lord Diplock said that the mischief rule should not be used in all cases, but only when the following circumstances apply:

❖ The mischief can be seen clearly from the Act.
❖ It was apparent that Parliament had overlooked the problem.
❖ The words required to be added could be identified with a high degree of certainty.

that compatibility, even though it was contrary to what Parliament had intended in s.41. In his book *The English Legal System*, Alisdair Gillespie argues that 'the 1998 Act does not provide the judiciary with an opportunity to turn its back on statutory interpretation but rather provides them with the ability to follow the legislature's desire that that the law should comply with the ECHR'.

Questions

1 Explain in your own words how the purposive approach differs from the mischief rule.

2 Identify a case in which the approach was used and one in which its use was felt to be inappropriate.

3 What view of the purposive approach did the Law Commission take?

4 What did Lord Scarman attempt to do? How successful was he?

5 In which two cases did Lord Denning appear to be arguing for the purposive approach?

6 Suggest one disadvantage of the purposive approach.

7 Why does UK membership of the European Union mean that the purposive approach is more likely to be used?

8 What does s.3 of the Human Rights Act 1998 require judges to do? Is this the same as using the purposive approach?

9 In *R* v *A* were judges following the intentions of Parliament?

Extension exercises

1 *Magor and St Mellons RDC* v *Newport Corporation* (1952)

Facts

❖ There was some reorganisation of local authority boundaries.

❖ Under s.34 of the Newport Extension Act 1934, the county borough of Newport was extended to take in parts of two rural districts — Magor and St Mellons.

❖ The Act provided for reasonable compensation to be paid to the two rural district councils (RDCs).

❖ Immediately after the Act took effect, the two RDCs were amalgamated by an order made by the minister. As the two RDCs mentioned in the Act no longer existed, the question for the court was whether the new RDC was entitled to the compensation instead.

❖ The task for the judges was to decide how to interpret the Act and apply it to the case.

Lord Denning in the Court of Appeal noted:

We do not sit here to pull the language of Parliament to pieces and make nonsense of it… We sit here to find the intention of Parliament and of Ministers and carry it out, and we do this better by filling in the gaps and making sense of the enactment than by opening it up to destructive analysis.

I think that Parliament has really made its intention plain enough. The Act which conferred the title to compensation conferred it on each of the district councils, not in its own right, but in the right of its ratepayers... The district council was the hand to receive the compensation, but it only received it so that it might give relief to the ratepayers for the increased burden which the change of boundaries cast on them. The amalgamation changed the legal identity of the two councils, but it did not change the ratepayers at all, nor did it relieve them of their burdens; and there is no reason why the amalgamated council should not claim the compensation due to the ratepayers.

Questions

1 Summarise Lord Denning's argument in your own words.

2 Which of the rules of interpretation does he appear to be using?

Viscount Simmonds in the House of Lords noted:

The duty of the court is to interpret the words that the legislature has used. Those words may be ambiguous, but, even if they are, the power and duty of the court to travel outside them on a voyage of discovery are strictly limited.

The proposition that the court must proceed to fill in the gaps cannot be supported. It appears to me to be a naked usurpation of the legislative function under the thin guise of interpretation, and it is the less justifiable when it is guesswork with what material the legislature would, if it had discovered the gap, have filled it in. If a gap is disclosed the remedy lies in an amending Act.

Questions

1 Summarise Viscount Simmonds' argument in your own words.

2 Which of the rules of interpretation does he appear to be using?

3 What solution does he propose to the financial hardship being suffered by the ratepayers?

2 Three decisions in the 1960s

Read through each of the extracts from judgements which were all made by the same judge.

1 Everybody knows that this was an Act intended to clean up the streets, to enable people to walk the streets without being molested or solicited by common prostitutes. Viewed in that way it can matter little whether the prostitute is soliciting while in the street or is standing in a doorway or on a balcony or at a window.

2 It is perfectly clear that according to the ordinary law of contract the display of an article with a price on it in a shop window is merely an invitation to treat. It is in no sense an offer for sale...in those circumstances I am driven to the conclusion that no offence was here committed. At first sight it sounds absurd that knives of this sort cannot be manufactured, sold, hired, lent or given, but apparently they can be displayed in a shop window. [But] it is not for this court to supply the omission.

3 Here is a section in an Act of Parliament designed to prevent interference with members of Her Majesty's forces. It would be extraordinary, I venture to think it absurd, if an indictable offence was...created when the obstruction took place outside the precincts of the station, albeit in the vicinity, and no offence at all was created if the obstruction occurred on the station itself.

Order Act 1986, the House of Lords referred expressly to the Law Commission report on which the Act was based.

Hansard

Wording might also be explained by examining what was said in the debates in Parliament (found in *Hansard*, which prints transcripts of House of Commons debates). In *Davis* v *Johnson* (1979), Lord Denning argued that *not* to refer to *Hansard* was like groping around in the dark without putting the light on. While the House of Lords initially rejected this, Lord Denning's view was eventually accepted — subject to strict conditions — by the House of Lords in *Pepper* v *Hart* (1993). *Pepper* v *Hart* overruled *Davis* v *Johnson* and allowed reference to *Hansard* when:

❖ wording in a statute is ambiguous, obscure or leads to an absurdity
❖ the material relied upon consists of one or more statements by a minister or other promoter of the bill, together if necessary with such other parliamentary material as is required to understand such statements and their effect
❖ the statements relied upon are clear

The Law Lords did not anticipate frequent use to be made of *Hansard*. In the leading judgement, Lord Browne-Wilkinson said that, in most cases, reference to parliamentary material would not throw any light on the matter. However, the judgement has been criticised by commentators such as Aileen Kavanagh, who argue that restricting the use to statements by ministers confuses the distinction between the executive and the legislature (which is dealt with in more detail in Chapter 2) and fails to acknowledge that the intention of Parliament in the wording it chooses may not reflect the wishes of the minister or other sponsor of the bill.

In *R* v *Deegan* (1998), an application to consider *Hansard* was rejected because what ministers had said was not sufficiently clear, and Lord Bingham noted in *R* v *Secretary of State for the Environment ex parte Spath Holme* (2001) that:

> *Unless parliamentary statements are indeed clear...the court is likely to be drawn into comparing one statement with another, appraising the meaning and effect of what was said and considering what was left unsaid and why. In the course of such an exercise the court would come uncomfortably close to questioning the proceedings in Parliament contrary to Article 9 of the Bill of Rights 1689 and might even violate that important constitutional prohibition.*

Recent cases have suggested that the courts may limit the use of *Pepper* v *Hart* to those cases against the government. In *R* v *A* (2001), Lord Hope said that essentially reference to *Hansard* is 'available for the purpose only of *preventing* the executive from placing a different meaning on words used in legislation from that which they attributed to those words when promoting the legislation in Parliament'.

Lord Mackay, dissenting in *Pepper* v *Hart,* argued that use of *Hansard* would increase the expense of litigation without contributing much of value to the quality of decision-making. On the other hand, in considering such objections to the use of *Hansard*, Lord Bridge said that he found it 'difficult to suppose that the additional cost of litigation or any other ground of objection can justify the court continuing to wear blinkers which...conceal the vital clue to the intended meaning of an enactment'.

When dealing with cases involving Acts that introduced either an international convention or a European directive into English law, it was held in *Three Rivers DC* v *Bank of England* (1996) that the *Pepper* v *Hart* principle did not have to be applied so narrowly because it was important to construe the statute purposively and consistently with any European materials, such as directives.

In conclusion, it seems that with the increasing use of the purposive approach, it is likely that use of external aids will also increase. However, using external aids will always be more controversial than using internal aids, partly because the courts are in danger of treating materials that are not part of the Act as having the same status as the Act itself, and also because of the danger referred to above of blurring the distinction between the intention of the executive and the intention of Parliament.

Questions

1 Identify a case in which reference to a dictionary was helpful.

2 Explain what is meant by 'unanimity' and name a case in which reference to a dictionary did not achieve unanimity.

3 For how long have explanatory notes accompanied Acts? What does Alisdair Gillespie mean when he describes them as 'a creature of the executive'?

4 What view did Lord Denning express in *Davis* v *Johnson* (1979) about the use of *Hansard*?

5 Under what circumstances in *Pepper* v *Hart* (1993) did the House of Lords say that *Hansard* could be referred to?

6 What limitation on the use of *Hansard* was suggested by Lord Hope in *R* v *A* (2001)?

Extension exercise

Read the following comments.

1 From a lecture given by Lord Steyn, May 2000:
Arguably the House may have had in mind in Pepper v Hart *that an intention derivable from the Financial Secretary's statement ought to be imputed to Parliament. If that were the case, the reasoning would rest on a complete fiction. My view is that the only relevant intention of Parliament can be the intention of the composite and artificial body to enact the statute as printed.*

Chapter 6

The doctrine of precedent

What is judicial precedent?

Judicial precedent is the idea that a decision made in one court must be followed by other courts in the future if there is a similar case. It is sometimes referred to as *stare decisis* — stand by the decision. Michael Zander describes precedents as the raw material from which lawyers and judges distil rules of law. In simple terms, when deciding a case, judges will look at previous cases that appear to be based on similar principles. If the rule created in a precedent seems to apply to the case being considered, then it will be followed. For instance, in the case of *Nettleship* v *Weston* (1971), the Court of Appeal decided that the standard of care required of a learner driver was the same as that required of any other driver, namely that of a reasonably competent and experienced driver. It is clear therefore that in any cases where a driver causes an accident, they are to be judged by this standard and not on the basis of how much driving experience they actually have.

In *Nettleship* v *Weston* (1971), the Court of Appeal decided that the standard of care required of a learner driver was that of a reasonably competent and experienced driver

However, this simple description does not fully explain how precedent works. There is a hierarchy of courts, for example, meaning that not all courts are equal in their ability to make precedents.

The development of common law

The phrase 'common law' is used to describe the law that is developed by judges. We refer for example to murder having a 'common law definition'. By this we mean that the definition of murder has developed through the decisions of judges in various cases and has never been defined by Parliament. In contrast, we talk about theft having a 'statutory definition' because the definition has been drawn up by Parliament in a statute (the Theft Act 1968).

The idea of 'common law' originates from the time of King Henry II (1154–89). Until then much of the law in remote parts of the country was based on local custom. Henry was anxious to extend his rule over the whole country and therefore he divided it into 'circuits' or areas for judges to decide cases in. Gradually, judges administered justice in different parts of the country, using rules and customs that were being applied in other places as well. The result was that the law became uniform or 'common' throughout the land.

There are many areas of law where nearly all of the rules are made by judges. For example, most of the main rules on the **formation and discharge of contract** are judge-made, as are the main rules covering the **tort of negligence**. Both areas of law are explored in later chapters.

We shall also see in Chapter 15 that some of the most significant principles of criminal law are derived from judicial decisions, including the definitions of both recklessness (from *R v Cunningham*, 1957) and intention (from *R v Mohan*, 1976). Most of the rules in the offence of murder are judge-made and, even in other areas of criminal law, where there are statutory rules, judges have developed these rules through precedent. For instance, in Chapter 16 when we explore non-fatal offences, you will notice how the definitions of the offences in sections 18, 20 and 47 of the Offences Against the Person Act 1861 have been amplified significantly by judicial decisions.

The mechanics of precedent
Hierarchy

In order for the system of judicial precedent to work, there must be some rules that judges are required to follow to ensure some consistency in the law. One way of doing this is to have a system of **hierarchy**, where decisions in the higher courts bind the lower courts. Some of the courts are also bound by their own previous decisions.

European courts

Since joining the EU in 1973, on matters of EU law (e.g. interpretation of treaties), decisions made by the European Court of Justice (ECJ) are binding on all the courts in the UK. The ECJ is not bound by its own previous decisions and can overrule them. This flexibility is a reflection of the practice in most European countries and is in contrast to the approach used in the UK. In addition, under the Human Rights Act 1998, decisions of the European Court of Human Rights (ECHR) must be applied by UK courts.

The House of Lords

The House of Lords is currently the highest appeal court in England. Under s.23 of the Constitutional Reform Act 2005, the jurisdiction of the Appellate Committee of the House of Lords will be removed and transferred to a new **Supreme Court for the United Kingdom**. The House of Lords is bound by the decisions of the ECJ, but as the highest appeal court, its decisions bind all the other English courts.

The House of Lords hears only a few cases each year (74 in 2005), and there are only 12 Law Lords altogether. As a result, there are few major law changes each year and there should be consistency between decisions — five of the 12 judges will usually hear each case, though in exceptional cases as many as nine may sit, as happened in *A and others* v *Secretary of State for the Home Department* (2004).

Originally, except where a decision was made **per incuriam** ('in error'), the House of Lords was bound by its own previous decisions. This was established in *London Street Tramways* v *London County Council* (1898), and ensured certainty in the law. The only way that the law could be changed was by Parliament. For example, in *DPP* v *Smith* (1961), the House of Lords ruled that someone could be guilty of murder if a reasonable person would have foreseen that death or serious injury would result. While this decision was criticised widely, it could not be changed by the courts. In the event, Parliament changed the law by legislating in 1967.

However, in 1966 the Lord Chancellor issued a **Practice Statement** (or Direction) that stated:

> *Their Lordships regard the use of precedent as an indispensable foundation upon which to decide what is the law and its application to individual cases. It provides at least some degree of certainty upon which individuals can rely in the conduct of their affairs, as well as a basis for the orderly development of legal rules. Their Lordships nevertheless recognise that too rigid adherence to precedent may lead to injustice in a particular case and also unduly restrict the proper development of the law. They propose therefore to modify their present practice and, while treating decisions of this house as normally binding, to depart from a decision when it appears right to do so.*

In a press release accompanying the statement, the Lord Chancellor added that 'an example of a case in which the House might think it right to depart from a precedent

is where they consider that the earlier decision was influenced by the existence of conditions which no longer prevail, and in modern conditions the law ought to be different'.

This power has been used sparingly. In *Jones* v *Secretary of State for Social Services* (1972), four of the seven Law Lords hearing the case felt that the earlier House of Lords decision in *Re Dowling* (1967) was wrong, but all seven judges agreed that the mere finding that an earlier decision was wrong was not enough to justify overruling it. Another example is the case of *R* v *Knuller* (1973), in which, despite criticising the decision in an earlier case (*R* v *Shaw,* 1962), Lord Reid and the other Law Lords followed it, arguing that the Practice Statement did not mean that 'whenever we think a previous decision was wrong we should reverse it'.

In various cases between 1966 and 1975, Lord Reid devised criteria to determine when the Practice Statement should apply, and these had the effect of restricting its use. Research by Alan Patterson found that between 1966 and 1980, it had the option of overruling itself in 29 cases, but it chose to do so in only eight. Interestingly, he commented that in a further ten cases at least one Law Lord had been willing to overrule the previous decision, and that in a considerable number of others, the House of Lords had been able to get round earlier cases by distinguishing them (i.e. deciding that the facts are sufficiently different to allow a different decision to be reached).

However, the House of Lords has used its power to overrule its own previous decisions in a number of cases:

1 *British Railways Board* v *Herrington* (1972) overruled *Addie* v *Dumbreck* (1929) on the duty of care owed to a child trespasser. Lord Diplock's justification for using the Practice Statement was 'the general development of legal concepts since 1929 as to the source of one man's duty to take steps for the duty of another'.

2 In *Murphy* v *Brentwood District Council* (1990), the House of Lords, with seven judges sitting, overruled *Anns* v *Merton London Borough Council* (1977) on the duty of care owed by local authorities.

3 *Pepper* v *Hart* (1993) overruled the previous House of Lords ruling in *Davis* v *Johnson* (1979), which banned the use of *Hansard* in statutory interpretation.

4 *R* v *Shivpuri* (1986) was the first criminal case in which the power under the Practice Statement was used. The House of Lords overruled *Anderton* v *Ryan* (1985) on attempting the impossible in theft. The earlier case had been widely criticised and Lord Bridge argued that, if a serious error had distorted the law, the sooner it was corrected the better.

5 Within 10 months, the Lords used the power again in a criminal case. *R* v *Howe* (1987) overruled *DPP* v *Lynch* (1975) on whether it was open to someone to use duress as a defence to a murder charge. In *Lynch*, the Lords had decided by 3 to 2 that it was; it was held unanimously in *Howe* that it was not.

The Court of Appeal

This Court of Appeal is divided into two divisions, which deal solely with either **civil cases** or **criminal cases**. Both divisions are bound by decisions of the House of Lords and the ECJ, but the decisions of one division do not bind the other.

The Court of Appeal (Civil Division)

Lord Denning had long argued that the Practice Statement should apply to the Court of Appeal. Initially, he tried to argue that the Court of Appeal should not be bound by earlier House of Lords decisions if it believed them to be wrong. Inevitably, these attempts were doomed to fail. In the case of *Broome* v *Cassell & Co. Ltd* (1972), for example, Lord Hailsham rebuked Denning, saying: 'It is not open to the Court of Appeal to…ignore decisions of the House of Lords.'

The Civil Division of the Court of Appeal is also bound by its own previous decisions. The case of *Young* v *Bristol Aeroplane Co. Ltd* (1944) confirmed this, but set out three exceptions that would allow the Civil Division to depart from its own previous decisions:

1 *The previous decision was made* per incuriam. In other words, the precedent was made in ignorance of some authority, either statutory or case law, which would have led to a different conclusion, e.g. the decision was made without considering a relevant Act of Parliament. In *Rakhit* v *Carty* (1990), the Court of Appeal declined to follow earlier decisions on the **Rent Act 1977** because they had been made in ignorance of a relevant provision of the Act.

2 *There are two Court of Appeal decisions that conflict.* An example of this occurred in *Tiverton Estates Ltd* v *Wearwell Ltd* (1974), which concerned the meaning of s.40 of the **Law of Property Act 1925**. The Court of Appeal chose to follow older precedents rather than the decision in *Law* v *Jones* (1974).

3 *A later decision of the House of Lords overrules a previous decision in the Court of Appeal.* In *Family Housing Association* v *Jones* (1990), the Court of Appeal felt obliged to ignore earlier Court of Appeal precedents, because they seemed to be in conflict with later House of Lords decisions.

Lord Denning tried to challenge the rule in *Young* on the basis that the Court of Appeal had imposed this limitation on itself so it could also remove it. The House of Lords took a different view and in both *Gallie* v *Lee* (1969) and *Davis* v *Johnson* (1979) overruled Denning. One argument the Lords used was that there were more judges in the Court of Appeal than in the House of Lords, and it heard more cases. The result of giving more power to the Court of Appeal would be to have more conflicting decisions, more uncertainty in the law and more confusion.

Note however that there are now two additional exceptions to the rule. It seems clear following s.3 of the **European Communities Act 1972** that the Court of Appeal can ignore a previous judgement which is inconsistent with European Community law or a decision of the ECJ.

Similarly, in s.2 of the **Human Rights Act 1998**, the courts are bound to take into account judgements of the ECHR, and presumably apply them rather than a previous Court of Appeal judgement.

The Court of Appeal (Criminal Division)

The Criminal Division of the Court of Appeal is usually bound by its own previous decisions, but is allowed to take a more flexible approach. Besides the exceptions in *Young*, it is clear from the case of *R v Spencer* (1985) that the Criminal Division is allowed to depart from its earlier decisions in the interests of justice or where a person's liberty is at stake. In *R v Simpson* (2003), a five-person Court of Appeal decided that it would overrule an earlier decision, not because the liberty of the defendant was at issue, but rather to ensure justice for the public at large and maintain confidence in the criminal justice system. LCJ Woolf said that the discretion to depart from a previous precedent was not to be exercised lightly, but he ruled that the defendant should not be allowed to rely on a wrongly-decided case to provide a technical defence to a confiscation order made following his conviction for VAT fraud.

Divisional court

It appears that, following the decision in *R v Greater Manchester Coroner ex parte Tal* (1985), the divisional court is in the same position as the Criminal Division of the Court of Appeal.

The High Court

The divisional court and the ordinary High Court are all bound by the decisions of the Court of Appeal, the House of Lords and the ECJ. The Family Division and the Chancery Division, civil courts, are bound by their own previous decisions. There is more flexibility in the Queen's Bench Division when hearing appeals on criminal cases. The ordinary High Court is bound by the decisions of the divisional courts but not by its own previous decisions. However, if High Court decisions are reported, they are regarded as persuasive. This means that another High Court judge in a similar case is expected to follow the previous decision, unless there are good reasons not to.

Mark Dyball/Alamy

The ordinary High Court is bound by the decisions of the divisional courts but not by its own previous decisions

The Crown Court

The Crown Court is bound by the decisions of all the higher courts. Its decisions are not binding precedent, although the decisions of High Court judges sitting in the Crown Court could form persuasive precedent if reported, but Crown Court cases rarely are. The court is not bound to follow its own decisions.

Magistrates' and County Courts

These courts are bound by the courts above them, but their own decisions do not form binding or persuasive precedent, as they are courts of inferior jurisdiction.

Tribunals

Some tribunals have their own system of precedent. For example, decisions of the Employment Appeal Tribunal are binding on employment tribunals.

Questions

1 What is the general principle of hierarchy?

2 What does the Practice Statement 1966 enable the House of Lords to do?

3 Give an example of the Lords refusing to use the Practice Statement.

4 Name two cases in which it was used.

5 Which judge tried to get the same power for the Court of Appeal? How successful was he?

6 In which case were circumstances set out that enabled the Court of Appeal to depart from its earlier decisions?

7 Under what circumstances is the Criminal Division of the Court of Appeal allowed to depart from its own earlier decisions?

Extension exercise

Read the following extract adapted from the judgement of Scarman LJ in *Tiverton Estates Ltd* v *Wearwell* (1974).

> *The Court of Appeal operates a central but intermediate position in our legal system. To a large extent, the consistency and certainty of the law depend on it. If therefore, throwing aside the restraints of* Young v Bristol Aeroplane Company Ltd, *one division of the court should refuse to follow another because it believed the other's decision to be wrong, there would be a risk of confusion and doubt arising where there should be consistency and certainty. The appropriate forum for the correction of the Court of Appeal's errors is the House of Lords.*

Questions

1 Explain what is meant by 'central but intermediate position'.

2 Explain the restraints of *Young* v *Bristol Aeroplane Co. Ltd* (1944).

3 What benefits does Scarman LJ see in having these restraints?

4 In which case in 1978 did Lord Denning attempt to challenge the view being taken by Scarman LJ?

5 What was the outcome of this challenge?

6 To what extent do the restraints identified by Scarman LJ apply to the Criminal Division of the Court of Appeal?

Ratio decidendi

On deciding a case, a judge will set out his or her reasons in a **judgement**. This judgement sets out the facts of the case and the legal principles that the judge has used to reach his or her decision. These are known as the *ratio decidendi* ('the reason for deciding') and they are what become the precedent (rather than the facts of the case). Sir Rupert Cross described *ratio decidendi* as 'any rule…treated by the judge as a necessary step in reaching his conclusion'. Michael Zander defines it as 'a proposition of law which decides the case, in the light or in the context of the material facts'.

An example of *ratio decidendi* is the rule in *R* v *Nedrick* (1986), confirmed in *R* v *Woollin* (1997), that if a jury considers that the defendant foresaw death or serious injury as a virtual certainty, oblique intention may be inferred. Another example is the judgement in *R* v *Cunningham* (1957) that to be reckless you have to know there is a risk of the unlawful consequence and decide to take the risk.

Nonetheless, identifying the *ratio* (as it is usually termed) is not always easy — in part because judges do not always make it clear *why* they have reached their decision or draw attention to the parts of their judgement that they regard as significant. They may give several reasons and the situation can be even more complicated when — as in the appeal courts — more than one judge may deliver a judgement.

If there is more than one proposition of law that decides the case, there will be more than one *ratio*. The idea of multiple *ratios* is one of the difficulties that lawyers and law students face if they try to identify what the *ratio* is of a particular case. For instance, the case of *Rylands* v *Fletcher* (1868) formed the basis of a new tort, but as Dugdale et al. point out there were actually three possible *ratios* and it was only evident from future cases which one was being adopted. Alisdair Gillespie identifies the case of *R (R)* v *Durham Constabulary* (2005) as a similar example. The House of Lords was unanimous in its decision, but Lord Bingham and Lady Hale gave very different reasons for their decisions. Although the majority of the Lords agreed with Lord Bingham's reasoning, this is no guarantee that future courts will reach the same conclusion.

Binding precedent

The *ratio* becomes a **binding precedent** for future cases where the facts of the second case are sufficiently similar and where the original case is decided in a court more senior (or in some cases, at the same level) in the hierarchy. A binding precedent is one that must be followed.

Obiter dicta

Not all of a judgement forms the *ratio decidendi*. A judge may say many things in the course of a judgement speech and only a small part of the speech may constitute the *ratio*. Sometimes, for example, the judge may speculate on what the decision *might have been* if the situation was different. This is known as ***obiter dicta*** ('things said by the way'). Although this is not part of the case law, it may influence judges in later cases as persuasive precedent.

This happened in *R* v *Howe* (1987), which was a murder case. The House of Lords commented that duress was not a valid defence (*ratio*) but they also said that it would not be a defence to someone charged with attempted murder either (*obiter*).

One of the difficulties in practice is that it is not always easy to distinguish different parts of a judgement and separate the binding part — the reasons for the decision from other parts.

Donoghue v Stevenson (1932)

The 'neighbour' principle in *Donoghue* v *Stevenson* (1932) has been regarded as the foundation of the modern law of negligence. In this case, Mrs Donoghue became ill after drinking ginger beer contaminated by a decomposing snail. Lord Atkin in the House of Lords gave judgement in her favour and stated that 'you must take reasonable care to avoid acts or omissions which you can reasonably foresee would be likely to injure your neighbour', and 'your neighbour would be anyone so directly affected that you should have had them in mind'. Not many cases with similar facts to *Donoghue* v *Stevenson* are likely to occur, but the principle on which the decision was made is applicable to many kinds of case.

However, Lord Atkin's comments are of a general nature and do not really go to the decision in the case. Therefore, they are almost certainly *obiter* comments rather than part of the *ratio*, and yet it is they rather than the reasons for the decision itself that have been accepted as providing the precedent for future cases.

Persuasive precedent

There are situations where a judge is not bound by an earlier decision, but may feel it is right and be persuaded by it.

Obiter dicta statements

As discussed before, when delivering their judgements, judges sometimes speculate on what their decision would have been if the facts had been slightly different. These *obiter* statements are persuasive and may become the *ratio decidendi* of future cases. For example, the statement in *R* v *Howe* (1987) on duress and attempted murder was followed in *R* v *Gotts* (1992).

In *R* v *Brown* (1993), the defendants, who had engaged in sadomasochistic activities, were unable to rely on the defence of consent when prosecuted under the **Offences Against the Person Act 1861**. However, the Lords stated in *obiter* that consent could be a defence to painful practices such as tattooing and piercing. In *R* v *Wilson* (1996), the defendant husband was able to rely on this defence when he used a hot knife to brand his initials onto his wife's buttocks at her request. The Court of Appeal held that the defendant was engaged in body decoration, which was similar to body piercing or tattooing.

Another good example is in *Hall* v *Simons* (2000), which concerned allegedly negligent advice given by solicitors. Lord Hoffman's statement, that the rule giving advocates immunity for alleged negligence was no longer appropriate and should be abolished, is technically *obiter*, but it has been treated as authoritative and will almost certainly be followed in future cases.

Courts lower in the hierarchy

Persuasive precedent may also arise from the lower courts. The House of Lords agreed with the reasons that the Court of Appeal gave in the case of *R* v *R* (1991) when deciding that a man could be found guilty of raping his wife.

Decisions of the Judicial Committee of the Privy Council

Decisions of the Judicial Committee of the Privy Council (JCPC) are made as a result of the judges' role as a court of final appeal for some Commonwealth countries (many of the judges in the court are members of the House of Lords and therefore very senior judges). These decisions are not binding on the English courts but they can also form persuasive precedent. The Court of Appeal in *Doughty* v *Turner Manufacturing Co. Ltd* (1964) chose to follow the JCPC decision, involving liability and remoteness of damage in the tort of negligence, in *The Wagon Mound No. 1* (1961), rather than its own earlier decision in *Re Polemis* (1921).

In *Daraydan Holdings Ltd* v *Solland International Ltd* (2004), Collins J said: 'The system of precedent would be shown in a most unfavourable light if a litigant... were forced by the doctrine of binding precedent to go to the House of Lords...in order to have the decision of the Privy Council affirmed. That would be particularly so where the decision of the Privy Council is recent, where it was a decision on the English common law [and] where the Board consisted mainly of serving Law Lords.'

Lord Cairns and Lord Cranworth stated the argument used by Blackburn J in a lower court, that Rylands should succeed because 'a person who brings on his land anything likely to do mischief if it escapes, must keep it at his peril, and if he does not do so he is *prima facie* liable for all the damage which is the natural consequence of its escape'. Lord Cairns repeated the Blackburn formula but added that liability should only arise if the use to which it is put is a 'non-natural' one. Lord Cranworth went on to present a wider principle, namely that 'when one person in managing his affairs causes, however innocently, damage to another, it is obviously just that he should be the party to suffer'.

In fact, judges in later cases chose to adopt the narrowest of the arguments used in *Rylands* v *Fletcher* and decided that the precedent would only apply where the use was a non-natural one, thus greatly restricting the range of cases to which it could apply. Lord Cairns did not define what he meant by 'non-natural', though he was presumably thinking of it in a physical sense — a reservoir doesn't just appear naturally, it is artificial. In *Rickards* v *Lothian* (1913), the House of Lords interpreted 'non-natural' to mean non-natural in a social sense, so that it was able to decide that piping water to the upper floor of a building was a natural use and therefore there was no liability for the escape of water to lower floors as a result of a blocked sink.

Questions

1 What would the effect have been on cases like *Rickards* v *Lothian* if the only *ratio* in *Rylands* v *Fletcher* had been the wider principle put forward by Lord Cranworth?

2 Explain with reasons whether the House of Lords in *Rickards* v *Lothian* could have overruled *Rylands* v *Fletcher*.

3 What is your view of the idea in *Rickards* v *Lothian* that 'non-natural' should be interpreted in a social sense?

Original precedent

Original precedent is where there are no similar cases and the point of law has not been decided before. In cases like these, judges have to try to find cases that seem to be closest in principle and argue from analogy. For instance, in *Hunter* v *Canary Wharf Ltd* (1997), the question was whether people had an action in respect of interference with television reception caused by Canary Wharf. By analogy, there was no actionable claim because there was no claim for loss of a view, arguably the closest parallel situation, caused when a new building was constructed.

Law reports

Precedent would be impossible without a system of **law reporting**: decisions made in cases must be written down in order for future courts to know about them. In

earlier times, the reporting of cases was haphazard, and it is only since the development of modern law reporting in 1865 that systematic reporting has allowed the proper development of the system of precedent.

Even today, there is no 'official set' of law reports, nor is there any official selection of the cases to be reported. The most authoritative set of reports are those produced by the **Incorporated Council for Law Reporting** (ICLR), set up for this purpose by the Law Society and the Inns of Court in 1865. They are known simply as 'The Law Reports' or as the 'Appeal Cases' (AC), and they report cases from the House of Lords, the Court of Appeal and the divisional courts of the High Court. These reports are checked for accuracy by the judges in the cases reported, and are always cited if available in preference to any other report. A separate volume of *Weekly Law Reports* is also published by the ICLR. The *All England Law Reports* are also published weekly and may report cases that do not appear in the ICLR Law Reports.

There are also specialised reports, such as the Family Law Reports or the Criminal Appeal Reports that deal with particular aspects of law, and often include cases not reported in the general reports. One problem is that it may take several months for reports to be published, but newspapers like *The Times* publish brief summary law reports of cases the same week that they are heard.

Many recent cases are now reported on the internet or on CD-ROMs. There are also subscription services, such as LexisNexis (the oldest of its kind) and Justis, and many case reports are available free. All High Court, Court of Appeal and House of Lords cases are now reported on the internet and are available within hours of their being handed down.

> ### Exam hint
> Students often fail to explain the importance of law reports when answering questions on precedent. Law reports are crucial in the mechanics of precedent and without them there would be no workable system of precedent.

Questions

1 Why are law reports important?

2 When did the modern system of law reporting begin?

3 Give two examples of law reports.

4 What is the advantage of featuring law reports in newspapers like *The Times*?

5 How has modern technology improved the reporting of cases?

How judges can develop and change the law

If there is a binding precedent, judges are expected to follow the decision, but there are ways that judges can avoid following the precedent.

Victoria Gillick sought a declaration from the courts that the policy of her Area Health Authority to prescribe contraception for and perform abortions on underage girls without parental consent was illegal

Another example is *Sweet* v *Parsley* (1970). Here, the defendant was convicted in the magistrates' court, her conviction was upheld in the divisional court and then reversed by the House of Lords.

The ability of higher courts to overturn decisions of lower courts is an important element of precedent, because it allows for decisions to be changed — but in a controlled way. Allowing the House of Lords to overturn its own earlier decisions means that the law can develop, but not allowing the Court of Appeal the same freedom ensures that some degree of certainty will remain. It could be argued, however, as Lord Denning did, that it is expensive to appeal to the House of Lords and many deserving cases will not be appealed, and therefore precedents will remain which should have been changed.

Incompatibility with European law

Because s.3 of the **European Communities Act 1972** requires courts either to refer cases dealing with Community law to the European Court of Justice (ECJ) or to decide the cases themselves in the light of a previous decision of the ECJ, it seems clear that the Court of Appeal can ignore a previous decision of its own that is inconsistent with European Community law or with a later decision of the ECJ. In addition, s.2 of the **Human Rights Act 1998** requires all courts to take into account any judgement of the European Court of Human Rights. It seems, therefore, that the Court of Appeal will overrule its own decisions where those are in conflict with the provision of the European Convention on Human Rights.

Questions

1 Copy and complete the following table:

Way of avoiding precedent	Meaning	Case example

2 Explain what is meant by *res judicata* and how it affects overruling.

3 How do s.3 of the European Communities Act 1972 and s.2 of the Human Rights Act 1998 affect the Court of Appeal?

1 Reversing and overruling

In the case of *R (on the application of Godmanchester Town Council) v Secretary of State; R (on the application of Drain) v Secretary of State (2007)*, the House of Lords reversed the decision of the Court of Appeal and overruled the decision of the High Court in *R v Secretary of State ex parte Dorset Country Council* (1999). The court was engaging in statutory interpretation. The case hinged on the meaning of s.31 of the Rights of Way Act 1932.

1932 The Rights of Way Act was passed. Under the Act, the law was always understood to be that if the general public used a path freely for 20 years or more then a public right of way was created. The exception to this (s.31) was when a landowner put up a sign saying 'no right of way', or locked gates or ordered the public off the footpath. Through these actions, which made his or her intention clear to the public, the route remained private.

1999 *R v Secretary of State ex parte Dorset County Council*. The High Court ruled that a landowner could, even after 20 years of uncontested public use, defeat a claim that a right of way had come into existence by producing evidence of virtually any sort of which the public were totally unaware — for example, letters to his or her solicitor, directions to staff to keep people off the path and so on. Indeed, a mere retrospective assertion by a landowner that he never intended a path to become public seemed sufficient to defeat a claim.

Two applications for public rights of way failed because of the High Court ruling in 1999. The Ramblers Association took on both cases in a joint action.

2004 The divisional court followed the 1999 ruling.

2005 The Court of Appeal upheld this decision.

2006 The Ramblers Association was granted permission to appeal to the House of Lords because there was an arguable point of law of general public importance.

June 2007 The Law Lords unanimously allowed the appeal.

In the leading judgement, Lord Hoffman said:

My Lords, in my opinion...the Court of Appeal was wrong. I think that upon the true construction of s.31(1), 'intention' means what the relevant audience, namely the users of the way, would reasonably have understood the landowner's intention to be. The test is...objective: not what the owner subjectively intended nor what particular users of the way subjectively assumed, but whether a reasonable user would have understood that the owner was intending.

Questions

1 Why might the Ramblers Association and other walkers have been upset about the decision of the High Court in *R* v *Secretary of State ex parte Dorset County Council* (1999)?

2 Was the Court of Appeal obliged to follow the 1999 decision in 2005?

3 Explain why Lord Hoffman thought that the Court of Appeal and the original High Court decision in 1999 were wrong.

2 Distinguishing cases

The following cases concerned the principle of whether the actual identity of a person was important in deciding whether a valid contract was made. They all involve a 'rogue' pretending to be someone else. In each case, the rogue disappeared leaving the two innocent parties — the person who sold the goods to the rogue and the person who bought the goods from the rogue — to fight it out.

Cundy v *Lindsay* (1878)

A person calling himself Blenkarn pretended to represent the respectable firm of Blenkiron & Co. and obtained goods on credit and never paid for them. He then sold the goods to an innocent third party. The House of Lords decided that the original supplier was entitled to recover the goods from the third party because there was no valid contract between the supplier and Blenkarn. They thought they were dealing with Blenkiron & Co. and therefore ownership had never passed to Blenkarn.

Philips v *Brooks* (1919)

A man went into a jewellers and pretended to be Sir George Bullough. He then paid for jewellery using a cheque in that name. The cheque bounced, but meanwhile the jewellery had been sold to an innocent third party, who was sued by the jeweller for recovery of the goods. The judge rejected the jeweller's claim and distinguished *Cundy* v *Lindsay* on the basis that it involved a transaction through the post, whereas in this case the jeweller sold face to face and intended to sell to the person in the shop, even though he was mistaken as to the person's identity

Ingram v *Little* (1961)

Two sisters advertised a car and a man bought it, giving the name Hutchinson and an address which the sisters checked in the telephone directory. He paid for the car by cheque and sold the car to an innocent third party; the cheque bounced. The Court of Appeal distinguished *Philips* v *Brooks* and decided that the offer to sell had only been made to the man because they believed him to be Mr Hutchinson and therefore the contract was void and the sisters were entitled to the car.

Lewis v *Averay* (1972)

A student advertised a car for sale and a man pretending to be a well-known actor bought the car, using a cheque in the actor's name and showing a studio pass as evidence of his identity. The cheque was dishonoured and the car was sold on to an innocent third party. The student's

6

claim for recovery of the car was rejected by the Court of Appeal, and distinguished from *Ingram* v *Little*. The basis on which it was distinguished was not entirely clear, though it may be that they felt that in *Ingram* the sisters had made more effort to check the identity and therefore they regarded the identity of the purchaser as more important. A more likely explanation is that the court in *Lewis* v *Averay* simply thought that *Ingram* v *Little* had been wrongly decided!

Shogun Finance Ltd v *Hudson* (2004)

A man bought a car on hire purchase, using a driving licence in a false name. The finance company carried out checks against the name on the licence and approved the loan. The man defaulted on the loan and sold the car to an innocent third party. Both the Court of Appeal and the House of Lords decided that the finance company was entitled to the car because they had only intended to hire the car to the person named on the licence.

Questions

1 In which cases were the third party made to return the goods and in which were they allowed to keep them?
2 How could a judge in *Phillips* v *Brooks* not follow a House of Lords decision in *Cundy* v *Lindsay*?
3 Lord Denning said in *Lewis* v *Averay*: 'A mistake as to identity, it is said, avoids a contract; whereas a mistake as to attributes does not. But this is a distinction without a difference. A man's very name is one of his attributes. It is also a key to his identity. If then he gives a false name, is it a mistake as to his identity or a mistake as to his attributes? These fine distinctions do no good to the law.' What did he mean? Do you agree?
4 What should the Court of Appeal in *Lewis* v *Averay* have done if it thought that *Ingram* v *Little* had been wrongly decided?
5 Referring to other decided cases, explain briefly what Lord Denning believed the Court of Appeal should be able to do in situations like this.
6 Which earlier precedent did the Court of Appeal in *Shogun Finance Ltd* v *Hudson* appear to be following?
7 Which precedent should it have followed?

Advantages of precedent

Flexibility

One of the advantages of the common law system is that the law is able to respond to new situations. Within the limits set by precedent and the rules of statutory interpretation, judges are able to develop the law in ways that reflect changing social and technological circumstances. For instance, the law has been adapted to deal with the effect of life support systems on the exact point of death *(R* v *Malcherek and Steel,* 1981).

It takes many months for an Act of Parliament to be passed. However, the courts may respond immediately to a novel situation. In *McLoughlin* v *O'Brian* (1983), the House of Lords extended the law on nervous shock to cover situations where the secondary victim came upon the 'immediate aftermath'.

Certainty

Certainty allows people to know what the law is, allowing lawyers to be able to predict the likely outcome of a case. Without a system of binding precedent, people could not be sure that the law would remain the same and this would make planning for the future much more of a risk. Sir Rupert Cross, in *Precedent in English Law,* points out that 'English justice, if it were not to remain fluid and unstable, required a strong cement. This was found in the common law doctrine of precedent with its essential and peculiar emphasis on rigidity and certainty'. The 1966 House of Lords Practice Statement refers to precedent as 'an indispensable foundation…providing at least some degree of certainty upon which individuals can rely for the conduct of their affairs'. In the case of *Knuller* v *DPP* (1972) in which the Lords had to decide whether they should overrule an earlier case that was widely believed to be wrongly decided, Lord Reid said that 'in the general interest of certainty in the law we must be sure that there is some very good reason before we so act'.

Consistency

Consistency occurs because similar cases are dealt with in the same way. In order for the law to be fair and credible, it is important that people feel that their case will be decided in the same way as other cases that are similar.

Real-life situations

Case law deals with situations that arise in practice — real facts in real situations — unlike statutes, which can only set out theoretical legal rules. If an unforeseen situation arises, judges can refer to existing precedents and adapt the law to meet the new situation. Over time, detailed and thorough rules will be built up, covering the whole range of situations that have occurred.

Prevents Parliament having to legislate

Parliament can legislate very quickly when it wants to. For instance, in 2001 an Elections Bill to postpone local elections because of the foot-and-mouth crisis passed through all its parliamentary stages in only 6 days. But it is unrealistic to expect

Parliament to legislate in all the situations where the courts currently overrule precedents.

The government will be intent on pushing through a legislative programme that fulfils its political goals. Furthermore, in contrast to judges who have only one case before them at any one time, MPs and peers have many conflicting priorities to attend to, and inevitably the non-controversial, politically insignificant reforms to the law are often left for many years. For example, despite the work of the Law Commission, the laws on non-fatal offences and corporate manslaughter remain unreformed. Similarly, moral issues are often not included in the legislative programme and the judiciary is consequently left to determine whether development of the law is required. This was clearly the case with husband rape. It had long been regarded by society as unacceptable, but successive Parliaments had not found time for statutory change. The long-awaited decision was made by the House of Lords in *R* v *R* (1991).

Although Parliament legislated quickly to postpone local elections during the foot-and-mouth outbreak in 2001, it is unrealistic to expect it to legislate in all situations where the courts currently overrule precedents

Law made by lawyers/experts

Judges have the further advantage over Parliament in that they are legal experts and thus better equipped to develop the law. Because they are trained to apply existing principles and relate developments to the existing law, the law is more likely to remain consistent and coherent. However, the development by judges of gross negligence manslaughter, based as it seems to be on civil law principles, has arguably not made the law of involuntary manslaughter either consistent or coherent.

Disadvantages of precedent

Complexity and volume

There are nearly half a million reported cases and this number is growing continually. This makes it difficult to know all of the cases that might be relevant. The judges in each case may only be aware of those precedents which each of the parties concerned bring to their attention. There is also the problem that in some cases it may be difficult to determine the *ratio decidendi* because of the complex way in which the judgement is written.

Rigidity and slowness of growth

Judges have to wait for cases to be brought before them, which means that reform may be delayed for many years. The strict hierarchy means that judges must follow binding precedent. Therefore, bad or inappropriate decisions cannot be changed unless they are heard in a higher court that can overrule them. As you have seen, the Court of Appeal is bound by its own earlier decisions and in practice few cases are appealed to the House of Lords. One of Lord Denning's arguments in *Davis* v *Johnson* (1979), for allowing the Court of Appeal to overrule its own earlier decisions, was that few litigants have the financial resources or determination to take a case to the House of Lords

Retrospective effect of decisions

The effect of a court overruling an earlier precedent is that people cannot rely on the law. They may act in the knowledge of what the law is at the time, only to have it changed if the case is appealed to a court that can change the precedent. This is what happened in *R* v *R* (1991) for example, the effect of which was to turn an act, which was lawful at the time it was committed, into a serious criminal offence. This partly explains why judges have been so reluctant to use the Practice Statement.

Constitutional position

While judicial law making may be desirable for a number of reasons, we have seen that it is the constitutional position that Parliament creates law and that judges apply it. There are two key reasons for this. First, the formulation of policy is the role of a democratically elected parliament who will recognise the will of the electorate. The judiciary are unelected. Second, it can be argued that the judiciary are not representative of the population. They are drawn from a narrow social group and this raises the possibility, identified by Professor Griffith, that they will inevitably have views reflecting this narrow social background. Women and people from minority ethnic groups are under-represented, especially among the senior judiciary. For instance, until the appointment of Lady Hale in January 2004, there were no female Law Lords.

The personal views of judges

Lord Denning made no secret of his approach to cases. He wanted to achieve what he believed to be justice and he was prepared to challenge the rules of precedent to try to achieve this. Little is known about the process that determines which judges hear which cases, but research by David Robertson into decisions by House of Lords judges between 1986 and 1995 suggests that it is predictable which way a case will be decided, by reference simply to the combination of judges hearing the appeal.

Lack of research

When Parliament wants to introduce a new piece of legislation, there is considerable opportunity for comprehensive research. Often, legislation will be the result of recommendations from the law reform bodies, which possess the expertise to research an area thoroughly. The Law Commission is a permanent law-reform body and has had considerable success in having recommendations recognised in Acts of Parliament. Examples of such legislation include the **Contracts (Rights of Third Parties) Act 1999** and the **Computer Misuse Act 1990**. The Green Paper stage allows for interested parties to be consulted and the passage of the bill through Parliament will involve many debates among people who are able to research the relevant issues. Judges, however, cannot be so comprehensive in their approach. Their decisions will be based on the evidence presented to them by the parties involved in the case. They cannot consider arguments about the general social, economic or moral aspects, even though their decision, as in *Gillick* (see page 109) for example, may inevitably have implications for society generally.

Judge-made law is incremental in nature

Judges can only make law on the facts of the case before them. They cannot lay down a comprehensive code to cover all similar situations. Some areas of law (e.g. negligence) might be well suited to this case-by-case approach. However, with other areas it is not helpful when one small change is made, such as the introduction of gross negligence manslaughter in *R* v *Prentice* (1994) and *R* v *Adomako* (1994), when really the whole area of involuntary manslaughter needs to be reformed properly.

Judge-made law thus develops in an unstructured, random way. It is dependent on cases being brought and then appealed through to a court sufficiently senior to make a new precedent.

Illogical and technical distinctions

One argument often used against precedent as a law-making process is that judges make technical distinctions between the case they are deciding and the precedent in order to avoid following the precedent. The result of this is that the law becomes complex and confusing, with many minor technical distinctions.

Problems with law reports

On the whole, the present law-reporting system works reasonably well, though there is a degree of duplication. However, it remains the case that surprisingly few cases are reported. According to Michael Zander, it has been estimated that only about a quarter of the decisions of the Court of Appeal Civil Division appear in the *Weekly Law Reports*, and probably only 70% of House of Lords cases and 10% of Court of Appeal Criminal Division cases are reported.

There is also the concern that the decision about which cases to report rests with the editor of the publication producing the law report. It could be argued that a wider group, more representative of those involved in that area of law, should be involved.

Questions

1 Suggest the three advantages of precedent that you consider to be the most important. Give reasons for your choices.

2 Explain what is meant by each of these words: 'rigidity'; 'retrospective'; 'incremental'.

3 Explain why each word could be considered to be a disadvantage of precedent.

Extension exercises

1 The problem of retrospective application of cases

The decision in *R* v *R* (1991) that a man could be found guilty of raping his wife was upheld by the ECHR. In *SW and CR* v *United Kingdom* (1995), the European Court of Human Rights held that the UK had not been in breach of Article 7 of the Convention, which provides that no one should be found guilty of an offence which was not an offence at the time it was committed. The court's reasoning was that judicial law making was well entrenched in legal tradition and the development of the law in this case had been reasonably foreseeable.

This problem does not arise with legislation, which operates prospectively. It is usually the case that legislation comes into effect on a fixed date after the Act has received the royal assent, in order to allow time for people to prepare for the law change.

In some countries, including the USA, cases only apply prospectively. This concept has been considered in relation to the English legal system. In a speech in 1987, the then Lord Chancellor, Lord Mackay, discussed the possibility of allowing prospective overruling, whereby the court might uphold the existing precedent in the instant case but declare it overruled for the future. The main problem with the idea is that while most litigants are prepared to accept defeat if the judge decides the law is against them, they would find it hard to accept that they had won their case only for future litigants, not for themselves. There would seem little point in going to court at all.

Questions

1 In your own words and referring to *R* v *R* (1991), explain what is meant by saying that 'case law operates retrospectively'.

2 How was the decision in *R* v *R* challenged and what was the outcome?

3 What are the strengths and weaknesses of Lord Mackay's proposal?

2 Lord Denning on precedent

Let it not be thought...that I am against the doctrine of precedent. I am not. It is the foundation of our system of case law. This has evolved by broadening down from precedent to precedent. By standing by previous decisions, we have kept the common law on a good course. All that I am against is its too rigid application — a rigidity which insists that a bad precedent must necessarily be followed. I would treat it as you would a path through the woods. You must follow it certainly so as to reach your end. But you must not let the path become too overgrown. You must cut out the dead wood and trim off the branches, else you will find yourself lost in thickets and brambles. My plea is simply to keep the path to justice clear of obstructions which would impede it.

Questions

1 What does Lord Denning seem to be arguing for in this quotation?

2 What criticisms could you make of Lord Denning's approach?

Sample exam questions

1 Identify and briefly explain the key features of the doctrine of precedent. (15 marks)

Suggested reading

Cross, R. and Harris J. W. (1991) *Precedent in English Law*, Clarendon Press.

Dugdale, T. et al. (2002) '*A' Level Law*, chapter 6, Butterworth.

Gillespie, A. (2007) *The English Legal System*, Oxford University Press.

Ingman, T. (2006) *The English Legal Process*, chapter 9, Oxford University Press.

Turner, C. (2006) 'Precedent', *A-Level Law Review*, Vol. 2, No. 1, pp. 10–12.

Zander, M. (2004) *The Law-Making Process*, chapters 4–6, Cambridge University Press.

Chapter 7

Juries

This chapter discusses how juries are selected under various Acts of Parliament, including random selection. It also looks at who is disqualified from jury service, who is ineligible, who may have his or her jury service deferred until a later date, or who may be excused altogether. It outlines the function of juries in a serious criminal trial in the Crown Court. Finally, it examines what advantages and disadvantages juries bring to our legal system.

Although for most of you law is a new subject for study, juries are a topic that everyone knows something about. Your relatives may have served on a jury, and you may be familiar with the role and importance of juries from watching films and television programmes, such as *Kavanagh QC* or John Grisham's *The Runaway Jury*.

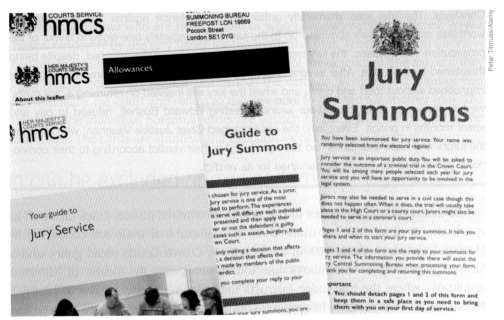

On receipt of summons papers, a citizen is required to attend court for jury service

under the Juries Act 1974 is eligible for jury service, with the sole exceptions of serious offenders and those suffering from a mental illness. This means that the former category of ineligibility, which precluded lawyers, judges, police officers and clergy, has effectively been swept aside.

The reason for this change is that before 2004, over 480,000 people a year were summoned for jury service, but of these, more than half were ineligible or were excused, either as of right or at the court's discretion. This meant that juries were no longer broadly representative — in particular, it was too easy for the professional middle classes to be released from this important civic duty. The Courts Minister in the Lord Chancellor's Department stated that this reform was designed to widen the pool of jury selection and to ensure that juries better reflect their communities and thus 'boost confidence in the system.'

However, a 4-year study of jury trials ('Diversity and fairness in the jury system'), undertaken by Professor Cheryl Thomas, Director of the Jury Diversity Project at Birmingham University, and published by the Ministry of Justice in June 2007, has demolished a number of myths about jury trials. Jury pools closely reflect the local population, ethnic-minority groups are not under-represented, and most people do not avoid jury service. In fact, the highest rates of jury service were among middle- to high-income earners.

The category of excusal 'as of right' has also been removed, although it is accepted that those serving in the armed forces will continue to be excused jury service, providing their commanding officer writes to the court to confirm that operational efficiency requires the person concerned to be excused. Doctors and nurses are also unable to be excused automatically. It is still be possible for people with a poor command of English or those whose religious beliefs would be in conflict with jury service to seek to be excused, but in general it is felt that excusal will be far more rarely granted. Holiday arrangements or business commitments will result in jury service being deferred, not excused altogether. In the first few months after this new law had been in force, over 10,000 deferral requests were granted and only 41 refused.

To summarise, a person can be excused from jury service on the following grounds:

* **Disqualification** — applies only to offenders who have received a custodial or community sentence, or who are on bail awaiting trial.
* **Ineligibility** — under the Criminal Justice Act 2003, only mentally disordered persons are ineligible for jury service. Such a person is one who suffers or has suffered from mental illness, psychopathic disorder or mental handicap and who is resident in a hospital or regularly attends for treatment by a doctor.
* **Excusal as of right** — with the exception of those aged between 65 and 70 this category was abolished by the Criminal Justice Act 2003. This change has the effect of enabling clergymen, lawyers, police officers and even judges to become jurors.

❖ **Excusal at the court's discretion** — applies to those with limited understanding of English, students doing public examinations, those with childcare problems, or those with holidays booked. In such cases, it is more likely that jury service will be deferred.

Is it wise to put a judge among the jurors?

The scandal of jury service was always that so many professionals could get out of it. Two-thirds of those summoned could find reasons to defer it or be excused altogether. The upshot was that, 'far from being representative, the jury was overloaded with housewives, the unemployed and those who could not think of an excuse'.

The changes have already been severely criticised by doctors and police officers — the police argue that defence lawyers are likely to complain that they are biased as jurors and will challenge their selection; doctors have warned that being called for jury service will disrupt an already overstretched National Health Service.

Soon after these changes were brought into force, a QC was summoned for jury service at the Old Bailey. However, having already been discharged from three other trials, he asked the presiding judge to excuse him from his last three days of jury service. The judge refused saying that knowing other lawyers in the trial was not a good enough reason for him to be discharged. However, on the fourth occasion he was chosen as a juror, he had finally to be excused, as the recorder said he knew him well. The trial judge — Judge George Bathurst-Norman — then stated: 'It deeply troubles me — I don't know how this legislation is going to work intelligently... It is not for me to undermine the will of Parliament but at the same time I have to ensure a fair trial.'

Anthony Scrivener QC argues: 'It's hardly fair to have people with specialist knowledge who know the rules of evidence...lawyers would know that the fact a defendant's character is not being put in evidence means it's likely he has previous convictions.'

Another lawyer, Romana Cannetti, who is a newspaper lawyer employed to check articles for potential libels, was summoned to sit on a civil libel jury: 'It's totally ludicrous', she said, 'I am bound to know the defendant — I advise ten different papers and broadcasters — as well as the lawyers because it is a small world and they come chiefly from two sets of chambers.' She continued, 'It would be totally inequitable for a lawyer to sit as a juror. I know too much about the workings of a trial, the techniques of cross-examination, why submissions are couched in a particular way...it makes a mockery of the idea of a panel of lay people coming along to judge a case on its facts.'

A final, humorous comment is provided by Anthony Scrivener, who said that there is only one sure way for a lawyer or judge to 'get off jury service', and that is to copy the example of one juror, whose experience of jury service was rapidly curtailed. As the usher brought the jury into court, this particular juror confided to her: 'I always find them "not guilty".'

Adapted from an article by Frances Gibb, *The Times*, 22 June 2004.

Questions

1 Why does the writer believe that a jury made up of housewives etc. would cause problems?
2 Summarise the arguments advanced by Scrivener and Cannetti as to why it is unfair for lawyers and judges to sit on juries.
3 On balance, do you think that these changes to jury eligibility will create injustice?

Lord Justice Dyson became the first serving judge to be summoned for jury service. This caused the (then) Lord Chief Justice — Lord Woolf — to issue a Practice Statement that points out that a judge serves on a jury as a private citizen, that excusal from jury service will only be granted in extreme circumstances and that judges must follow the legal directions given by the trial judge and must avoid the temptation to correct guidance which they believe to be inaccurate.

R v Abdroikov; Green and Williamson (2007)

This specific problem — that of lawyers, judges and police officers being eligible for jury service — formed the basis of an important appeal against conviction to the House of Lords. Three separate cases were heard together. In the first, there was a police officer on the jury where police evidence was not in issue. In the second, the crime victim was a police officer and the officer on the jury was from the same local police background (although he did not know the victim). In the third case, an experienced Crown Prosecution Service prosecutor was allowed by the judge to sit on the jury trying a serious rape case.

The House of Lord was anxious to emphasise that there was no evidence of any actual bias in any of these cases. However, as Lord Bingham explained, the principle was not only that justice must be done 'but should manifestly and undoubtedly be seen to be done'. Most adult human beings, he said, harbour certain prejudices and predilections because of their background, education and experience, but the court system does its best to neutralise the effect of these, not least by insisting that at least ten jurors should agree on a person's guilt. Nonetheless, Lord Bingham and a majority of the court held that in the police victim case and the Crown Prosecution Service prosecutor case, a reasonable onlooker would conclude that justice had not been seen to be done, because of the proximity of the jurors to the issues to be decided. These convictions were quashed — although in the serious rape case there may be a retrial.

As one of the dissenting judges, Lord Roger commented, this judgement drives a 'coach and horses' through Parliament's legislation as set out in the Criminal Justice Act 2003. But any attempt by Parliament to reassert its authority may well find itself challenged under Article 6 of the European Convention on Human Rights — the right of any accused person to a fair trial before an independent and impartial tribunal. 'Undoubtedly, guidance will now have to be issued for police officers, prosecutors and the like who will be routinely identified and vetted by the trial judge at the start of a case.'

Adapted from an article by Stephen Cragg, *The Times*, 23 October 2007.

Jury challenging

In the UK, challenging a juror is now a rare event, but there are three main ways that it can occur.

Stand by for the Crown

Prosecution can use 'Stand by for the Crown' without giving reason, although the Attorney General announced in 1988 that this right would only be used to remove 'a manifestly unsuitable' juror, or to remove a juror in a terrorist or security trial where jury vetting has been authorised.

Challenge for cause

Defence can challenge 'for cause', which in terms of a Practice Note issued by the Lord Chief Justice in 1973 may *not* include race, religion, political beliefs or occupation. A successful challenge is therefore only likely to occur where the juror is personally known. In *R v Gough* (1993), it was held that where a juror is challenged on the grounds of possible bias, the test is whether there is 'real danger' that he or she is biased. Note that the right of the defence to use a **peremptory challenge** (challenge without any reason being given) was abolished by the Criminal Justice Act 1988.

Challenge to the array

This is where both parties may challenge the whole jury panel on the grounds that the summoning officer is biased or has acted improperly. This happens very rarely. However, in 1993 the challenge was used in the *Romford Jury* case where, out of a panel of 12 jurors, nine came from Romford, with two of then living within 20 doors of each other in the same street. Another case where this challenge was successful was *R v Fraser* (1987) where, although the defendant was from a minority ethnic background, all the jurors were white. (Note, however, in *R v Ford* (1989) that it was held that if the jury was chosen in a random manner then it could not be challenged because it was not multiracial.)

Jury vetting

This process is usually conducted by the prosecution and involves checking the list of potential jurors to see if anyone appears 'unsuitable'. This matter first came to the attention of the public in 1978 in the *ABC* trial, a case brought under the Official Secrets Act 1911, when it emerged that vetting had been authorised by the Attorney General. Guidelines have since been published, which state that vetting is only justifiable in exceptional cases, such as those involving terrorism, the Official Secrets Acts and 'professional' criminals. Vetting in these cases requires the consent of the Attorney General. As Alisdair Gillespie notes:

A particular difficulty with this whole exercise is that although the guidlelines are published they are not particularly clear and are open to interpretation in a way that would allow the state to 'rig' a jury if they so wished. It has been noted that the guidelines do not place an obligation on the prosecution to 'stand by' a juror who would be biased against the defendant and yet the defendant would have no real way of knowing that they were.

Vetting would involve checking Criminal Record Office records, Special Branch and Intelligence Services' records and the knowledge of local CID officers.

> ### Exam hint
>
> 'How jurors are selected' is a common topic for examinations. You must know the relevant statutory authorities, especially the Juries Act 1974 and the Criminal Justice Act 2003, together with the rules on disqualification and ineligibility. Be careful not to confuse the latter two terms. You also need to learn how the process of random selection works. If the exam question is worth 15 or 20 marks, you should include at least a paragraph on challenging and vetting juries.

The function of the jury

The jury's function is to weigh up the evidence and decide what are the true facts of the case. The judge directs it as to what is the relevant law, and the jury must then apply that law to the facts that it has found and thereby reach a verdict. The trial judge will often refer to the jury as 'masters of the facts', while the judge is the 'master of the law'.

Criminal cases

Juries are used in all serious criminal cases (i.e. indictable offences tried at Crown Court). The jury has the sole responsibility for determining guilt. Since the **Criminal Justice Act 1967**, majority verdicts are possible (a minimum of 10 out of 12 must agree). During the trial — after the jury has been sworn in — jurors will be present to hear all the evidence put forward in the case by the prosecution and defence counsel. Notes may be taken and jurors will have the opportunity to question witnesses through the judge.

At the end of the case for the defence and the closing speeches of counsel, the judge will summarise the evidence in the case and direct the jury on relevant legal issues. In some more complicated cases, the judge will also provide a structured set of questions to assist the jury in its deliberations. On retirement to a private room, a foreperson is chosen to speak for the jury. After a minimum period of

2 hours and 10 minutes, if the jury has not returned with a unanimous verdict, the judge may recall the jury and advise that a majority verdict may be made under the **Criminal Justice Act 1967** (about 20% of convictions each year are given by such verdicts).

The jury must weigh up the evidence and decide the true facts of the case

Directed acquittal

During the trial itself or at the end of it, the trial judge may rule as a matter of law that the prosecution simply has not provided enough evidence for the defendant to be convicted 'beyond reasonable doubt'. If that is the case, the judge will direct the jury to return a formal verdict of 'not guilty'. However, under no circumstances may a trial judge require a jury to bring in a verdict of 'guilty'.

This was confirmed in *R* v *Wang* (2005). A man found in possession of a martial arts sword and a ghurka-style knife was charged with having an article with a blade or point in a public place. He testified that he was a Buddhist and practised Shaolin (a traditional martial art), and that he had the articles with him for good reason. The judge decided that the defendant's explanation did not meet the requirements of the statutory defence and directed the jury to convict. This was upheld on appeal, but after reviewing the authorities and referring to cases such as *R* v *Ponting* (1985) (see page 135) the House of Lords quashed the conviction, noting that there are no circumstances in which a judge is entitled to direct a jury to return a verdict of guilty.

Are juries representative?

The basis of the use of juries in serious criminal cases is that the 12 people are selected randomly and should therefore comprise a representative sample of the population as a whole. This ideal has come closer with the abolition of the property qualification and the use of computers for random selection. It has been argued that random selection may make a jury less likely to be representative — if, for example, many women are excused through childcare commitments, summoning twice as many women as men might be a better way of achieving a representative section of the community.

Research carried out by Michael Zander in 1983 found that women were only slightly under-represented and that non-white jurors constituted 5% of juries, while they make up 5.9% of the national population. While this last point is encouraging, the Commission for Racial Equality has argued that consideration should be given to the racial balance in particular cases. The Commission suggested that where a case has a racial dimension and the defendant reasonably believes that he or she cannot receive a fair trial from an all-white jury, then the judge should have the power to order that three of the jurors come from the same minority ethnic group as the defendant or the victim. This was endorsed by the Runciman Royal Commission on Criminal Justice but it has never been implemented. The decision in *R* v *Ford* (1989) that there is no principle that a jury should be racially balanced, still holds. This recommendation, although endorsed by Lord Justice Auld in his criminal justice review, has not been accepted by the government.

The refusal by both Parliament and judges to consider the principle of racially balanced juries has given rise to some serious problems. In 1994, the Lord Chief Justice wrote: 'Race issues go to the heart of our system of justice which demands that all are treated as equals before the law. It is a matter of the gravest concern if members of the ethnic minorities feel they are discriminated against by the criminal justice system: more so if their fears were to be borne out in reality.' Although a survey by Professor J. Gobert in 1989 found that there was 'an under-representation of ethnic minorities' on jury selection, nonetheless judges and legislators alike have been reluctant to 'introduce measures which nibble away at the principle of random selection'.

Extension exercise

Jurors behaving badly

Imagine you are an Asian man on trial in the crown court facing the prospect of a long jail sentence if convicted. Your fate is in the hands of 12 men and women randomly selected. But what if some of these jurors are racist? Suppose they make disparaging remarks about your appearance, your clothing, your accent.

This is what happened during Sajid Qureshi's trial at Mold crown court in 2000, according to one of the jurors who convicted him and saw him sentenced to 4 years in prison. In a letter to the court 6 days after his conviction, the juror claimed that some of her fellow jurors seemed to have already decided their verdict from the start, that one juror fell asleep during the trial and that some jurors tried to bully others.

However, this material was not enough for the Court of Appeal, who refused permission for an appeal to be brought because of the Contempt of Court Act 1981, which bans anyone, including judges, from enquiring into the secrets of the jury room.

British society is riddled with racism. A study of West Midlands courts by Oxford University in 1989 found that seven judges were sentencing black defendants much more harshly than white defendants. If so much of the criminal justice system is racist, why should the jury be any different?

John Spencer, Law Professor at Cambridge University, has argued: 'If juries are composed of 12 people chosen from the electoral roll at random, it is inevitable that they will sometimes be dominated by people who are racists, or are irresponsible and silly. Our legal system is gravely deficient if it fails to guard against this obvious danger.' In the same article in the *Cambridge Law Journal*, Professor Spencer argued that the decision of the Court of Appeal in Qureshi's case 'is to put it mildly, questionable' and 'almost certainly incompatible with Article 6 of the European Convention on Human Rights' (which guarantees defendants a fair trial before an independent tribunal).

In a later case — *Sander v United Kingdom* — brought before the European Court of Human Rights, this opinion was upheld. In the trial of Mr Sander, before the judge completed his summing up to the jury, a juror handed a court usher a written complaint that some jurors were not taking their duties seriously: 'At least two have been making openly racist remarks and jokes and I fear we are going to convict the defendants not on the evidence but because they are Asian.' The jury was told of this complaint, which was then refuted by a letter signed by all 12 jurors given to the judge. The judge rejected the defence request that the jury be discharged and the case retried before a different jury. The jury then convicted Mr Sander, who received a 5-year sentence. The Court of Appeal, dismissing the appeal, said the judge had been right to confront the jury with the problem, and had not erred in reaching the conclusion that there was no risk of bias. The European Court of Human Rights, however, concluded that the trial judge should have discharged the jury and ordered a retrial on the grounds that the original juror's note had raised the real fear of lack of impartiality, which was not dispelled by the judge's direction to the jury.

Adapted from C. Dyer: 'Jurors behaving badly', *Guardian*, 25 June 2002 and M. Zander: 'The complaining juror', *New Law Journal*, 19 May 2000.

Questions

1 What complaint was made by one juror about the jury in the trial of Sajid Qureshi?

2 Why did the Court of Appeal refuse permission for the appeal to be heard?

3 In *R v Sander*, why did the European Court of Human Rights overturn the Court of Appeal decision?

Advantages of juries

Public participation

Juries allow the ordinary citizen to take part in the administration of justice, so that verdicts are seen to be those of society rather than of the judicial system, satisfying the constitutional tradition of judgement by one's peers. Lord Denning described jury service as giving 'ordinary folk their finest lesson in citizenship'. A survey commissioned by the Bar Council and the Law Society found that over 80% of those questioned were more likely to have confidence in juries than other players in the justice system, and that juries were more likely to reflect their views and values. In addition, 85% trusted juries to reach the right decision and believed that juries improved the quality of the justice system.

It is also relevant that judges themselves retain considerable confidence in the jury system — in 1974, Lord Salmon estimated that no more than about 2% of defendants were wrongly acquitted by the jury. These findings have particular importance when one considers the background of magistrates, who are often white and middle class.

However, there is a growing body of evidence to suggest that this rosy picture of juries is questionable. In 1979, research by Baldwin and McConville suggested that about 5% of jury convictions were 'doubtful', and more recent research in 2001 by Gary Slapper shows that while acquittal rates remained static at about 32% from the mid-1970s to the end of the 1980s, they shot up during the 1990s. In 1999, 43% of all jury verdicts were 'not guilty', the highest percentage since the start of the survey. Slapper stated:

> The public is so much more critical and socially and politically aware... And so juries are more likely to think for themselves. They are less prone to be reverential towards police officers, because it is more common knowledge in 2001 than it was in 1959 that police officers are capable of lying, that lawyers are capable of covering up evidence and that judges can be less than wholesome characters.

Home Office data support this concern — acquittal rates for some crimes, such as criminal damage, are as high as 79%. In robbery cases, where the defendant pleads not guilty, 61% are acquitted, as are 69% of those on charges of violence against the person.

It should be borne in mind, however, that 70% of defendants plead guilty at the Crown Court and it can be inferred that those who plead not guilty are likely to have a strong case, which may go a long way to explaining (if not justifying) the high acquittal rates.

Layman's equity

'Layman's equity' is the idea that a jury can reach a decision on the basis of 'simple fairness' rather than on the law — effectively 'bending the law'. Neither judges nor magistrates can ever do this. Because juries have the ultimate right to find defendants innocent or guilty, it is argued that they act as a check on officialdom and are a protector against unjust or oppressive prosecution by reflecting the community's sense of justice. Michael Mansfield QC argues that: 'It is the most democratic form of justice in the world, a protection against the use of overbearing and arbitrary power by governments.' Juries, unlike judges and magistrates, have the power to acquit a defendant where the law demands a guilty verdict by 'bending the law'. There are several well-known cases of juries using this right to find according to their consciences, often concerning issues of political and moral controversy. Such cases include *R* v *Owen*, *R* v *Kronlid* and *R* v *Ponting*.

R v *Owen* (1992)

Stephen Owen was acquitted of all six charges brought against him, including attempted murder, wounding and possessing a gun with intent to endanger life. His son had been killed in a road traffic accident involving Mr Taylor who had knocked him off his bicycle with a 30-tonne truck. Kevin Taylor's lorry was not insured and was unroadworthy. He had never passed a driving test and he was blind in one eye. He was convicted of reckless driving and received an 18-month prison sentence. On his release from prison, Stephen Owen traced him to his home address and confronted him there, shooting him in the back. On the facts of the case, Owen was undoubtedly guilty of the charges of wounding and possession of a gun with intent. However, despite the judge's clear instruction 'to approach the evidence, not stop to consider whether we have feelings of liking, disliking or even loathing for Kevin Taylor', the jury acquitted Owen on all counts.

R v *Ponting* (1985)

Clive Ponting was a senior civil servant in the Ministry of Defence who sent confidential documents on the sinking of the *Belgrano* in the Falklands War to Tam Dalyell, a senior and well-respected Labour backbencher. These sensitive documents were used in Parliament to criticise the actions of the prime minister Margaret Thatcher, and she was severely embarrassed by the leak. The leak was traced to Ponting and he was charged under the Official Secrets Act 1911. Like Stephen Owen, in strict law he was certainly guilty, and the trial judge directed the jury that his conduct did amount to the offence charged, but nevertheless, the jury acquitted him, arguably taking the view that his prosecution was politically inspired.

The importance of this aspect of the jury's involvement in criminal justice is difficult to assess. In high-profile cases such as *Ponting*, it can be a valuable statement of public feeling to those in authority, but even in this kind of case, it cannot always be relied upon. In *R* v *Tisdall* (1984), the defendant, Sarah Tisdall, exposed government wrongdoing, and it was admitted that the leak was no threat to national security, yet she was convicted, unlike Ponting.

powerfully supports the perhaps surprisingly unanimous view of all the trial judges that juries can cope even in long and complex cases'.

Who is to blame when the jury is out to lunch?

James Comyn QC once told the story of the Irish jury which acquitted the defendant against the clearest evidence pointing to his guilt. Out of curiosity, the judge asked them why. 'Insanity,' replied the foreman. 'What?' responded the judge, 'all 12 of you?' While this tale is probably apocryphal, there are a number of well-documented cases where juries have been less than thorough in arriving at their verdict. In a case at Newcastle-upon-Tyne, a juror had to be discharged by the judge after asking for the defendant's date of birth so that he could prepare an astrological chart to help decide the case. In Canada, a woman was convicted of obstructing justice by having a love affair with a man on trial for murder while she was serving on the jury that acquitted him.

In a case at Luton, the judge discharged the whole jury after a juror told the defendant from the jury box, 'Why don't you plead guilty? You are ****ing guilty'. At Northampton, another jury had to be discharged when a juror told the usher that the defence barrister was 'such a rude little man' that she wanted to hit him, and the same result was achieved at Exeter where two jurors complained to the judge that one of their colleagues had fleas!

Adapted from an article by D. Pannick, *The Times*.

Probably the oddest example of a jury using a forbidden method of determining the verdict arose in *R v Young* (1995), a murder trial, where, after a lengthy deliberation in court, the jury was sent to a hotel to continue its deliberation. While there, one of their number claimed to be a spiritualist who could communicate with the dead. She obtained a ouija board from room service and proceeded to hold a séance with the other jurors. During this séance, communication was allegedly made with the deceased victim who confirmed the guilt of the defendant. The jury then returned to court where a guilty verdict was delivered. Fortunately, rumours reached the defence counsel as to the manner in which the jury had arrived at its verdict and an appeal was duly lodged, which resulted in a retrial, at the end of which the new jury also convicted the defendant. Presumably, the judge ensured no ouija boards or any other spiritualist materials were allowed into the jury room. Who says there is no humour in the law?

Jury nobbling

Despite the introduction of majority verdicts in the Criminal Justice Act 1967, it is believed that nobbling remains a major weakness. Jury nobbling is an attempt made by means of threats or bribery to 'persuade' a juror to return a 'not guilty' verdict.

In 1982, several Old Bailey trials had to be stopped because of attempted nobbling. In 1984, jurors in the *Brinks-Mat* trial had to have police protection to and from the court, and their telephone calls were intercepted. Sir Ian Blair, the Metropolitan Police Commissioner, has stated that the cost to the police force of protecting juries runs to £4.5 million per year, which underlines the significance of the problem.

A new criminal offence was introduced in the Criminal Procedure and Investigation Act 1996 to try to give additional protection to the jury, creating the offence of intimidating or threatening to harm a juror. More radically, in s.54 of that Act, it is provided that where a person has been acquitted and someone is later convicted of interfering with or intimidating jurors or witnesses in the case, then the High Court can quash the acquittal and the person can be retried.

Bias

Ingman suggests that jurors may be biased for or against certain groups — the police, for example. However, it could also be argued that such *individual* bias will be cancelled out in a group of 12 jurors.

Cost

An argument against juries is that, compared to trials in Magistrates' Courts, jury trials in the Crown Court are much more expensive. However, by far the greatest cost elements in the Crown Court are the costs of lawyers, the judge and other court personnel. As most criminal trials last no more than 1 day, the maximum jury cost will be only £500. Nonetheless, there is some foundation for the cost argument in lengthy fraud trials, where much of the evidence will be in documentary form. If a judge was trying these cases alone, he or she could read these reports, but a jury has to hear such evidence from witnesses, which takes up a great deal of additional time.

Difficulties with appeals

When judges sit alone, their judgement consists of a detailed and explicit finding of fact. When there is a jury, it returns an unexplained verdict, as under s.8 of the Contempt of Court Act 1981, jury deliberations are secret. Sir Louis Blom-Cooper QC has argued that 'the universal, formulaic and therefore inscrutable verdict of the jury' must constitute 'an ever-present worry to the administrators of criminal justice'. Under the Human Rights Act 1998, people involved in trials have a right to know the grounds upon which a court decision is based. Where does this leave due process in trial by jury? Blom-Cooper concluded that 'the jury is the high point of amateurism, potentially a recipe for incompetence and bias'.

Chapter 8

Magistrates

There are about 30,000 lay magistrates trying over 2 million cases a year — over 96% of all criminal cases — which is 20 times the number tried in Crown Courts. As Marcel Berlins wrote in *The Law Machine*: 'If the English system of criminal justice had to depend on our professional judges, it would break down immediately. The magistrates are not just important cogs; they are the mainstay of the criminal justice system.'

This chapter looks at how magistrates are selected and appointed. It outlines how they are trained and examines the criminal jurisdiction of magistrates. Finally, it looks at the advantages and disadvantages of magistrates.

Over 96% of all criminal cases are dealt with by magistrates

The position of magistrate is historic — they were first appointed by Richard I in 1195, and their present powers were established in a statute of 1361, which empowered them 'to pursue, arrest, take and chastise offenders according to their trespass and offence'. Their present-day importance was acknowledged by Lord Irvine when, as Lord Chancellor, he wrote the Foreword to the *Magistrates Bench Handbook*: 'The lay magistrates are volunteers who give their time to the community they serve for no financial reward. They play a key role in our criminal justice system. At least 95% of the criminal business of the courts begins and ends with them.'

There are also about 130 district judges in Magistrates' Courts — formerly called stipendiaries — who are appointed by the Queen on the recommendation of the Lord Chancellor, and must have a general advocacy qualification.

Selection and appointment

Under the Justices of the Peace Act 1997, lay magistrates are appointed by the Lord Chancellor on the advice of county local advisory committees (in the Shire counties, these are often split into advisory sub-committees), each mirroring a local bench or Petty Sessional Division. Members of the advisory committees, who are appointed by the Lord Chancellor, comprise approximately two-thirds magistrates and one-third lay members. While good local knowledge is essential for members, the prime requirement is that they possess the aptitude to identify the key qualities essential in those appointed as magistrates. This in turn means they need to be able to to assess in a structured manner the evidence available from both documentation and interview. In fact, all members must complete a nationally organised training course before sitting on selection panels, even if they have substantial interviewing experience.

Until comparatively recently, candidates for positions as magistrates were nominated by various organisations, such as local political parties, voluntary groups and trade unions. However, nowadays candidates must make a formal application — either in response to an advertisement or by making an enquiry through the government website.

While there are few formal qualifications laid down for the appointment to the magistracy, applicants are expected to live or work within a reasonable distance of the court where they will normally sit, and be aged between 18 and 65. Until recently, Lord Chancellors had announced that they would be unlikely to appoint anyone under the age of 27, as it was felt they did not possess the necessary experience. However, after 2003, a small number of younger magistrates have been appointed. In Horsham, a 21-year-old disc jockey was appointed in 2005 and in 2006, a 19-year-old law student was appointed to the Pontefract Bench.

It should be stressed that magistrates are primarily determiners of fact rather than law: they are given structured guidelines for sentencing decisions and always sit with the benefit of an appropriately qualified legal adviser. Thus, generalised qualities and attitudes are sought rather than previous legal knowledge. Since they are drawn from, and reflect the demographic composition of, their local areas, it is inevitable that achieving a bench balanced on socioeconomic factors is a challenge. Other factors, such as easier access to additional paid leave for those working in the public sector, can also affect the mix of those applying to become magistrates.

Extension exercise

Are teenagers really mature enough to serve as magistrates?

The Lord Chancellor has been keen to emphasise that being a magistrate should be more than a hobby for middle-class white men of pensionable age. In practice, the evidence no longer totally supports this perception, with many benches, for example, finding it easier to secure a flow of female than male applicants. The North Sussex Bench recently provided a powerful symbol for a modern, more representative magistracy when it appointed the (then) youngest ever magistrate — a 20-year-old man described as a 'disc jockey of Asian origin'. Anand Limbachia's appointment was made shortly after the Department for Constitutional Affairs launched a £4 million advertising campaign to recruit 1,000 new magistrates. 'It is important that we get magistrates from every background to have a Bench that reflects the local community' said Lord Falconer. 'We want to recruit more young people, especially those in employment, to ensure that they too are represented in the magistracy.'

This appointment was welcomed by Simon Woolley, the National Co-ordinator of Operation Black Vote. However, there is still a long way to go. One in five people arrested by the police comes from an ethnic minority background, but only 8.5% of magistrates come from such communities. As for age, only 4% of magistrates are below the age of 40, and almost 80% are over 50.

The average age of magistrates is 55, 'but there is no question of appointing a lot of younger people to bring that age down', remarked Rachel Lipscomb, the chairman of the Magistrates Association. 'There are all sorts of issues that make the job quite an undertaking for anyone in their twenties and even in their forties'. In reality, career and family pressure often preclude many ideal candidates aged, say, between 25 and 35 from feeling able to make the substantial time commitment involved.

Understandably there are mixed views about the appointment of such young magistrates: One defence solicitor was enthusiastic about this appointment — 'it's long overdue'. The other point of view was expressed by another lawyer who said: 'We are asking people to sit in judgement on their fellow human beings, and to try to understand the difficulties that people might have in their lives...I think that you have to have a certain amount of living to have a fair perspective.'

Applicants must also be able to devote an average of half a day a fortnight to the task, for which only expenses and a small loss of earnings allowance are made. Certain people are excluded: police officers, traffic wardens, probation officers and members of their immediate families. Also excluded are members of the armed forces, those with certain criminal convictions and undischarged bankrupts.

Adapted from an article by J. Robins, *The Times*

Questions

1 What is the argument for having more ethnic-minority magistrates?

2 What reasons are given for magistrates having an average age of 55?

3 Do you agree with the statement in the article that 'you have to have a certain amount of living to have a fair perspective'?

Key qualities of magistrates

In 1998, the Lord Chancellor revised the procedures for appointing lay magistrates. These aimed to make the appointment criteria open and clear. Thus, a job description was introduced, which declares that the six key qualities defining the personal suitability of candidates are:

1 Good character — personal integrity, respect and trust of others, absence of any matter which might bring the magistracy into disrepute.

2 Understanding and communication — an ability to understand documents, identify and comprehend facts and follow evidence and arguments, and an ability to communicate effectively.

3 Social awareness — an appreciation and acceptance of the rule of law, an understanding of local communities and society in general, respect for people from different ethnic, cultural or social backgrounds, and experience of life beyond family, friends and work.

4 Maturity and sound temperament — an ability to relate to and work with others, regard for the views of others, willingness to consider advice, humanity, firmness, decisiveness, a sense of fairness, courtesy.

5 Sound judgement — common sense, an ability to think logically, weigh arguments and reach a balanced decision, openness of mind, objectivity and the ability to recognise and put aside prejudices.

6 Commitment and reliability — commitment to serve the community, willingness to undertake at least 26 and up to 35 half-day sittings or more a year, willingness to undertake the required training, in sufficiently good health. (Note that research commissioned in 2000 reported that the average magistrate sat 41 times.)

Selection process for magistrates

The advisory committee arranges interviews for candidates who have been short-listed after references have been checked. The interview panel usually comprises

If a defendant is charged with an either-way offence, there will be a preliminary hearing called **plea before venue** to determine which court — Magistrates' or Crown Court — will handle the case. If the defendant decides to plead 'not guilty', the choice of court is made by the defendant. However, in such cases, if the charge is a serious one and the magistrates believe their sentencing powers may not be sufficient to reflect the seriousness of the offence, they may overrule the defendant's choice of summary trial and remit the case to the Crown Court.

If the defendant's plea is one of 'guilty', the magistrates decide whether sentencing should be the responsibility of themselves or the Crown Court. It should be noted that, even if the eventual disposal is a community order, it may be better for that to be imposed by the Crown Court, as their residual powers are far greater in the event of that order being breached.

During the trial itself, magistrates, who usually sit in panels of three, are advised on points of law by legally qualified clerks. In *R* v *Eccles Justices ex parte Farrelly* (1992), it was ruled that the magistrates' decision in a case could not be upheld because the legal adviser had retired with the magistrates and had spent 25 minutes out of a total 30 minutes in the retiring room. The argument by the defence was that there was a clear inference that the adviser gave the magistrates additional advice (which in law must be given in open court), and possibly that the adviser was involved in the actual decision-making process.

Another case that exemplifies the rule that only magistrates are to be involved in the actual decision-making process is *Guildford Magistrates ex parte Harding* (1981) where again the adviser retired with the magistrates. In this case, the chairperson of the bench suggested that the reason the adviser had been asked to come to the

Magistrates usually sit in panels of three and are advised on points of law by legally qualified clerks

retiring room was to advise on the standard of proof in a criminal case. However, the appeal against conviction was quashed on the simple ground that if the magistrates were not themselves well aware of the standard of proof, they should not have been sitting as magistrates in the first place.

Note that the procedure is rather different in the Family Proceedings Court, where the chairperson has to deliver an often-lengthy written and reasoned determination, usually reading it out to the parties before the clerk gives them copies. In such cases, the clerk will typically join the bench in the retiring room and formulate a draft document on the basis of its deliberations.

If the defendant is found guilty, the chair of the bench will pronounce that verdict, but unlike jury verdicts, reasons for the verdict must be given. Unless the bench considers a fine or discharge appropriate, when sentencing will take place at the end of the trial, magistrates will usually defer sentencing pending the receipt of a pre-sentencing report from the Probation Service.

Magistrates' present sentencing powers are limited to a fine not exceeding £5,000 and/or a prison sentence up to 6 months. Where consecutive sentences are passed by magistrates for two or more separate either-way offences, their maximum powers are 6 months in aggregate. The Criminal Justice Act 2003 made provision for an extension to 1 year's imprisonment but, presumably because of serious prison overcrowding, this power has not been implemented. It remains an option for magistrates to remit a case after trial and conviction to the Crown Court for sentencing, where the offence justifies a heavier sentence than lies within magistrates' powers.

Procedure for indictable offences

Indictable offences are the most serious offences, such as murder, manslaughter, rape, armed robbery and inflicting grievous bodily harm with intent, which may only be tried at the Crown Court by a judge and jury. Section 51 of the Crime and Disorder Act 1998 states that, for indictable-only offences, adults appearing in the magistrates' court shall 'be sent forthwith' to the Crown Court. Submissions of no case to answer will become part of the pre-trial procedure at the Crown Court. This process removes the former committal powers of magistrates in such cases. Bail applications may, of course, be necessary.

Appeals

In ordinary appeals against conviction and/or sentence from the Magistrates' Courts to the Crown Court, magistrates (usually two) sit with a circuit judge. Care is taken to ensure that these magistrates are independent of those who made the original decision.

Warrants

Magistrates deal with requests for arrest and search warrants from the police.

Youth court

This court has the responsibility of trying all offenders aged between 10 (the minimum age of criminal responsibility) and 17 for all offences except murder (for which the only sentence is life imprisonment).

The procedure in the youth court is similar but less formal than in the adult courts, and is held in the presence of three magistrates and the justice's clerk. However, the magistrates concerned must have received additional training and there must be a mixed-gender bench. The court also requires the presence of a parent or guardian, and the youth may also have a legal representative or social worker present.

Unlike the adult court, the hearing is held in private and the defendant's name is not disclosed to the public unless deemed to be in the public interest. If found guilty, the young person will be bound over, receive a deferred sentence, community sentence or, if he or she is over 15, a sentence of detention in a Young Offenders Institution. If aged 12–14 and convicted of a sufficiently serious offence, and the offender is judged to be a **persistent offender**, a new sentence under the **Criminal Justice and Public Order Act 1994** may be given — a detention and training order (maximum 2 years, of which 12 months will require the defendant to be under supervision).

Other sentences include a fine, absolute or conditional discharges, or an attendance centre order (for 10–20 year olds). Another sentence is a referral order: this is relevant only for first-time offenders who have pleaded guilty. The length of this order is set between 3 and 12 months and is governed by the seriousness of the offence. The referral is to a local Youth Offender Panel, which draws up a 'contract' of aims targeted at addressing the offending behaviour. One further sentence is a supervision order, which can be issued against a defendant aged between 10 and 17, whereby a social worker is to 'advise, assist and befriend'.

District judges — Magistrates' Courts

District judges are legally qualified, paid judges, being barristers or solicitors of at least 7 years' standing. They are appointed to courts in large cities or within a county. There are at present 129 such judges. Retirement is at 70 unless the Lord Chancellor permits an extension. These district judges (and part-time deputy district judges) sit mainly in large cities, where they try more serious either-way cases. They also deal with extradition hearings, which raise complex legal issues.

Advantages of magistrates

Cost

In 1989, the magistrate system cost about £200 million a year to run, while it brought in a total income of almost £270 million in fines. Because lay magistrates are volunteers, the system is extremely cost-effective — in 2003/04 their expenses amounted only to £15 million for about 30,000 magistrates, an average of just £500 per magistrate.

Lay magistrates try the vast majority of criminal cases. To pay professional judges to deal with such an enormous caseload would be hugely expensive — at least £100 million per year in salaries alone, plus the cost of appointment and training. It would also take a long time to amass the required number of legally qualified candidates. Switching to Crown Court trials would be even more expensive. In 1999, the Home Office estimated the average cost of a contested trial by magistrates at £1,500, and a guilty plea at £500, whereas for Crown Court trials the figures were £13,500 and £2,500 respectively.

Lay involvement

This is substantially the same point that is cited in support of the jury, but the true value of lay involvement is open to doubt, given the restricted background of magistrates. In 2001, the Auld Report stated that 'the magistracy is not a true reflection of the population nationally or of communities locally'. Another commentator wrote that the magistracy 'is overwhelmingly drawn from professional and managerial ranks...and disproportionately middle class'. While this may be regarded as a criticism of lay magistrates, it must be remembered that the only alternative would be professional judges, and they are not remotely representative of the population at large or the local community. However, as Rupert Jackson noted in *The Machinery of Justice in England*: 'Benches do tend to be largely middle to upper class, but that is a characteristic of those set in authority over us, whether in town hall, Whitehall, hospitals and all manner of institutions.'

However, because magistrates usually live within a reasonable distance of the court, this may provide them with a better-informed picture of local life than judges. Lord Irvine, the Lord Chancellor, emphasised this in a speech made in 1999 to the Magistrates Association: 'Your role as lay justices is not just to decide cases but to represent to the offender the views of the community against which he has offended. Your local knowledge is again valuable here.'

Note that in recent years many more magistrates from minority ethnic groups have been appointed — the national figure is now almost 8.5%. In 2001/02, 9.3% of all new magistrate appointments were drawn from people with minority ethnic backgrounds, which indicates that the initiatives of the Lord Chancellor's Department to widen access to the magistracy have been successful. In terms of gender balance, magistrates have achieved parity between male and female appointments and, indeed, many benches will have a marginally higher female than male composition. It would be salutary to contrast this equality with the number of female judges — only 16% of judges are women.

Weight of numbers

The simple fact that magistrates must usually sit in threes may make a balanced view more likely — in a real sense they sit as a 'mini-jury'. In the absence of consensus, the majority view prevails, which can lead to chairpersons having to make pronouncements with which they personally disagree.

Few appeals

Because most defendants plead guilty, it is unsurprising that there are few appeals. In 2003, only 11,858 appeals were made to the Crown Court, of which only 2,811 were successful (out of a total workload of more than 1.9 million criminal cases). There were only 96 appeals by way of case stated to the Queen's Bench divisional court on a point of law, of which 43 were allowed. As Jacqueline Martin comments (in *AS Law*) 'it can be argued that despite the amateur status of lay magistrates they do a remarkably good job'.

Disadvantages of magistrates

Inconsistency

There is considerable inconsistency in the decision-making of different benches. This is particularly notable in the awards of legal aid and the types of sentences ordered. Research has confirmed that some magistrates' benches are more than ten times more likely to impose a custodial sentence than neighbouring benches for similar offences. In the White Paper *Justice for All*, analysis on the 2001 criminal statistics showed that for 'driving while disqualified', the percentage of offenders given a custodial sentence varied from 21% in Neath to 77% in mid-north Essex. For offenders convicted of receiving stolen goods, custodial sentences ranged from 3.5% in Reading to 48% in Greenwich. In spite of these findings, the use of the Common Guidelines and a structured approach would appear to achieve generally consistent decisions within the same area, irrespective of which individual magistrates hear the cases.

Bias towards the police

Police officers are frequent witnesses and become well known to magistrates, and it has been argued that this results in an almost automatic tendency to believe police evidence. In *R v Bingham JJ ex parte Jowitt* (1974), a speeding case where the only evidence was that of the motorist and a policeman, the chair of the bench said that where there was direct conflict between the defendant and the police 'my principle in such cases has always been to believe the evidence of the police officer'. The conviction was quashed because of this remark (which was criticised severely). However, many magistrates would strenuously refute the accusation of pro-police bias.

'Cheap/amateur' justice

Because the chances of acquittal are substantially higher in the Crown Court than in the Magistrates' Court, this creates the suspicion that the Crown Court is a fairer forum in which to decide cases, or even that magistrates are not as fair as they might be. It should be noted, however, that over 90% of defendants plead guilty and the nature of most cases depends more on factual issues than complex legal problems (e.g. drink-driving). This argument is weakened further by the fact that magistrates are given expert legal advice by a qualified legal adviser. This point has given rise to another criticism — that of undue reliance by magistrates on their legal advisers — but to counter these arguments is the fact there are so few successful appeals made against the decisions, both convictions and sentences. Some would also argue that magistrates inevitably become more experienced in assessing witness credibility and thus comfortable with reaching decisions than many jury members, for whom hearing a single, short trial may be a once-in-a-lifetime and onerous occurrence.

Increasing complexity of the law

More crimes are being down-graded to summary offences with new offences being created. Sentencing has also become much more complex in recent years, for example with the introduction of curfew orders and ASBOs. This increasing complexity is, however, reflected in the provision of more intensive training and appraisal schemes, as well as by the fact that legal advisers must have qualified and practised as solicitors or barristers. Certainly, the greater the number of sentencing options (especially with requirements within community orders), the longer and more complex the pronouncements become, but this applies whoever is doing the job.

Finally, it should be noted that in no other European jurisdiction do lay judges have so much power. To the question 'Are lay magistrates any longer justifiable?', Professor Dugdale in *A-Level Law* answered:

> *Whatever merits there may be in suggestions for that professional judges should replace lay magistrates, there seems no prospect of their coming to fruition. The lay magistracy has the emotional appeal of involving the ordinary person in the administration of justice and the practical appeal of dealing with the vast majority of criminal cases relatively cheaply. This is surely an unassailable combination.*

Questions

1 Who are disqualified from being appointed as magistrates?

2 Name three of the six key qualities laid down by the Lord Chancellor.

3 What body is responsible for organising training for magistrates?

4 What is the role of legal advisers?

5 Which Act regulates bail applications?

6 What are three conditions that may be imposed if bail is allowed?

7 Outline the procedure called 'Plea before venue'.

8 Which Act requires magistrates to send defendants charged with indictable offences to the crown court?

9 What are the main differences in procedure between the adult court and the youth court?

10 What are the maximum sentences that magistrates can impose in the adult court?

Sample exam questions

1 Explain the criminal jurisdiction of magistrates.   (10 marks)

Task

Read the following sample answers to this question, which have been assessed as 'fragment', 'limited' and 'some' respectively. Rewrite them as both a 'clear' and a 'sound' answer.

> *Magistrates try most criminal offences, including road traffic offences.*

This answer receives 1–2 marks only — 'fragment'.

> *Magistrates try 97% of all criminal offences, including all summary offences and the majority of either-way offences. They can sentence convicted offenders to 6 months in prison or a fine up to £5,000.*

This answer receives 3–4 marks only — 'limited'.

Magistrates try 97% of all criminal offences, including all summary offences such as drink-driving, and most either-way offences, for example theft. They will be advised by legal advisers about legal rules and if they decide to convict the offender, they can impose a prison sentence up to 6 months or a fine up to £5,000.

This answer receives 5 marks only — 'some'.

2 Explain and discuss the advantages and disadvantages of lay magistrates in the criminal justice system. (15 marks)

Task

Read the following sample answer to this question, which has been assessed as 'some', and the hints that follow. Rewrite the sample answer as both a 'clear' and a 'sound' response.

One advantage of magistrates is that they are local people and therefore are aware of local concerns. They are also representative of local people in a way that judges cannot be — for example, most benches have equal number of male and female magistrates, and they also have many more from ethnic minorities. Magistrates are much cheaper than judges since they do not get paid.

However, there are some disadvantages — first, their sentences can be inconsistent, with some benches being much more likely to impose custodial sentences than others.

Second, because the law is becoming much more complicated, it can be argued that they may make mistakes in cases brought before them.

Finally, it is sometimes said that magistrates tend to be biased towards the prosecution because they hear the same types of cases time and time again, and get to know the police officers who often attend as prosecution witnesses.

Overall, however, the advantages seem to outweigh the disadvantages.

This answer receives 8 marks out of 15.

Hints

The explanations in this sample answer are superficial — in effect, the candidate gives a simple list of advantages and disadvantages. This is a common weakness in such answers. It is much better to explain two issues in depth than list three or more. There are no cases cited to illustrate any particular point. The discussion is a 'one-liner' at the end, which rates as a 'fragment' only.

Appeals lie to the divisional court of the Queen's Bench Division of the High Court on a point of law by way of case stated, or to the Crown Court against sentence or conviction.

Crown Court

The main jurisdiction of Crown Courts is to hear all indictable offences, such as murder, rape, robbery and the more serious either-way offences, where jurisdiction has been declined by magistrates or where the defendant has elected to be tried on indictment by a judge sitting with a jury. It also acts as an appeal court hearing cases from Magistrates' Courts.

Cases are tried by different judges depending on the seriousness of the offence. All Class 1 offences (murder) must be tried by a High Court judge from the Queen's Bench Division. Such judges also try the majority of Class 2 offences (those that can result in a life sentence, e.g. rape, robbery, attempted murder). Other less serious offences are tried by circuit judges or recorders. In all cases heard in the Crown Court, the decision on the defendant's guilt or innocence is taken by the jury. If the jury finds the defendant guilty, the judge has the responsibility of sentencing the convicted offender.

Appeal courts

Court of Appeal (Criminal Division)

This is presided over by the President of Queen's Bench Division. Three judges make up the panel that hears appeals — usually a Lord Justice of Appeal accompanied by two senior High Court judges from the Queen's Bench Division. In more important appeals, all the judges will be Lord Justices.

Appeals may be made to this court by defendants against sentence or conviction from the Crown Court, providing that 'leave to appeal' has been granted. In appeals against sentence, the Court of Appeal may confirm or reduce the sentence imposed at trial.

The grounds for appealing against conviction are principally that the original conviction is 'unsafe or unsatisfactory', new evidence that was not available at the time of trial has come to light, or there had been a material irregularity in the course of the trial.

As regards such appeals, the court can uphold the original conviction, quash it (i.e. overturn it and release the defendant), substitute a lower-level conviction — for example, a manslaughter conviction where the original conviction was for murder — or order a re-trial.

Appeals by the Attorney General

Under s.35 of the Criminal Justice Act 1988, the Attorney General acting on behalf of the Crown Prosecution Service can, with the leave of the court, appeal to the Court of Appeal against 'an unduly lenient sentence'. In such appeals, it is then open to the Court of Appeal to increase the original sentence imposed by the trial judge.

The Attorney General can also refer a case to the Court of Appeal following an acquittal in the Crown Court, which he or she has reason to believe was the result of an error in law made by the judge in his or her directions to the jury. The purpose of such a referral is to verify the correct legal rule. The defendant, having been acquitted, is not identified in the citation, which is simply listed as 'Attorney General's Reference No... of 2008', and whatever decision on the law is made by the Court of Appeal, the acquittal is not affected in any way.

Appellate Committee of the House of Lords

Under the Constitutional Reform Act 2005, this court will be renamed the Supreme Court of the United Kingdom in 2010. The court is already effectively our Supreme Court — the judges are called **Lords of Appeal in Ordinary** or, more commonly, **Law Lords**. Only about 60 cases are heard by this court each year, most of them civil cases. Leave to appeal must be granted by the Court of Appeal, although if this is not given, the appellant may seek leave to appeal from the House of Lords itself. Only cases that raise legal issues 'of general public importance' will be considered (e.g. *A and others* v *Home Secretary*, 2004). No appeals against sentence are heard by this court.

If the issue in law concerns a possible breach of human rights as laid down in the European Convention of Human Rights, which was incorporated into English law by the Human Rights Act 1998, there is one further route of appeal — to the European Court of Human Rights (ECHR) in Strasbourg.

> **Suggested reading**
>
> Gillespie, A. (2007) *The English Legal System*, Oxford University Press.
> Turner, C. (2007) 'Criminal appeal routes', *A-Level Law Review*, Vol. 2, No. 2.
>   pp. 30–31.

the Bar), the barrister finally has to secure a tenancy in a set of chambers. Obtaining pupillage and a tenancy are both very difficult, with demand outstripping supply. (There are currently no more than 600 pupillages and 300–350 tenancies available, with over 1,700 students successfully completing the BVC each year). In *Counsel* (the monthly magazine published by the Bar Council), it was stated in an article by Peter Newman that 'currently, many more than half of the students who take the BVC will never practise at the Bar' (April 2006).

Barristers carry out most of their work in court-based advocacy

Equality and diversity

Like many people, I care very much about the Bar and about equality and diversity. In a modern society a profession is not sustainable if it is not open, and seen to be open, to the best people for the job. This is not simply to do with race, ethnicity and sex. It is about ensuring that people, whatever their circumstances and background, all have the same opportunities to become and practise as barristers, provided they have the necessary ability.

Accessibility to the profession must start early. At school, children select subjects based on career goals and on advice obtained from teachers and parents. If students do not see the profession as accessible, they are unlikely to see it differently at a later date. Even if they do, their opportunities for entering the legal profession might by then be limited by degree or university choice so that it is too late and they will be lost to the profession and the profession will be lost to them.

Lord Neuberger, *Counsel*, March 2007

Legal executives

Most firms of solicitors employ legal executives who do much of the basic work of solicitors — especially conveyancing and probate. Their qualifications are laid down by ILEX. This requires trainee legal executives to pass Parts I and II of ILEX, and then to work for 5 years in a firm of solicitors or other legal organisation (e.g. the Crown Prosecution Service) in order to become a Fellow of ILEX. Legal executives work in solicitors' firms, where they specialise in probate or conveyancing work under the supervision of solicitors. They also have limited **rights of audience** (the right to represent clients in court) in County Courts. It was announced in June 2006 that they would receive limited rights of audience in Magistrates' Courts for certain criminal cases, including bail applications. Barristers have full rights of audience — they can appear in any court, whereas solicitors, unless qualified as solicitor-advocates, only have rights of audience in Magistrates' and County Courts.

Legal executives would also be able to appear in the Crown Court for bail applications. Following the government's commitment to open up the judicial appointments system, it is likely that in the future legal executives could become eligible for appointment as district judges.

Exam hint

In questions on explaining how to become a solicitor and/or a barrister, it is essential not to confuse these two professions. Read the comments made in the Examiner's Reports about the problems candidates experience in this common type of question. For questions on barristers, ensure that you learn the chronology of the various stages thoroughly — (i) law degree (or non-law degree followed by GDL); (ii) application and entry to Inn of Court; (iii) admission to BVC course; (iv) 12 dinners; (v) call to the Bar; (vi) pupillage; (vii) tenancy.

Work of solicitors

Solicitors may work on their own as sole practitioners but, increasingly, they work with other solicitors in a firm. On qualifying, a solicitor will work as an **associate solicitor** within a firm. Once he or she becomes more experienced, they may become a **partner** in the firm, which means they will receive both a salary and a share of the profits the firm makes.

Most of a solicitor's work involves giving legal advice to clients and carrying out administrative tasks, including:

* **Conveyancing** — dealing with the legal requirements of buying and selling property.
* **Probate** — drafting wills and acting as executors for the estates of deceased persons.

After 10 years in practice, barristers may apply to the Lord Chancellor to become a **Queen's Counsel** or QC. This is known as 'taking silk', as they wear court gowns made of silk. About 10% of barristers are QCs — this is a required step for most barristers if they aspire to be circuit or High Court judges. QCs are those senior lawyers, still almost all barristers, who will appear in the most difficult civil and criminal cases, and appeals before the Court of Appeal and the House of Lords. Most judges, especially superior judges (High Court judges, Lord Justices of Appeal and Law Lords) are QCs.

Comparison between the work of solicitors and barristers

Quite often an examination question that requires candidates to explain the work of each branch of the legal profession also requires candidates to compare the work of each branch. If you look at the comments in the Chief Examiner's reports on such questions, you will find that this part of the question is often answered much less satisfactorily.

Main differences

- ❖ Solicitors are allowed to form partnerships and work for other solicitors, whereas barristers have to be independent and self-employed. Even though they join with other barristers in sets of chambers and share expenses, they do not share their income.
- ❖ Solicitors work across the country and there are solicitors' firms on most high streets. However, barristers' chambers are concentrated in one small area of London and in central areas of large cities that have Crown Courts — particularly those major cities that also have High Court sittings.
- ❖ Solicitors deal directly with members of the public, whereas barristers are a 'referral profession'. This means that members of the public have to consult a solicitor first.
- ❖ Solicitors are often described as 'general legal advisers'. They carry out a huge variety of office-based work — writing letters, drawing up documents (e.g. for the purchase, sale or lease of a house or factory), negotiating with other people on behalf of the client and completing the preparatory work for cases that will end up in court.
- ❖ Barristers, on the other hand, are usually thought of as 'specialists' who spend their time either on advocacy in court or writing counsels' opinions — advice to clients and their solicitors on specialist areas of law.

❖ Barristers have rights of audience in all the courts, whereas solicitors usually only have rights of audience in Magistrates' and County Courts.

❖ Barristers traditionally are appointed as superior judges, whereas solicitors rarely achieve higher judicial office than circuit judges. Most solicitors who become judges are appointed as district or deputy district judges.

Changes in working practices

There have been many changes to the ways in which both solicitors and barristers work. It is important to understand the nature of these changes because this provides the *evaluative* content to examination questions.

❖ The biggest change is that solicitors can now obtain rights of audience in the higher courts as solicitor-advocates. This radical change was introduced in the Courts and Legal Services Act 1990, and was extended in the Access to Justice Act 1999. Eventually, it is envisaged that most solicitors will qualify as solicitor-advocates. As a result of this change, solicitor-advocates now have the qualifications to be appointed as High Court judges. There have been two such appointments since 1993.

❖ The biggest change involving barristers concerns the issue of access to barristers, through Direct Professional Access and Direct Client Access.

❖ The Legal Services Act 2007 enacts the recommendations made in the Clementi Report. This will make multi-disciplinary partnerships possible, in which barristers and solicitors could find themselves working in the same law firm. It is even envisaged that firms such as supermarkets could employ lawyers to provide legal services directly to members of the public — the so-called 'Tesco law'.

❖ In terms of specialisation of work, it may no longer be the situation that solicitors can be compared to GPs in the medical profession, with barristers being likened to medical consultants. Today, many solicitors specialise in different branches of law — criminal, family, employment, sports law, personal injury, intellectual property (patents and copyright). Equally, many barristers, especially junior barristers, are just as likely to be general lawyers, being briefed in most kinds of law case.

While there are still two different professions, regulated by different professional bodies, the changes that have occurred since 1990 have allowed each profession to adapt and to do some of the things traditionally performed by the other. It would now be more accurate to say that rather than solicitors being general, office-based advisers and barristers being court-based specialists, they are increasingly in competition with each other for similar kinds of work. It is inevitable that the Legal Services Act 2007 will accelerate this process.

Questions

1 Why can QC status be regarded as an indication of merit only if there is continuing appraisal of QCs?

2 Why do QCs cause inflationary pressures?

3 Why would the abolition of the QC rank impact substantially on a new generation of women and ethnic-minority lawyers?

4 Do you agree with the final statement that the 'rank of QC actually promotes competition and drives up standards'?

The role of professional bodies

The Law Society

The Law Society has a number of functions:

❖ It regulates admission, qualifications and training (including continuing professional development) for all solicitors.

❖ It issues practising certificates.

❖ It promotes the interests of solicitors.

❖ It deals with disciplinary matters and complaints.

Following the publication of the Clementi Report in 2004 and the government White Paper (*The Future of Legal Services*) in 2005, the Law Society divided its roles of regulation and representation.

David Pearson/Alamy

The Law Society is the representative body for solicitors in England and Wales

Discipline

Following heavy criticism from the Legal Services Ombudsman and the Lord Chancellor about the Law Society's handling of client complaints, the Law Society decided to create a completely independent complaints handling service. This is now overseen by the **Solicitors Regulation Authority** (SRA), which was set up in 2007. This body is independent and has a governing body of 16 members — nine solicitors and seven lay members. Its budget of £50 million is raised from the practising certificate fee paid annually by all solicitors.

Complaints from the public are sent to the **Legal Complaints Service** (LCS). After investigation, if it is decided that the complaint is justified, the solicitor against whom the complaint was made can be ordered to reduce his or her bill, pay compensation or correct a mistake he or she has made and pay any costs involved. If the complaint is found to be serious, involving dishonesty or the breach of any other rule of professional conduct, it may be referred by the LCS to the SRA. In such cases, the complaint could then be referred to the **Solicitor's Disciplinary Tribunal**, which has statutory powers to discipline the solicitor by fining or even striking him or her off the Rolls of the Law Society, effectively 'sacking' the solicitor. In recent years, more solicitors are being struck off than ever before. Appeals from this tribunal go the High Court.

In 2004, the Lord Chancellor created the new position of the **Legal Services Complaints Commissioner** under s.51 of the Access to Justice Act 1999, with powers to investigate how effectively the Law Society is dealing with complaints. In 2006, the Commissioner (who is also the Legal Services Ombudsman) imposed a fine of £250,000 on the Law Society for its failure to impose effective targets to improve its handling of consumer complaints.

The Bar Council

The Bar Council is the body that has overall control of practising barristers. Its members come from all sections of the Bar and its functions include making general policy decisions, determining the consolidated regulations for the Inns of Court, dealing with disciplinary matters and making provision for the education and training of barristers.

Discipline

In 1997, the Bar Council appointed its first **Complaints Commissioner**, who can require barristers to reduce, refund or waive fees and order compensation of up to £2,000. More serious complaints will be referred to the **Bar Standards Board**, which can decide to dismiss the complaint or to find the barrister guilty of misconduct. In that event, it has the power to fine the barrister up to £5,000, and to suspend or disbar him or her. In 2000, in a major change of the law, the case of *Hall* v *Simons*

solicitors have not been awarded legal aid contracts and cannot provide any legal assistance to people living in that area who are unable to pay privately.

A 2002 Law Society survey showed that 28% of solicitors' firms had dropped some legal aid contracts. Among the greatest areas of concern were housing and employment law, where 25% of firms had dropped contracts, and welfare benefits and debt, where 23% of firms no longer did the work. This survey found no solicitor in the whole of Kent offering public-funded advice on housing matters, with very few offering legally aided divorce work, even in London.

How great is this unmet need? The 1973 book *Legal Problems & the Citizen* (by Brian Abel-Smith, Michael Zander and Rosalind Brooke) contained a study that compared people's perception of needing legal advice in certain areas with the steps they actually took to obtain such advice. In a large number of cases, no action was taken at all. This study also supported the view that people usually approach solicitors on a fairly narrow range of issues. Nearly all the respondents who needed legal advice in connection with buying a house consulted a solicitor, but only 3% sought advice on social security law. Sixteen percent sought advice from other sources such as Citizens Advice, but 81% sought no advice at all, even though they believed they had a problem.

Too many people remain as 'hidden need' — some may be unable to articulate their problem, and others may not appreciate that their problem is capable of being addressed through legal services. Essential to an inclusion agenda is the need for community-based resources to create the grass-roots structure through which the most marginalised can find a voice and thus gain access to the justice system. Key areas of legal need are those concerning welfare entitlements, housing law, discrimination, debt, employment, community care, mental health, immigration and education. All these problem areas have a significant bearing on the major political problem of social exclusion. This formed the centrepiece of a review commissioned by the Lord Chancellor and published by that department.

Despite efforts by the Community Legal Service to establish Community Legal Partnerships to widen the availability of access to legal advice by funding law centres, Citizens Advice and charities, this unmet need continues to grow.

Different ways of funding a civil case

A typical examination question might require you to explain how a claimant who has been injured in a road or workplace accident would be able to pay for the case to go to court. Here are some of these ways.

Paying a solicitor and barrister privately

This would, of course, be expensive, although some firms of solicitors do advertise a 'free first hour of interview'. Hourly rates of associate solicitors often exceed £150,

11

while senior partners will charge over £300. Barristers' fees are charged for the whole case — drafting pleadings and court advocacy — but even a short County Court case would cost several thousand pounds.

Receiving full or part legal aid

Under the Access to Justice Act 1999, the **Community Legal Service (CLS)** manages the **Community Legal Service Fund** provided by the government. This fund is capped: there is a fixed amount of money paid into it, and the government has laid down certain priority areas for the money. These include social welfare issues, domestic violence issues, cases involving children's welfare and proceedings against public authorities alleging serious wrongdoing. The entitlement to receive public funding is based on a means test, which assesses the claimant's income and capital. To qualify for full legal aid funding, both to cover initial advice and then legal representation in court, the claimant would have to be wholly dependent on social security benefits.

There is also a merits test to ensure that such funding is only given where the case has a good prospect of success. This takes into account the likely amount of damages that would be awarded. No assistance is available from the CLS in cases involving personal injury or damage to property, conveyancing, probate, boundary disputes or defamation.

Conditional fee litigation

Conditional fee litigation was first introduced into English law under the Courts and Legal Services Act 1990, and was greatly extended under the Access to Justice Act 1999. This scheme is commonly referred to as 'no win, no fee' because under it, the lawyers are only paid for their services if the case is won. To make it attractive to lawyers, under this scheme, they can charge a 'success fee' of up to 100% of their usual fee. The lawyers' fees are paid by the losing defendant. In the Naomi Campbell libel case, which was appealed to the House of Lords, the total fees of the claimant amounted to £1.5 million.

To ensure money is available to pay the other side's legal costs if the case is lost, lawyers will arrange for 'after-the-event' insurance to be provided, which the claimant will have to pay. This policy then pays the other side if they win, and the premium becomes a part of the claimant's costs payable by the defendant if the claim is successful.

In *Callery* v *Gray* (2001), the Court of Appeal laid down guidelines concerning the defendant's liability for both the success fee and the after-the-event insurance premium. Even where there is a high chance of the claim being successful, it is not unreasonable for the claimant when he or she first seeks legal advice to make such an agreement and take out insurance against the (unlikely) possibility of losing. The defendant is therefore liable for these additional costs, but in simple cases (as that was), the success fee should not be 100% but should be restricted to no more than 20% of the solicitor's normal fee.

This scheme has been extremely controversial on a number of points. First, research has shown that very few people are aware of it and how it actually works. Second, it has resulted in the argument that we now have a 'compensation culture' fuelled by claim management companies who advertise 'where's there's blame there's a claim'. Most lawyers will restrict such cases to claimants, with few prepared to defend a case on this basis. Finally, it raises the problem that lawyers only have an incentive to take cases on this basis if they are really strong. In the early days of this scheme, two large city firms of solicitors undertook a test case to recover damages for a claimant who had contracted lung cancer from smoking, and had then died. The case never made it to a full High Court hearing, and these firms lost over £1 million as a result.

The majority of civil cases are now funded through conditional fee agreements

Citizens Advice and law centres

Both of these are free of charge to the public and funded by the CLS. Although Citizens Advice staff are not legally qualified, they may refer clients to solicitors. In matters such as housing, welfare and debt counselling, they have as much experience as many solicitors and may be able to advise clients in a more accessible way.

There are about 60 law centres in England and Wales. Funded by local authorities and the CLS, they employ qualified solicitors and barristers to give advice to clients,

mainly regarding housing, employment, welfare and immigration matters. They do not deal with criminal law problems, conveyancing or probate.

Other ways of funding legal advice and/or representation

Pro bono

This is work undertaken by a solicitor and/or barrister for free. In recent years, both professions have encouraged solicitors and barristers to work a number of hours each year on a *pro bono* basis as part of a social responsibility programme.

Private legal insurance

This is much more common in other countries than in the UK, but it is expanding here as a source of funding for civil litigation. Most motor and house insurance policies now routinely include legal insurance cover.

Professional bodies or trade unions

These often provide legal advice to members and will even cover the cost of legal representation in a court case. For example, in *Pepper* v *Hart* (1993), the Association of Teachers and Lecturers funded a case all the way to the House of Lords.

Charities

Certain charities, such as Shelter and Age Concern are able to provide some legal advice for the public, but only within the limits of their charitable responsibilities. For example, Shelter can advise on housing benefit claims or whether a landlord could be made responsible for replacing a leaky roof. Age Concern can advise elderly people about claiming for benefits.

Local authorities

All local authorities, through the trading standards or environmental health departments, can offer specialist legal advice regarding consumer problems. Some authorities also fund housing advice or welfare rights units to help the public with legal advice.

Criminal legal aid

Under the Access to Justice Act 1999, criminal legal aid is administered by the Criminal Defence Service (CDS). Unlike civil legal aid, this scheme is uncapped — there is no set budget — and is 'demand led'. The CDS is tasked with 'securing that individuals involved in criminal investigation or proceedings have access to such advice, assistance and representation as the interests of justice require'. The following schemes are provided and funded by the CDS.

Duty solicitor scheme at police stations

This scheme was first provided under the Police and Criminal Evidence Act 1984 (PACE). This is available to anyone who has been arrested and is being held in custody at a police station, providing that the solicitor has a contract with the CDS. However, this scheme no longer automatically provides that a solicitor will actually visit the arrested person in the police station.

Since May 2004, duty solicitors may not attend the police station where the client has been detained for a non-imprisonable offence (e.g. for drink-driving offences or if the client is in breach of bail conditions). Instead, legal advice in these cases may only be given by telephone, unless the client is vulnerable (e.g. a youth, someone who cannot speak English, or who is mentally ill). Because of the low 'fixed-fee' nature of this scheme, many qualified solicitors do not participate in it. A survey by McConville and Hodgson in 1993 revealed that, of a total of 180 advisers attending police stations, 44 were solicitors, 28 were trainees and 108 were clerks (including 38 ex-police officers).

Advice and assistance

This scheme provides for 1 hour's work and may not include advocacy (legal representation in court), unless the solicitor has applied for a representation order. The scheme is means tested, so only those clients on low incomes or in receipt of benefits will qualify. However, the scheme does cover all defendants in custody at the Magistrates' Court, where it is available for bail or full legal aid applications, or a plea in mitigation if the defendant chooses to plead guilty.

Assistance by way of representation

Assistance by way of representation (ABWOR) is intended to provide limited representation in the Magistrates' Court for an otherwise undefended defendant. It is available free for those whose incomes are below income support level and with capital under £3,000. Those with higher incomes must contribute to the cost. In *Benham* v *United Kingdom* (1996), when the defendant was imprisoned for non-payment of poll tax, it was held by the European Court of Human Rights that, where deprivation of liberty was a real possibility, the defendant had a right to legal representation. Following this decision, the government amended the ABWOR rules so that anyone facing a real prospect of imprisonment for failure to obey a court order is entitled to the assistance of the duty solicitor in court, or to the assistance under the ABWOR scheme.

Representation in court

This scheme is means tested, and is also subject to a merits test, which involves asking whether the defendant is 'likely to face a sentence depriving him of his liberty or loss of livelihood or serious damage to reputation'. This test effectively means that most if not all defendants facing trial at a Crown Court will receive legal representation under this scheme, but the position at the Magistrates' Court will be much more variable. It is argued that this is wrong in principle, since anyone convicted, even by magistrates, will have their reputation ruined.

The defendant can usually choose his or her own solicitor and/or barrister from those employed by or under contract to the CDS, subject to the level of representation appropriate to the case.

At the end of the case, the court must decide whether the defendant should be required to pay some or even all of the costs of his or her representation, although the court equally has the power to order the prosecution to pay the defence costs where the defendant has been acquitted.

Questions

1 What is the present level of government expenditure on all forms of legal aid?
2 Which body provides legal aid for civil cases?
3 Which Act regulates legal aid?
4 Which Act introduced conditional fee litigation?
5 What was decided in *Callery* v *Gray*?
6 What is the main difference between Citizens Advice and law centres?
7 Which body provides legal aid for criminal cases?
8 Briefly explain what is meant by '*pro bono*' work.
9 Which Act created the duty solicitor scheme in police stations?
10 What was decided by the European Court of Human Rights in *Benham* v *United Kingdom*?

Sample exam questions

1 **Briefly discuss the advantages and disadvantages of both private funding and conditional fee litigation.** (10 marks)

2 Outline how someone injured in a workplace or road traffic accident would pay for his or her case to be taken to court (10 marks)

A 'sound' answer to question 2 simply requires the various options to be explained and applied briefly. A sample answer is given below.

The injured person would be well advised to consult a solicitor as quickly as possible, as personal injury claims can often be complicated. He or she could pay for this advice privately, or if the person is receiving social security benefits or is on a very low wage, an application could be made to the Community Legal Service fund for legal aid. It would be necessary for the solicitor to have a contract with the Community Legal Service to be able to submit this application.

Alternatively, under the Access to Justice Act 1999, the injured person could approach a solicitor and ask for the case to be dealt with on a conditional fee basis. This means 'no win, no fee', and is becoming a more common way of funding such cases, especially because civil legal aid has been sharply reduced for personal injury cases. If the case is successfully contested, the claimant receives the full amount of compensatory damages, with his or her legal costs being paid for by the losing side. To encourage more lawyers to deal with cases under this scheme, they are allowed to increase their fees by up to 100% as a 'success fee'.

However, given that the injuries occurred through a workplace or road traffic accident, the injured person may be able to have all the legal costs involved in obtaining advice, plus the costs of court representation, paid under his or her trade union membership benefits or, for the road traffic accident, from his or her car insurance policy. Equally, if the person has bought a private legal insurance policy, this will pay for his or her legal costs.

In terms of obtaining free advice only, rather than legal representation, the person could contact Citizens Advice and/or a law centre. These facilities will provide initial legal advice concerning his or her claim, and will also advise whether legal aid may be available.

*Finally, the injured person may be able to persuade a solicitor and then a barrister to accept the case on a **pro bono** basis — in other words, to provide legal advice and representation in court free of charge.*

This answer satisfies all the criteria for a 'sound' answer:
* It is generally accurate.
* The material is supported by relevant authority — the **Access to Justice Act 1999**, and reference to the Community Legal Service.
* It deals with the content of this question competently and coherently.

Suggested reading

Dugdale, T. et al. (2002) *'A' Level Law*, Butterworth.

Gillespie, A. (2007) *The English Legal System*, Oxford University Press.

Martin, J. (2005) *AQA Law for AS*, Hodder Arnold.

Mitchell, A. and Dadhania, M. (2006) *AS Law*, Routledge-Cavendish.

Appointment procedures

Created by the Constitutional Reform Act 2005, the **Judicial Appointments Commission** (JAC) was set up in April 2006 under the chair of Baroness Prashar. This body is responsible for the selection of all judicial office holders — judges and tribunal members. It is possible that, in the future, magistrates will also be selected by this commission. There are 15 commissioners in the JAC, drawn from the judiciary, both legal professions, tribunals, the magistracy and lay public. Twelve commissioners, including the chair, are appointed through open competition and three are selected by the Judges' Council.

It is the JAC's responsibility to select candidates for judicial office on merit. They do this independently of government, through open competition and by encouraging a wide range of applicants.

To become a deputy district judge or a district judge, suitably qualified candidates respond to advertisements placed in newspapers and professional journals, or on the website of the Lord Chancellor's Department (LCD) and complete an application form. References are taken up and shortlisted candidates are invited to a 1-day selection procedure, during which they are interviewed and take various tests to measure legal and procedural knowledge. They also participate in mock trials. Successful candidates are nominated by the JAC to the Lord Chancellor for appointment.

For recorders and circuit judges, the procedure is broadly the same. Advertisements are placed by the JAC in newspapers and professional journals, and on the LCD's website. Suitably qualified candidates apply by filling in an application form providing a number of personal referees. After taking up these references, candidates are shortlisted and interviewed by a panel of members from the JAC. Successful candidates are nominated to the Lord Chancellor, who makes the appointment formally.

For appointment as a High Court judge, candidates are again required to apply to the JAC and provide references. Referees will be interviewed by a panel chosen from the JAC, further references will also be taken up and then shortlisted candidates are interviewed by a panel chosen from the members of the JAC. The JAC then nominates one candidate to the Lord Chancellor for appointment. In the first batch of High Court appointments, 144 candidates applied — 123 men and 21 women. Ninety-four were barristers, 43 were circuit judges, and 7 were solicitors. Only 3 applicants were from minority ethnic groups. The commission shortlisted 57 — 44 men and 13 women. All

were interviewed by a panel, which was chaired by Lady Prashar (chair of the JAC) and included Lord Justice Auld and Sara Nathan, a lay commissioner. The panel chose 21 'to wait in the wings' — this means they are in a waiting pool from which future High Court vacancies will be filled as they arise. The Lord Chancellor can accept the nomination, reject the nomination or ask the panel to reconsider the selection. In the case of High Court judicial appointments, the JAC has the power to decide that none of the applicants was suitable for appointment but the Lord Chancellor can ask the commission to reconsider that decision. Since April 2006, the JAC has made 161 recommendations to the Lord Chancellor and none has been rejected.

Appointments of Lord Justices of Appeal are similar to the procedure followed for High Court appointments. The only significant difference is in the constitution of the panel that considers the applications. Under the Constitutional Reform Act 2005, this panel must contain:

❖ the Lord Chief Justice (LCJ) (or a nominee of the LCJ, who must be either a Head of Division or a Lord Justice of Appeal)
❖ a Head of Division or Lord Justice nominated by the LCJ
❖ the chair of the JAC
❖ a lay member of the commission

In practice, all appointments of Lord Justices of Appeal are made from the ranks of High Court judges.

Appointments to the House of Lords Appellate Committee — to be renamed the Supreme Court under the Constitutional Reform Act 2005 — are made under a different procedure because, unlike all the other courts in which judges sit (County, Crown, High Court, Court of Appeal), the Supreme Court is a court of the UK, not merely of England and Wales. By convention, two members are from Scotland and one from Northern Ireland and, although the Act does not explicitly enact this convention, under s.27(8): 'the commission must ensure that between them the judges will have knowledge of, and experience in, the law of each part of the United Kingdom'.

No specific process is laid down in the statute, and therefore it is for the commission to decide the nature of any competition for such an appointment. The Act does, however, require that part of the appointment procedure involves consulting:

❖ the Lord Chancellor
❖ the First Minister of Scotland
❖ the First Secretary of the Assembly of Wales
❖ the Secretary of State for Northern Ireland

The selection panel must comprise the president of the Supreme Court, the deputy president and one member each of the JAC for England and Wales, Scotland and Northern Ireland.

Having received a nomination of one candidate, the Lord Chancellor has the same options open to him or her as for appointments to the post of High Court judge or Lord Justice of Appeal. However, Supreme Court appointments are recommended to the Queen by the prime minister and under s.26(3), the prime minister must accept the name provided by the Lord Chancellor. Before the Constitutional Reform Act 2005 was passed, the prime minister could — and occasionally did — reject the candidate recommended by the Lord Chancellor, as Lord Hailsham (Conservative Lord Chancellor from 1979 to 1987) made clear in his autobiography.

Training

The **Judicial Studies Board** (JSB) was set up following the Bridge Report. This identified that the key aim of judicial training was to 'convey in a condensed form the lessons which experienced judges have acquired'. The JSB's activities include advising on and producing materials for the training of magistrates and judicial officers in tribunals, training members of the judiciary on appointment, and providing continuing training on specific changes in law and procedure that directly affect the management and conduct of cases. Judicial training generally takes place at the lower end of the judicial scale and is not therefore relevant for senior judges.

As all judges were formerly either barristers or solicitors, it is argued that they are already highly skilled, both in legal knowledge and in court procedure. This professional background has in the past led judges to believe that further training is not necessary. It is the case that in the UK judges receive much less training to be judges than is the case in other countries, where there are 'career judges' — law graduates who decide to train as judges without first qualifying as lawyers. This problem is compounded by the fact that many judges are appointed to try cases where they have no particular expertise. Recorders, whose principal duty is to try either-way offences in the Crown Court, are often selected from barristers or solicitors who have little criminal court experience. High Court judges are sometimes assigned to a division in which they have little direct experience.

The training regime for recorders (known as the Criminal Law Induction Course) lays down the requirement that recorders should undertake a 4-day residential course before sitting in a Crown Court. The course includes lectures, sentencing and summing-up exercises, mock trials and equal treatment training. Visits to penal institutions (i.e. prisons), observations of serving judges and meetings with probation officers will also be provided to supplement the training. Further training is given in the form of a criminal conference 18 months later. Before presiding over a Crown Court trial, recorders in training will sit alongside an experienced circuit judge.

In recent years, the JSB has received large increases in its operating budget, and has arranged significantly more training for judges and magistrates, including courses in ethnic awareness, human rights and computer use. The Civil Procedure Rules — reforms to the civil justice system — have also prompted further judicial training.

Functions

In civil courts, judges preside over the court, decide legal issues concerning admissibility of evidence and give a reasoned decision in favour of one of the parties. If the defendant is held liable, the judge will decide the award of damages. In criminal cases tried in the Crown Court, the judge will ensure order is maintained, decide legal issues in the absence of the jury (such as rules governing admissibility of evidence), summarise evidence to the jury and direct them on relevant legal rules. If the defendant is convicted, the judge will decide the sentence to be imposed. In appeal cases, judges have an important law-making role, through the operation of the doctrine of precedent and statutory interpretation.

District judges work in County Courts, where they preside over small claims cases and have administrative responsibilities, and in Magistrates' Courts, where they sit by themselves. Recorders work in both Crown Courts and County Courts, as do circuit judges.

High Court judges are assigned on appointment to a specific division of the High Court. Queen's Bench judges go on circuit to Crown Courts, where they try all Class 1 offences (such as murder) and most Class 2 offences (all other serious offences for which a life sentence could be imposed.) Such judges also sit in the Court of Appeal (Criminal Division), together with a Lord Justice of Appeal.

Lord Justices of Appeal sit in the Court of Appeal, either in the Civil or Criminal Division, and usually in a panel of three. Only those judges who had formally sat in the Queen's Bench Division are able to sit in the Criminal Division of the Court of Appeal.

Law Lords sit in the House of Lords (Appellate Committee), where they hear final appeals that must involve a point of law of 'general public importance'. Only about 60 cases are heard each year, the majority being tax cases. These same judges also sit in the Judicial Committee of the Privy Council to hear cases from the few Commonwealth countries that allow such appeals to the UK. Under the Constitutional Reform Act 2005, the present Law Lords will preside over the new UK Supreme Court when the Middlesex Guildhall is refurbished in October 2009.

Senior judges are asked by government ministers to preside over judicial or public enquiries — examples are the Dunblane Enquiry (Lord Cullen), the Hillsborough Football Disaster Enquiry (Mr Justice Taylor) and the Arms-to-Iraq Enquiry (Lord Scott).

Dismissal

The **Supreme Court Act 1981** states that High Court judges and Lord Justices of Appeal hold office (until retirement at the age of 70) 'during good behaviour, subject to a power of removal by Her Majesty on an address presented to her by both Houses of Parliament'.

This has never happened to an English judge. The only occasion when the procedure was invoked was in 1830 when an Irish judge, Sir Jonah Barrington, was dismissed for embezzlement. It would be unlikely for any judge to achieve this distinction, since most judges would prefer to resign rather than be subjected to this procedure.

The only recent example of a High Court judge resigning was that of Mr Justice Harman, who resigned following serious criticism made of him in the Court of Appeal in a case in which he had taken over 18 months to deliver a reserved judgement.

It is possible for a judge to be removed on grounds of incapacity — through physical or mental ill-health — but this depends on the discretion of the Lord Chancellor. Lord Widgery, then LCJ, became seriously ill towards the end of his judicial career, and although he suffered from a serious degenerative nervous disease, he remained in his job. The Lord Chancellor has the power, first introduced in the **Administration of Justice Act 1973** (and now incorporated in the **Supreme Court Act 1981**), to declare vacant the office of any judge who through ill-health is incapable of discharging his or her duties and of taking the decision to resign.

High Court judge Mr Justice Harman resigned in 1998

Many lawyers and organisations — such as Justice — have argued for the establishment of a Judicial Complaints Commission, which would be an independent body with powers to investigate whether a judge had acted injudiciously. If serious allegations against a judge were upheld, the commission would then present these to a tribunal, which could recommend to the Lord Chancellor that a judge should be suspended or dismissed. Such arguments are dismissed by judges on the grounds that judicial independence would be undermined. However, under the Constitutional Reform Act 2005, the **Office for Judicial Complaints** (OJC) was established in 2006.

Office for Judicial Complaints

The OJC was established in April 2006 under the Constitutional Reform Act 2005, under which 'the Lord Chancellor and the LCJ have joint responsibility for a new system for considering and determining complaints about the personal conduct of all judicial office holders'. The OJC handles these complaints and provides assistance and advice to the Lord Chancellor and LCJ in the performance of their new joint role.

Complaints may be made to the OJC about the personal conduct of any judge, tribunal member or coroner. Examples of personal misconduct would be the use of insulting, racist or sexist language. The OJC cannot deal with complaints about a judge's decision or about how he or she has handled a case — these matters are properly within the jurisdiction of the appeal process.

On completing its investigation of a complaint made against a judge, the OJC advises the Lord Chancellor and LCJ of its findings. They may then decide what action to take against the judge. They have the power to advise the judge as to his or her future conduct, to warn the judge, to reprimand, or even to dismiss an inferior judge. No disciplinary action may be taken against a judge unless both the Lord Chancellor and the LCJ agree the case merits it.

Racism, drink-driving and improper conduct...the case against judges

There have been a record number of complaints against judges and magistrates. The Office for Judicial Complaints has looked into 1,434 cases in its first 10 months. Eight judges and magistrates were removed from the Bench and a further 10 reprimanded. Only allegations of misconduct or behaviour that may bring the judiciary into disrepute are taken up by the OJC. Nearly 400 complaints have yet to be considered. This number is much higher than in 2005, when 250 complaints were investigated by the Department for Constitutional Affairs.

Among the most serious complaints directed against judges include the case of two immigration judges who had employed a Brazilian cleaner who was an illegal immigrant, and the case of Lord Justice Richards, who was arrested following a complaint about a serious incident on a train. In this latter case, Lord Justice Richards was acquitted of this charge and continues to sit in the Court of Appeal.

Adaption from R. Verlaik (2007) 'Racism, drink-driving and improper conduct...the case against judges', *Independent*, 28 March.

Judicial Appointments and Conduct Ombudsman

This new post was created under the **Constitutional Reform Act 2005** with responsibility for the investigation of complaints about the judicial appointments process and the handling of matters involving judicial discipline or conduct. It is completely independent of the government and the judiciary.

The Ombudsman will consider individual complaints from candidates for judicial office who are unhappy with some aspect of the handling of their application by the JAC or the Lord Chancellor's Department.

The Ombudsman will also consider individual complaints from members of the public who are unhappy with some aspect of the handling of their case by the OJC, the Lord Chancellor, the LCJ, a Magistrates' Advisory Committee or a tribunal president.

The Ombudsman may make recommendations to the Lord Chancellor and the JAC about what steps should be taken in relation to a complaint that has been upheld. He or she may also offer advice on changes to procedures that have come to his or her attention as a result of a complaint. The Ombudsman also has the power to recommend compensation be paid to successful complainants for loss suffered as a result.

However, the Ombudsman has no power to rebuke or reprimand a judge, or to decide to trigger procedures for removing a judge from office.

Evaluation

The judiciary has often been attacked for being out of touch with society and being made up of a white, male, middle-class elite. The findings of J. A. G. Griffith in his book *The Politics of the Judiciary* confirm this view. Judges, he points out, are largely homogeneous in background and attitude and therefore perpetuate a conservative attitude that can best be described as 'corporate prejudice'. It is certainly true that judges are predominantly white males drawn from the barristers' profession. It is also true to say that the senior members of the judiciary have certain common traits, such as an Oxbridge education, that might also account for a perceived judicial mindset that places certain conservative values above other factors. Research undertaken by the Labour Research Department in 1999 confirms that a public school and Oxbridge bias in appointments remains. It is submitted, however, that at times criticism should be reserved for what the judges do, rather than what they represent.

Gary Slapper has argued in the *Student Law Review* that Griffith's position only has relevance if it can be used to show either that: (a) the judges are delivering defective judgements because of such a background; or (b) that such a background reduces public confidence in the administration of justice. Otherwise, to attack the judges just because they represent a privileged elite is meaningless, because the outcome, in legal terms, is unimpaired.

As to the representation of women and members of ethnic minority groups in the judiciary, it is clear from the statistics, as Darbyshire (2001) points out, that 'women, solicitors and members of the ethnic minorities are not reflected in the Judiciary in the proportions in which they populate the legal profession'. However, the Lord Chancellor has said that the proper measure is not of the number of women in the profession today compared with the number appointed to judicial posts. Instead, he suggests, it is the number of women in the profession 20 years ago compared to the number of women in judicial posts today. This does seem a more relevant measure because it considers the amount of women in the profession who would have become eligible for judicial office.

Lady Hale — the only Lady of Appeal in Ordinary

Furthermore, it seems that women and minority ethnic applicants for judicial posts are on the increase (as illustrated by the recent Judicial Appointments annual reports). Slapper has welcomed this trend as indicative that the 'social composition of the judiciary is beginning to change'. The judicial statistics, however, continue to show how few female and minority ethnic judges are appointed (see Table 12.2). It remains to be seen how seriously the JAC will take its responsibility to consider the need for far greater judicial diversity when nominating candidates to the Lord Chancellor.

Table 12.2 Judicial statistics, 1 April 2007

Judicial rank	No. of judges	Men	Women	Minority ethnic groups	Barristers	Solicitors
Law Lords	12	11	1	0	12	0
Heads of Division	5	5	0	0	5	0
Lord Justices of Appeal	37	34	3	0	36	1
High Court judges	108	98	10	1	107	1
Circuit judges	639	566	73	9	547	92
Recorders	1,201	1,022	179	53	1,097	104
Recorders in training	5	2	3	0	5	0
District judges — civil	450	349	101	14	36	414
District judges — Magistrates' Court	139	106	33	7	47	92
Superior judges — High Court to Law Lords	162	148	14	1	160	0
Inferior Judges — district to circuit judges	2,427	2,039	388	100	1,930	0

Whether judges should reflect the social mix of the wider community more accurately is a question that continues to provoke considerable debate. A previous Lord Chancellor, Lord MacKay, Lord Irvine's predecessor, took the view that the judiciary was distinct from the legislature and therefore did not have to reflect a democratic and representative social group, a view that Griffith deplored. Slapper has provided an interesting example to illustrate the problems with the sort of position adopted by MacKay: 'During the last millennium right up to 1992 (the case of *R* v *R*) it was not a crime for a man to rape a woman if she was his wife. The people who fabricated this rule and perpetuated it for centuries were all judges (not MPs) and they were all men, many of whom regarded women as inferior beings.' However, this point loses its impact when it is considered that the judges who reversed this rule, and did so without waiting for Parliament, were also white men from a shared cultural, economic and academic background. That such judges, from such a narrow background, were capable of radical law making suggests that perhaps more emphasis needs to be placed on the judicial role of objective decision-making. This should flourish in any condition where people of merit and intellect are involved.

Lord Irvine adopted the view that judicial appointments should be merit-based above all, though welcoming to eligible candidates from both genders and all ethnic and social backgrounds. This was complemented by the view, supported by the Bar in particular, that the legal profession as a whole should be more representative of wider society, thus in time supplying the judiciary with a wider pool of candidates. The changes introduced by the Constitutional Reform Act 2005, especially the creation of the JAC together with the revised appointment system for QCs, should lead to a much more representative judiciary, which at the very least will begin to reflect the make-up of the legal profession. Women already form 54% of the entrants to the solicitors branch and 50% of those to the Bar, while those from minority ethnic groups are well represented in both branches of the profession.

Why are so few women appointed to the High Court?

Should we worry about the fact that no women have been appointed as High Court judges for more than 2 years, or that more than 3 years have passed since the only black High Court judge first took her place on the bench?

Eleven white male ex-barristers have been appointed to the High Court from the first shortlist drawn up by the new Judicial Appointments Commission. There are another seven men and three women on the list — all white and barristers.

The commission 'must have regard to the need to encourage diversity in the range of persons available for selection for appointments.' Those who set it up are disappointed that it has not found more candidates from the ethnic minorities. Dame Heather Hallett, who joined the commission at the beginning of 2006 and is now vice-chairman, says these candidates are simply not there. 'I have been worried for some years about the available pool, and of course, we can only fish in the available pool.'

Adapted from an article by Joshua Rozenberg, *Daily Telegraph*, 7 February 2008.

Judicial independence

In our legal system great importance is attached to the idea that judges should be independent from any pressure from the government, and from any political or other pessure groups. This is to guarantee that they are free to decide cases impartially. For instance, Article 6 in the European Convention of Human Rights, which was incorporated into UK law by the Human Rights Act 1998, guarantees that every citizen has the right to be tried by a 'fair and impartial tribunal'. Judicial independence is also

Constitutional Reform Act 2005

Under s.3 of the Constitutional Reform Act 2005, 'the Lord Chancellor, other ministers of the Crown and all with responsibility for matters relating to the judiciary or otherwise to the administration of justice must uphold the continued independence of the judiciary.' In s.3(6), the Lord Chancellor must have regard to:

❖ the need to defend that independence
❖ the need for the judiciary to have the support necessary to enable them to exercise their functions
❖ the need for the public interest, in regard to matters relating to the judiciary or otherwise to the administration of justice, to be properly represented in decisions affecting those matters

Tenure of office

In England, all judges of the Supreme Court hold office during good behaviour, subject only to removal by the monarch on an address presented by both Houses of Parliament. This has never happened to an English judge. Under the Constitutional Reform Act 2005, the Office for Judicial Complaints (OJC) was appointed to investigate complaints made against judges. However, the OJC has no power to dismiss judges or even to reprimand them — instead, it makes recommendations to the LCJ who will decide what, if any, action is to be taken after further discussions with the Lord Chancellor.

Judicial immunity from suit

No judge may be sued in respect for anything done while acting in his or her judicial capacity. There continues to be a distinction between inferior and superior judges — the latter have immunity from all actions even when acting outside their jurisdiction, providing that their words or actions were done in good faith, whereas inferior judges only receive immunity in respect of actions conducted within their jurisdiction. The reason for this immunity is that it protects judges from vexatious litigants and provides finality in litigation — subject only to possible appeals.

Immunity from parliamentary criticism

No criticism may be made in either House of an individual judge except by way of a substantive motion. Political neutrality is also preserved — judicial salaries are charged upon the Consolidated Fund, which removes the opportunity for an annual debate. Note that full-time judges are excluded from membership of the House of Commons.

However, in the House of Lords, all Law Lords and the LCJ are able to speak during debates on particular bills and to vote. In recent years, there have been a number of well-known examples where serving Law Lords have become involved in politically contentious debates concerning the administration of justice, penal policy and civil liberties. For instance, the present LCJ opposed the provision in the Criminal Justice Bill 1997 for mandatory sentences. Such examples raise the obvious difficulty that these judges who were actively involved in the passage of legislation in the House of Lords may in the future be the same judges who have to decide these issues in their judicial capacity.

However, under the Constitutional Reform Act 2005, when the new Supreme Court is established, the judges of that court (all currently Law Lords and, as such, life peers) will lose their right to sit in the House of Lords and speak and vote in legislative debates.

The value of judicial independence is highlighted by the recent increase in judicial review cases, whereby judges are required to examine the legality or procedural correctness of government decisions. There have been many instances where government ministers have had their decisions overruled by judges. Since the passage of the Human Rights Act 1998, which came into force in 2000, there have also been many important cases where judges have had to consider whether the government has legislated in breach of that Act, most notably in *A and others* v *The Home Office* (2004). In this case, the Law Lords roundly condemned the government for breaching individuals' rights by detaining them without limit of time and with no charges having been made against them under anti-terrorism legislation.

In August 2007, there was another key example of judicial independence when the Asylum and Immigration Tribunal ruled that Learco Chindamo, the murderer of the British headmaster Philip Lawrence, could not be deported on the completion of his prison sentence to his country of origin, Italy, because to do so would breach Chindamo's right under Article 8 of the European Convention on Human Rights to family life. This decision went directly against the wishes of the home secretary to deport Chindamo. (At the time of writing, the government has made it clear it intends to appeal against this decision.)

The independence of the judiciary is also relevant when one considers the need for judges to chair inquiries into major national events — for instance, the Stephen Lawrence murder, Dunblane shootings, Hillsborough disaster, Arms-to-Iraq and Profumo scandals.

In our legal system, great importance is attached to the idea that judges should be independent from any pressure from the government or pressure groups. This is to guarantee that they are free to decide cases impartially. Judicial independence is also essential to the theory of 'the rule of law'. This important concept was analysed by A. V. Dicey in the nineteenth century. He commented that 'no person is punishable except for a distinct breach of the law established in the courts', and that 'no man is above the law, but that every man, whatever be his rank, is subject to the ordinary law of the realm'.

Ministry of Justice

A new Ministry of Justice was created in May 2007. This new ministry has responsibility for courts, tribunals, legal aid and judges (from the former Lord Chancellor's Department/Department for Constitutional Affairs), together with responsibility for prisons and probation (from the Home Office). This combination of responsibilities has given rise to a fierce controversy over the issue of judicial independence, with judges arguing that 'safeguards must be put in place to protect the due and independent administration of justice' (Lord Phillips CJ). As Joshua Rozenberg commented in the *Daily Telegraph*:

> *With a single minister responsible for both the penal system and the judiciary, judges were bound to come under improper pressure to save money by releasing people who should be in prison. This matter is regarded as so important by Lord Phillips that he has considered using the 'nuclear option' of making a formal complaint to Parliament under the Constitutional Reform Act 2005 that justice is at risk.*

According to Lord Phillips: 'Judicial independence cannot exist on its own — judges must have the loyal staff, buildings and equipment to support the exercise of the independent judicial function.' This view echoes that of Lord Brown-Wilkinson, a former Law Lord, who himself argued that 'control of the finance and administration of the legal system is capable of preventing the performance of those very functions which the independence of the judiciary is intended to preserve...the right of the individual to a speedy and fair trial by an independent judge'.

Questions

1 What are the statutory qualifications required to become a circuit judge and a High Court judge?

2 What is the name of the body that organises the appointment of judges?

3 Which body is responsible for the training of judges?

4 Briefly explain some criticisms that could be applied to our system of judicial training.

5 What is the responsibility of the Judicial Appointments and Conduct Ombudsman?

6 What is the responsibility of the Office for Judicial Complaints?

7 Why do you think that it is argued that our judges are not representative, and that in future they should be?

8 Briefly explain the theory of separation of powers.

9 To what extent does the UK constitution follow this theory?

Sample exam questions

1 Explain how inferior judges are appointed. (10 marks)

Task

Read the following sample answer to this question, which has been assessed as 'limited'. Work out what omissions there are (e.g. there are no references to other kinds of inferior judges), and rewrite it as a 'clear' answer.

Inferior judges, like district judges, have to be solicitors or barristers and are appointed by the Judicial Appointments Commission. This body will take up references and interview candidates. The actual appointment is made by the Lord Chancellor.

2 Explain how superior judges are appointed. (10 marks)

Task

Applying the same process used in question 1, write a 'clear' answer to this question.

3 Explain what is meant by the principle of judicial independence. Discuss the importance of this principle. (20 marks)

Task

Read the following sample answer to this question, which has been assessed as 'some'. Rewrite it as a 'sound' answer.

Judicial independence means that judges must be able to decide cases without being subject to any pressures, particularly from government. This principle is illustrated in the following ways. First, through the independence of the Judicial Appointments Commission, which is responsible for selecting judges. Also, under the Act of Settlement 1701, judges are given security of tenure, which makes it difficult for judges to be dismissed. Judges are also granted immunity from being sued for their decisions in court. It is not possible for an individual judge to be criticised in Parliament, and judges are not allowed to become MPs.

The principle of judicial independence is important because under the European Convention of Human Rights, everyone is entitled to a fair trial 'before an independent and impartial tribunal.' Also, because of the theory of separation of powers, it is vital that judges are not part of the government or in any way subject to political pressures. That way, the public can continue to have confidence in the quality and fairness of judicial decisions, many of which nowadays concern actions taken by individuals against governments. This principle means that judges are able to uphold the rule of law, and to hear judicial review cases taken against government actions.

Suggested reading

Berlins, M. and Dyer, C. (2000) *The Law Machine* (5th edn), Penguin.

Blood, P. (2007) 'Exploring legal theory: separation of powers', *A-Level Law Review*, Vol. 3, No. 1, pp. 2–4.

Lee, S. (1989) *Judging Judges*, Faber and Faber.

Mitchell, A. (2008) *AS Law*, Routledge-Cavendish.

Mitchell, A. (2005) 'Judging the judiciary', *A-Level Law Review*, Vol. 1, No. 1, pp. 2–5.

Rivlin, G. (1999) *First Steps in the Law*, Blackstone.

Chapter **13**

Civil courts

This chapter explains the work of the civil courts: the trial (or first instance) courts, where cases actually begin, and the appeal courts, where the losing party may either appeal against the decision made in the trial court or argue that the damages awarded were too high.

Given the obvious disadvantages of taking a case to court — high costs, delay, formality and the requirement for solicitors and barristers to prepare and argue the case — there have been many attempts to improve the ways in which the courts operate. Judge Learned Hand of the American Supreme Court once famously stated: 'I must say that, as a litigant, I should dread a lawsuit beyond almost anything short of sickness and death.' Mr Justice Lightman made a similar comment in a *New Law Journal* article (6 February, 2004), in which he wrote:

> *Litigation has always been high risk, and no more so than today in terms of uncertainty of outcome and cost...on the negative side, the outcome is unpredictable with no necessary relationship to the merits, and the cost of the experience for the parties can prove totally debilitating, if not fatal.*

The most far-reaching reform was initiated following Lord Woolf's Access to Justice report, which led to the creation of the **Civil Procedure Rules** in 1999. While these have certainly brought about significant improvements in civil court procedures, they have also served to underline the growing importance of alternative dispute resolution.

Civil disputes involve individuals bringing claims against other individuals, who could be private citizens or companies; a claim could even be made by a private citizen against a government department or other public body, such a local council or the National Health Service. Such claims could arise from a breach of contract, for example where a consumer has bought a product from a shop that turns out to be faulty, or where two companies have agreed a contract and one argues that the other

High Court

The High Court is based in London but can also sit in major cities; Birmingham effectively has a permanent High Court in session. This court is presided over by High Court judges (or deputy High Court judges) and is organised into three divisions:

* The **Queen's Bench Division** is by far the busiest and has the greatest number of High Court judges assigned to it. Most of the cases it hears are contract or tort.
* The **Chancery Division** hears cases involving company law, partnership actions, patent and copyright law, and tax and trust cases.
* The **Family Division** deals with defended divorce actions and other matrimonial cases. It is also concerned with the welfare of children under the Children Act 1989; judges may have to decide cases involving adoption, guardianship and the custody of and access to children.

Appeals procedure

The unsuccessful party in a civil case can appeal the decision to a higher court, but leave to appeal must be obtained from the trial judge. In most cases, the grounds for appeal relate to legal issues rather than arguments about the facts of the case.

If the appellant is successful in his or her appeal, the decision of the trial judge may be overturned, or damages may be reduced. In *Sutcliffe* v *Pressdram* (1991), the wife of the Yorkshire Ripper was originally awarded £600,000 in damages against *Private Eye*. The magazine appealed, and the damages were reduced by 90% to £60,000 in the Court of Appeal.

The routes for appeal are:

* from Small Claims Court to a single circuit judge in the County Court
* from fast-track cases in the County Court to a single High Court judge
* from multi-track cases in the County Court to the Court of Appeal (Civil Division), presided over by two Lord Justices of Appeal
* from the High Court to the Court of Appeal (Civil Division), presided over by three Lord Justices of Appeal
* from the Court of Appeal to the House of Lords, provided leave to appeal has been given, either by the Court of Appeal itself or after application to the House of Lords; such leave will only be given if the case raises issues of 'general public importance'

Questions

1 What is the financial limit for cases in the Small Claims Court?
2 Why is there a lower figure for personal injury cases in the Small Claims Court?
3 Name three types of case that would be tried by the County Court.
4 Which cases cannot be heard in the County Court?

5 Name the divisions of the High Court.

6 Which division of the High Court is the busiest?

7 Which division of the High Court deals with guardianship and adoption of children?

8 Give three examples of cases that would normally be heard by the Chancery Division.

Civil justice system: pre-Woolf reforms

Lord Woolf was appointed to carry out a far-reaching review of the civil justice system. In his Access to Justice report in 1996, he stated that a civil justice system should be:

❖ just in the results it achieves

❖ fair in the way it treats litigants

❖ understanding to those who use it

❖ responsive to the needs of those who use it

❖ effective, adequately resourced and organised

It should also:

❖ offer appropriate procedures at a reasonable cost

❖ deal with cases at a reasonable speed

❖ provide as much certainty as the nature of particular cases allows

Lord Woolf concluded that the system at the time failed to achieve all these goals. It is possible that this failure was inevitable, due to conflicting aims:

In 1994, Lord Woolf was appointed by the Lord Chancellor to carry out a review of the civil justice system in England and Wales

❖ A system based on cost efficiency would make it difficult to justify claims for small sums, yet those cases are important to the parties involved.

❖ Promoting efficiency can conflict with the need for fairness.

❖ Making the courts more accessible could lead to a flood of cases, which would make it impossible to provide a speedy resolution.

In addition, changes made to the system may have effects outside it. For example, making it easier to bring personal injury actions could push up the cost of insurance, and it has been suggested that in the USA this has led to unwillingness on the part of doctors to perform any risky medical treatment.

It is therefore impossible to resolve all the conflicts or to reconcile the separate aims. Lord Scarman once commented:

To be acceptable to ordinary people, I believe the legal process in litigation must be designed to encourage, first, settlement by agreement; secondly, open and speedy trial if agreement is not forthcoming. In other words, justice, not truth is its purpose. It is against the criteria of justice and fairness that the system must be assessed.

Advantages of the civil courts

While most students are able to state the problems of civil courts in terms of 'delay, expense and formality', comparatively few can explain the advantages that these courts have over any other form of dispute resolution.

Compulsory process

There is no other process by which you can effectively compel the other side to come to a forum to resolve a dispute. The other party could, of course, decline to lodge a defence or even to appear in court, but in that case a default judgement would be issued against it.

Formality of procedures

Rules of evidence, disclosure and legal argument all ensure a fair process. This process is supervised by a judge, who is a trained and qualified expert in the law and legal processes.

Appeals process

No other dispute-resolution process allows for appeals. In many tribunals, there is no appellate tribunal, and an appeal to the Queen's Bench Divisional Court is only allowed on a point of law. This is also the position with arbitration. Such appeals are rare, however.

Legal aid

Although civil legal aid has been greatly reduced in recent years, particularly as a result of reforms in the **Access to Justice Act 1999**, it is still more widely available for court litigation than for any alternative. It is also true that lawyers are far more likely to litigate on a conditional fee basis in court than in tribunals, arbitration or mediation.

Law making and development

Only courts, and especially the Court of Appeal and the House of Lords, can make and develop legal rules through the doctrine of precedent. Any decision given in arbitration, and even in tribunals, applies only to the case in question. It is essential in the world of business and taxation for companies and individuals to understand the relevant legal rules, and to be able to challenge these through the appellate system to allow the law to develop.

Enforcement of decision

Courts have much greater powers to enforce their decisions than any other dispute-resolution agency.

Chapter **14**

Alternative dispute resolution

The problems of cost, delay and complexity, which are inherent in the civil court system and which the Civil Procedure Rules have largely failed to resolve, have resulted in many individuals — and, increasingly, companies — turning to alternative dispute resolution (ADR) procedures. While a court decision offers certainty and finality (subject to rights of appeal), ADR is generally quicker, cheaper and far less complicated.

ADR schemes have been in use in the USA, Australia, Canada and New Zealand for many years, and have been endorsed by Lord Woolf's civil justice reforms, which expressly laid emphasis on litigants considering alternatives to courts.

Most forms of ADR attempt to involve the client in the process of resolving the dispute. They do not rely on adversarial approaches but instead concentrate on reaching an agreement; the parties must even concur on hearing times and places. Each case is decided on its merits without reference to previous cases, and the common ground between the parties should be emphasised, rather than focusing on points of disagreement. ADR offers a confidential process, and the outcome will not be published without the consent of both parties.

The aim of ADR is to facilitate settlement, whereas the aim of litigation is to obtain judgement, but note that judges are increasingly becoming involved with ADR, as are barristers and solicitors. In 1993, a Practice Statement issued by the Commercial Court (of the Queen's Bench Division) stated that parties should be encouraged to consider using ADR as an additional means of settling disputes. Judges of this court can offer arbitration but not mediation or conciliation, although the clerk to the court retains a list of bodies offering such services. The Committee on Alternative Dispute Resolution, established by the Bar Council and chaired by Lord Justice Beldam, published a report in 1991 that advocated courts embracing ADR to support the judicial process. Consequently, potential litigants or their legal representatives should undertake such procedures before resorting to litigation. In his Access to Justice report, Lord Woolf recommended greater use of ADR, e.g. the use of neutral experts to assist in reaching a pre-trial settlement, and independent mediation, separate tribunal or specialist arbitration schemes for small claims involving medical negligence.

The main types of ADR are:

❖ tribunals
❖ arbitration
❖ mediation
❖ conciliation

Exam hint

AS examination questions regularly ask for advantages and disadvantages of ADR, but they are rarely answered well. The main reason is the failure of candidates to recognise that ADR is effectively a collective noun, covering several different methods of resolving disputes without going to court. Unless some reference is made to individual forms of ADR, it is hard to avoid the trap of writing little more on advantages than 'ADR is much cheaper, faster and less formal than litigation'. While this statement is generally true for all forms of ADR, there are many issues that need to be explored in greater detail.

Tribunals

The twentieth century has seen considerable growth in the potential for disputes between individuals, groups and state agencies.

To begin with, the expansion of agencies set up for the implementation of state interventionist policies (as in the field of welfare provision) has created, in turn, the potential for disputes between individuals and social welfare officials, and between property owners and planning authorities. Frequently, the legislation that established the machinery for implementing such policies has also set up the institutional framework within which disputes in particular fields are to be resolved. It is significant that in many such cases, the dispute-solving mechanisms adopted have not been ordinary courts of law but rather specialised tribunals. Examples include:

❖ Mental Health Review Tribunal (MHRT)
❖ Employment Tribunal (ET)
❖ Social Security and Child Support Appeals (SSCSA)
❖ General Commissioners of Income Tax (GCIT)
❖ Criminal Injuries Compensation Appeals Panel (CICAP)
❖ Lands Tribunal

If all disputes created under this weight of social legislation had to be settled in ordinary courts, the court system would collapse under the enormous workload.

Consultant cardiologist Robin Roberts took Kingston NHS Trust to a tribunal in 2007; he was sacked for using a procedure to save a patient's life that was not approved by the Trust, even though it is used regularly in the NHS

Furthermore, the courts are, for many of these cases, inappropriate organs to deal with the dispute. For example, it would be completely out of place for a County Court to hear a social security claim for a few pounds a week, where the usual delays affecting court cases would operate harshly on the claimant who needs an immediate decision. The importance of tribunals was reflected in a statement made by Carnwath LJ as Senior President of Tribunals (Designate):

> There is no doubt...that tribunals represent one of the most important pillars of the system of justice in this country... It is fair to say that more people bring a case before a tribunal than go to any other part of the justice system.

In order to provide a system whereby disputes may be resolved without the trappings of law courts, various governments have, through legislation, introduced a network of administrative tribunals designed to provide instant justice cheaply, efficiently and with minimum delay and formality. Instead of highly paid judges, these tribunals comprise panels, with a chairman who is (usually) legally qualified and two non-legally qualified people who have expertise in the particular field over which the tribunal has jurisdiction. In all, there are about 70 different types of tribunal, hearing over 1 million cases per year.

Too complex

The 1979 Royal Commission on Legal Services (the Benson Commission) recommended a review of tribunal procedures, with a view to simplifying the process so that applicants could as far as possible represent themselves. However, if anything, tribunal procedures have become more legalistic. The research by Genn and Genn appears to confirm that self-representation is difficult before some tribunals and therefore improved legal or lay representation will become even more necessary.

Lack of accessibility

The recommendation of the Franks Report that tribunals should be 'open' requires more than the issuing of a rule that hearings should usually be held in public; it also demands that citizens should be aware of tribunals and their right to use them. In cases where the dispute is between a citizen and the government, the citizen will usually be notified of procedures to be followed, but in other cases more thought needs to be given to publicising citizens' rights.

Lack of appeals

There is no absolute right to appeal from a tribunal; such rights exist only when laid down by statute. Consequently, there is no uniform appeals system, and some tribunals offer no appeal rights at all, for example those concerning vaccine damage.

Some tribunal appeals may only be made to the relevant minister, allowing for bias. Appeals to the High Court (when allowed) are expensive and complex. Under the Tribunals, Courts and Enforcement Act 2007, which gives effect to many of the recommendations made by Sir Andrew Leggatt, a new system of upper tribunals has been created to act in an appellate capacity from the first instance (now named 'first-tier') tribunals.

Arbitration

Arbitration is often referred to as 'privatised litigation': 'privatised' in the sense that parties to the dispute have much more control over procedures than would be the case if they went to court, and 'litigation' insofar as the decision by the arbitrator is legally binding.

Arbitration is governed by the Arbitration Act 1996, s.1 of which states: 'The object of arbitration is to obtain the fair resolution of disputes by an impartial tribunal without unnecessary delay or expense.' It also enacts that people 'should be free to agree how their disputes are resolved' and that the court 'should not intervene'.

Arbitration is favoured by the commercial world and by trade unions as an alternative to a court trial. Some trade associations have even set up their own mediation and arbitration services to deal with consumer complaints, usually on questions of poor-quality goods or services. Examples include schemes run by the Association of

14

ACAS was involved in the resolution of the firefighters' pay dispute in 2002

British Travel Agents (ABTA), the trade associations for electrical retailer or house-builders, and even funeral directors. Often, companies in dispute with a trade union on issues of pay seek arbitration by reference to the Advisory, Conciliation and Arbitration Service (ACAS).

The Arbitration Act 1996 provides for the appointment of arbitrators and lays down procedures for them to follow. The conflicting parties have to agree in writing for their dispute to go to arbitration. It is quite common for commercial contracts to contain a *Scott* v *Avery* clause, whereby any disputes arising under the contract can *only* be resolved through arbitration. With such a clause present, neither party may start court proceedings against the other. Under s.9 of the Act, a party against whom court action has been started may apply to the court to enforce the arbitration clause and to stay the court action pending an arbitration award.

An arbitrator does not have to be a judge or a lawyer, although he or she is expected to be a legal expert in the particular field in which the dispute arises. The arbitrator must conduct the proceedings in accordance with the stipulated rules and in a judicial manner. Such industries as construction, re-insurance and shipping have traditionally used arbitration as their favoured method of resolving disputes.

Recent arbitration cases include the following:

❖ In a serious dispute over cost overruns in the contract between Transport for London and Metronet, the dispute was referred to arbitration where it was decided the contractor was responsible for the additional costs (and, consequently, it went into administration).

❖ Possibly the biggest financial arbitration in recent years was the dispute between Eurotunnel and the consortium of building contractors, which resulted in Eurotunnel having to pay over £2 billion for the costs of extra engineering work.

❖ At time of writing, a major dispute between Tesco and John Laing has been referred to arbitration following the collapse of a railway tunnel during the construction of a new supermarket.

Although the parties usually have to agree on the choice of an arbitrator, the arbitrator has the final say in the procedures to be adopted. There is normally a preliminary meeting between the parties where the arbitrator decides on these procedures. In that meeting, the arbitrator usually tries to achieve a consensus between the parties so that he or she can issue a consent order, which should reduce the risk of the ultimate arbitral award being challenged in the courts.

Arbitrations can be fixed at a time and place to suit all the parties, so there are no long delays caused by court waiting lists. The dispute can either be resolved or else the parties can come to some other form of understanding. However, arbitrations may break down, and the only recourse for the parties may be to begin again in court. Some trade associations insist on a condition that bars the aggrieved consumer from seeking a remedy in court. Note that in the Small Claims Court, the arbitrator is the district judge.

The decision in an arbitration case is immediate, unless a point of law is raised that has to be referred to the High Court. Arbitrators have discretion to refer a complex legal problem arising in the course of arbitration to the Queen's Bench Divisional Court for a judge to determine. Under s.69 of the Arbitration Act 1996, the award itself may be challenged in court on a point of law, but only after being granted leave to appeal — and this is rarely granted. Alternatively, an application may be made to the Queen's Bench to set aside or remit the award on the grounds that the arbitrator lacked jurisdiction or that there was a serious irregularity affecting the arbitration process.

Evaluation of arbitration

Advantages of arbitration

❖ The parties have greater control than if the case were pursued in court, for example they can choose the arbitrator, the procedure to be adopted, the time and place and the length of arbitration, and they may also be able to limit the arbitrator's powers.

❖ Arbitration is totally private — an important consideration for commercial disputes.

❖ In addition to having legal knowledge of the issue in dispute, an arbitrator will also be an expert in that area.

❖ Small claims arbitration by a district judge in the Small Claims Court has become the most popular forum for consumer arbitration.

Disadvantages of arbitration

❖ As for all forms of ADR, there is no legal aid available.

❖ The opportunity to appeal the decision is much more restricted than it would be from a court decision.

❖ Just as with mediation and other consensual forms of ADR, if the parties' positions are entrenched, arbitration is not a realistic possibility for dispute resolution.

❖ As with all forms of ADR, an arbitrator's decision is more difficult to enforce than a court-backed order.

Mediation

Mediation is an informal procedure that assists disputing parties in their negotiations. It involves an independent, neutral third party acting as a go-between to facilitate cooperation and agreement. The mediator will often discuss the disputed matter with each party in separate rooms. Where the relationship between the parties needs to be preserved, as in family disputes or those involving commercial matters, mediation ensures that the relationship is not soured, as it would be by litigation. Mediation is a voluntary process and the parties feel in control.

Mediation is often used in the USA in family and corporate disputes. It can also be used to settle priorities before the start of litigation, or in some cases in place of litigation. However, its use presupposes a degree of cooperation between the parties, and one of the major criticisms is that where parties are entrenched, mediation is inappropriate.

Mediation is only successful when the parties reach an agreement, and that agreement is only binding once it has been drawn up, usually by lawyers.

Commercial mediation is used in the UK, where it is promoted and organised by companies such as International Resolution Europe Ltd and the Centre for Dispute Resolution, founded in 1990 under the auspices of the Confederation of British Industry.

Research from the Centre for Effective Dispute Resolution (reported in the *New Law Journal*, November 2007) claimed that the commercial mediation profession saves businesses more than £1 billion each year in wasted management time, damaged commercial relationships and legal fees. Furthermore, these savings are achieved at a cost of only £8.2 million in terms of total fee income to the mediation profession, with individual mediation fees now averaging £3,120.

Mediation in family disputes is available from the National Association of Family Mediation and Conciliation Services, which offers support to those who wish to conduct their own negotiations and only refer to lawyers in an advisory capacity. Some 300 mediators throughout the UK offer family counselling and legal advice; these are trained solicitors and counsellors, and their aim is to arrive at a mutually agreed settlement. Note the importance attached to mediation in the Family Law

Act 1996, which aimed to take divorce settlements out of the courts and establish family mediation centres throughout the UK.

Call in the referee to end disputes

Chris Robson was furious when his best customer refused to pay him for the sandwich filling he had supplied to a food manufacturer. His demands for an explanation were met with indifference and he decided he had nothing to lose by suing for the £20,000 payment due. However, before the claim was formally made, he was asked by a friend if he had considered mediation to resolve this dispute. When this procedure was explained to him, he agreed to 'give it a try', as did the food manufacturer.

Within two days, the mediator whom they had appointed had brought both sides together. After the mediator had separated the sides and talked to each side alone and in confidence, it emerged that the food manufacturer had wrongly ordered the sandwich filling, but that the manager concerned couldn't admit his mistake. He also admitted that the business relationship between the two firms had previously been good. Chris Robson in turn admitted to the mediator that he was much more upset about the loss of a valuable customer than the £20,000 unpaid bill. The mediator then tried to find some way of re-establishing the broken business link rather than apportioning blame. A new deal was worked out in which the £20,000 was written off by Chris in return for a long-term contract of at least three years, which would cover the supply of additional product lines. 'Both sides agreed and were immensely relieved', said the mediator. 'The manufacturer had been worried that his mistake would come out in court, Robson was worried about the future of his company without the manufacturer's business. They walked away far happier that they would have done had the case gone to court.'

The mediation had taken just 6 hours and cost £1,400 divided between both parties.

In Britain, where mediation is still a relatively new science, the success rate stands at an impressive 90% according to the Centre for Effective Dispute Resolution (CEDR). Research showed that British businesses spent an estimated £1.3 billion a year on legal action, with cases dragging on for years with no guarantee of a successful outcome. 'Mediation, on the other hand, is a fraction of the cost and aims to find a resolution within days.'

Adapted from an article by Louise Armistead in the *Sunday Times*, 29 September 2002.

Evaluation of mediation

Advantages of mediation

❖ Unlike other forms of ADR, mediation seeks to reflect the *interests* of both parties, not their legal rights — see the article above. Because of this, only mediation offers a 'win, win' solution — indeed, mediation can only work in this way. It therefore allows the relationship between parties to be preserved. This is important in both family and commercial disputes.

❖ Mediation is usually the quickest and cheapest form of ADR.

❖ Mediation is the form of ADR most actively encouraged by the courts under the Civil Procedure Rules.

❖ As with arbitration, if mediation fails to produce a resolution to the dispute, the parties retain their right to pursue their claims in court.

Disadvantages of mediation

❖ As with arbitration, mediation cannot work if the parties are entrenched.

❖ There is no legal aid available

Conciliation

Conciliation falls somewhere between arbitration and mediation, the former being the most formal, the latter the least formal, although in many cases differentiating between mediation and conciliation is not easy. Both forms of ADR are consensual, and both reflect the interests rather than the rights of the parties concerned.

Conciliation usually involves the parties being seen separately by the conciliator, who shuttles between them with offers and counter-offers. This means that conciliation can be used even where the positions of the two parties are entrenched or where there is a misunderstanding as to the facts of the case. Since the two sides are kept apart, there is less risk of them 'play acting' by trying to destabilise the other side. At the end of the process, the conciliator offers a non-binding opinion, which may lead to an agreed settlement between the parties (as in mediation).

Conciliation is often used in the USA to settle commercial disputes. Lawyers representing each side present the arguments in the case to the parties and a neutral adviser, who may be a judge or senior lawyer. This enables the parties to assess the strengths, weaknesses and prospects of the case, and to have the opportunity to enter into settlement discussions on a realistic, business-like basis.

Questions

1 How many cases are dealt with by tribunals each year?

2 What are the three main elements that Lord Franks stated should be characteristic of tribunals?

3 Name one tribunal for which legal aid is available.

4 Which Act regulates arbitration?

5 What is a *Scott* v *Avery* clause?

6 Which professional body can provide trained arbitrators?

7 To which court can an appeal be made from arbitration?

8 What are the grounds for an appeal against an arbitration decision?

Sample exam question

Explain any three forms of alternative dispute resolution (ADR).
Include a description of the types of case they deal with. (20 marks)

Task

Read the following sample answer to this question, which has been assessed as 'some'. Rewrite it as a 'clear' and 'sound' answer.

> *Tribunals were set up by statute to handle disputes between citizens and the government. There are about 70 different kinds of tribunal dealing with tax and welfare benefits disputes. Cases are heard by a panel of three people, the chairman being legally qualified, and at the end of the case, a binding decision is given. Another tribunal is the employment tribunal, which hears cases involving unfair dismissal and discrimination.*
>
> *Arbitration involves the parties to a dispute agreeing to let a third party decide the case between them. The arbitrator need not be legally qualified but will know the law in the area of dispute. Arbitration is governed by the Arbitration Act 1996, and this procedure is used to resolve business disputes. Small Claims Courts use a form of arbitration that is less formal than courts.*
>
> *Mediation is the least formal ADR procedure and involves a mediator being appointed by both parties who will assist the parties themselves to reach an agreement. Types of case that can be resolved by mediation include family and business disputes.*

Suggested reading

Dugdale, T. et al. (2002) *'A' Level Law*, Butterworth.
Elliott, C. and Quinn, F. (2000) *Law for AQA*, Longman.
Gillespie, A. (2007) *The English Legal System*, Oxford University Press.
Mitchell, A. and Dadhania, M. (2008) *AS Law*, Routledge-Cavendish.

Unit 2
The concept of liability

Chapter **15**

Introduction to criminal liability

The traditional basis for criminal liability — the liability to be prosecuted in a criminal court and, if convicted, to be punished by the state — is an *actus reus* (the physical element) accompanied by the appropriate *mens rea* (the mental element). This chapter looks at these two important concepts in detail.

A general principle of criminal law is that a person may not be convicted of a crime unless the prosecution has proved beyond doubt that he or she:

❖ has caused a certain **event**, or that responsibility is to be attributed to him or her for the existence of a certain **state of affairs**, which is forbidden by criminal law
❖ had a defined **state of mind** in relation to the event or state of affairs

The event or state of affairs is called the *actus reus* and the state of mind the *mens rea* of the crime.

Actus literally means 'act'. However, while most crimes involve the accused committing a certain act, this is not always the case. Criminal liability may also arise through a failure to act (an omission) from a certain type of conduct. *Actus reus* means 'prohibited act', but few crimes can be adequately described simply by reference to the act — most require proof of accompanying circumstances and some proof of a particular consequence. For example, in criminal damage the offence consists of destroying or damaging property that belongs to another (the act), and for there to be no lawful excuse (the circumstances).

Each separate crime has its own specific *actus reus* — for battery, it is the infliction of unlawful personal violence. For assault occasioning actual bodily harm, it is both the original assault or (more usually) battery and the actual bodily harm suffered by the victim as a consequence.

Note also that while *mens rea* may exist without an *actus reus*, if the *actus reus* of a particular crime does not exist or occur, that crime is not committed.

Actus reus

Ordinarily, the prosecution must prove that the accused person voluntarily brought about the ***actus reus*** of the crime — that is, the act or omission must have occurred because of the defendant's **conscious exercise of will**. If in an assault case the defendant's arm was physically forced by another to strike the victim, or if the defendant was pushed against the victim by another person, then there would be no crime by the defendant, although it is probable that the perpetrator of the force would be guilty of crimes against both the defendant and the victim. A useful case example is *Hill* v *Baxter* (1958). This was a driving case, where the defendant claimed to have become unconscious as a result of being overcome by a sudden illness. He was convicted and, in his appeal, the Queen's Bench divisional court found that the facts showed the defendant was driving, 'as he was controlling the car', and upheld the conviction. What is memorable in this case was the *hypothetical* example given of a swarm of bees flying through an open car window and causing the driver to lose control of the car. This would be an instance of an involuntary act, and therefore there would be no *actus reus*.

Another famous case involving this rule that the act must be involuntary is *Bratty* v *Attorney General for Northern Ireland* (1963), where the defendant strangled a girl in his car. He gave evidence that a 'blackness' came over him and that he didn't know what he was doing. There was some evidence that he might have been suffering from epilepsy. Following his conviction for murder, there was an appeal to the House of Lords, but this was dismissed. Lord Denning stated:

> The requirement that the defendant's act should be voluntary is essential. No act is punishable if it is done involuntarily, and an involuntary act in this context means an act which is done by the muscles without any control of the mind such as a spasm, a reflex or a convulsion... The term 'involuntary act' is, however, capable of wider connotations: and to prevent confusion it is to be observed that in the criminal law an act is not to be regarded as an involuntary act simply because the doer does not remember it.

Circumstance crimes

In **circumstance** crimes, the *actus reus* refers not to an act but to circumstances. For example, the *actus reus* of driving while under the influence of alcohol is simply the circumstance that the defendant is in control of the car and is drunk. Other such offences are **possession** crimes — possession of stolen property, illegal drugs, knives or handguns.

Crimes of omission

As well as actions, such as hitting someone over the head or stealing a wallet, an *actus reus* can also be an **omission** or failure to act. In most criminal prosecutions, the prosecutor will be seeking to prove that a prohibited situation or result has been brought about by the defendant's acts. However, in certain situations it will be the fact that the defendant failed to act that led to the prohibited event occurring.

Most jurisdictions, including that of England and Wales, have not adopted a general principle of liability for failing to act. If the defendant witnesses a child drowning in a shallow paddling pool and fails to go to that child's assistance, and the child drowns, then the defendant cannot be convicted of any offence. Though we might recognise the existence of a strong moral duty to act in such circumstances, no legal duty to do so is recognised in law — unless the defendant is the child's parent or in some way responsible for the child. In other countries, such as France, there exists what is known as a 'Good Samaritan' law which obliges everyone to go to the help of a person in danger.

Instead, in England and Wales, the law has defined certain factual situations in which persons are under a duty to act. If they fail to act in these situations, thereby causing a prohibited criminal result, they shall be liable for that result.

There are six areas where such liability for omissions exists.

1 Contractual duty to act

In *R* v *Pittwood* (1902), a railway crossing gate-keeper opened the gate to let a cart through and went off to lunch, forgetting to shut it again. Ten minutes later a hay-cart, while crossing the line, was struck by a train and the driver was killed. The gate-keeper was convicted of manslaughter on the ground that there was gross and criminal negligence, as the man was paid to keep the gate shut and protect the public. Therefore, it is possible to incur criminal liability from a duty arising out of contract.

2 Failure to act

Statute can make it an offence in defined circumstances to fail to act, for example s.1(1) of the **Children and Young Persons Act 1933**. The *actus reus* of this offence is simply the failure for whatever reason to provide the child with the necessary medical care.

3 Assumed responsibility

One can be made liable where there is an assumed responsibility for the care of an aged or infirm person, as in the case of *R* v *Stone and Dobinson* (1977), where an unmarried cohabiting couple (Stone and Dobinson) invited Stone's middle-aged sister, who was anorexic, to come and live with them. Although they were aware that the woman was neglecting herself and was deteriorating rapidly, Stone and Dobinson did nothing to assist her or to summon medical help or inform social services. Three years after she came to live with them, she was found dead in her bed, naked and severely emaciated. The cause of death was toxaemia from the infected bed sores and prolonged immobilisation. Stone and Dobinson were convicted of her manslaughter — they had assumed a duty of care for her, a duty which they could easily have discharged by calling for help or by providing basic care.

4 Omissions

Statute can make certain omissions an offence, such as failure to wear a seat belt or to stop after a road accident and report it.

5 Creation of a dangerous situation

Liability also exists where the defendant has by his or her own acts created a dangerous situation. In the case of *R* v *Miller* (1983), Lord Diplock had no doubts that the defendant had been convicted correctly. This was because the *actus reus* of the offence of arson is present if the defendant accidentally starts a fire and fails to take any steps to extinguish it or prevent damage, due to an intention to destroy or damage property belonging to another or being reckless about whether any such property would be destroyed or damaged. In this case, by his own admission, Miller became aware of the fire and chose to do nothing; this case is *not* suggesting liability for purely accidental fire. It should be noted here that if, when Miller realised he had started a fire, he had tried to phone for the fire brigade or had alerted neighbours, he would not have incurred criminal liability, even if in the meantime the fire had spread to an adjoining gas-holder and half the town had blown up.

The *actus reus* of arson is present if the defendant accidentally starts a fire and fails to take any steps to extinguish it or prevent damage.

6 Requirement to protect others

A defendant may have a particular occupation that requires him or her to act in such a way to protect other people — see *R* v *Dytham* (1979). In this instance, a police officer was held guilty of a crime when he failed to perform his duty to preserve the Queen's Peace by not protecting a citizen who was being kicked to death.

> **Exam hint**
>
> In most of these rules, a case is used to show an example of the type of omission that results in a defendant being convicted of a crime. It is essential that you learn these cases — this is one of the key points that examiners are looking for.
>
> The most common examples of omissions in exam questions are those of 'assumed responsibility', where a relative or other responsible adult takes on responsibility for the care of a child, and the *R* v *Miller* 'dangerous situation', where the defendant has accidentally created a dangerous situation and has thus simultaneously put himself or herself under a duty of care to do something about it.
>
> In any question that asks you to explain what is meant by *actus reus*, the best strategy is to deal quickly with the definition as the physical element of a crime and the need for the act to be voluntary, but then to concentrate on omissions and the cases referred to above. One of the reasons for this is that omissions provide the opportunity to use case examples effectively, which should gain you extra marks. Note too that the rules of causation should not be included unless the question specifically includes causation. In a general *actus reus* question, it is not uncommon for candidates to write over a page on causation, which will receive no marks at all because it is not relevant.

Causation

Another *actus reus* issue is **causation**. This occurs in so-called 'result' crimes — those that need an act which then goes on to cause a specific result. In murder, for example, to be guilty the defendant must not only have attacked the victim in some way but must also have caused the victim to die.

Factual causation

The first rule to be considered is the factual rule of causation, referred to as the 'but for' rule, which simply requires the prosecution to prove that 'but for' the defendant's act, the event would not have occurred. This is well illustrated by the case of *R* v *White* (1910), where the defendant put potassium cyanide into a drink called 'nectar' with intent to murder his mother. She was found dead shortly afterwards with the glass, three-quarters filled, beside her. The medical evidence showed that she had died not of poisoning, but of heart failure. The defendant was acquitted of murder and convicted of attempted murder. Although the consequence that the defendant intended had occurred, he did not *cause* it to occur and therefore there was no *actus reus* of murder.

Legal causation

While it is usually easy to prove the 'but for' rule, there are many situations where the question of causation is much more difficult to establish clearly. Tony Dugdale in 'A' Level Law lists some examples:

❖ A points a gun at B and B dies of a heart attack.
❖ A knocks B unconscious and leaves him lying in a road, where he is run over by a car and killed.
❖ A injures B, who is taken by ambulance to the hospital. The ambulance crashes, killing all the occupants.
❖ A knocks B unconscious and she remains lying in a street for several hours, where she is robbed, raped or assaulted further.

In all the above examples, it could be argued that A caused the consequences on the basis that none of these events would have happened 'but for' the initial attack by A on B. The obvious difficulty with this approach, however, is that it can link an initial cause (the attack) with consequences that are both highly improbable and unforeseeable. This has been a particular problem in cases of unlawful killing — murder and manslaughter — where there is a less direct link between act and effect.

In such cases one has to consider what the responsibility of the defendant is for the victim's death. At one time, the legal position was that the defendant was liable for all natural and probable consequences of his or her voluntary acts, but this presumption has now been overturned on the grounds that this formula could link together events that are connected too remotely. In *R v Marjoram* (1999), the trial judge instructed the jury to consider the legal cause — there must be something which could reasonably be foreseen as a consequence of the unlawful act. Nowadays it is accepted law that the defendant need only have made 'a significant contribution' to the unlawful result, as in *R v Cheshire* (1991), or have been an 'operative and substantial cause of harm'.

Further rules that occur in causation address the question of what constitutes a new intervening act (*novus actus interveniens*). This requires something that cannot be foreseen, and it must be so overwhelming as to invalidate the original *actus reus*. For example, A shoots at B and causes B serious internal injuries which could be treated successfully if immediate and specialised medical treatment were provided, but the ambulance takes 10 minutes to arrive and as a result B dies. This is a foreseeable result and A is guilty of murder. However, if C knocks D down and leaves him unconscious in a building that collapses in a sudden earthquake, and D dies as a result, then C would not be liable for D's death. It seems generally to be accepted that an 'act of God' — such as an earthquake or a tidal wave — which by definition could not reasonably be foreseen will break the causal chain.

Medical treatment

What is the legal position where the defendant has inflicted serious injuries on the victim, but the victim later dies in circumstances where it can be proved that the medical treatment received was poor? If the victim had been promptly and correctly treated, would he or she have made a full recovery?

Questions

1 What is the meaning of the rule that an *actus reus* has to be a voluntary act?

2 What is the general rule regarding omissions as a form of *actus reus*?

3 Give an example of a 'circumstance' crime.

4 Why was Miller held liable for accidentally starting a fire?

5 Why were Stone and Dobinson held liable for the death of their relative?

6 Which case could be used to illustrate the 'but for' rule of causation?

7 Which case states that the defendant's acts must have made a 'significant contribution' to the outcome?

8 Why was Jordan's conviction quashed?

9 Which case confirmed the 'thin skull' rule?

10 Briefly explain what the 'thin skull' rule means.

Mens rea

Having looked at issues of *actus reus* — the physical element in a crime — we now need to examine the even more important areas dealt with under *mens rea* — the mental element necessary for all serious crimes. Criminal law does not exist to punish a person who has simply committed some kind of wrongful action — to be criminally liable, that person must have done that wrongful act in circumstances in which blame can be attached to his or her conduct. To put it more simply, a criminal is punished not so much on account of what he or she has done, but because of *why* he or she did it. All the crimes which form part of Unit 2 — non-fatal offences — and those that are included in later A2 units have both a separate *actus reus* and *mens rea*. The following states of mind are used to denote *mens rea*:

❖ **Intention** — where the offender has made a decision to break the law.

❖ **Recklessness** — which applies to those who act while realising that there is a possibility that their action could cause the illegal outcome.

❖ **Gross negligence** — which covers those situations where the defendant did not foresee causing any harm, but should have realised the risks involved. An example is *R* v *Adomako* (1994), where an anaesthetist failed to recognise and deal with the problems that arose when the breathing tube slipped out of a patient's mouth. As a result, the patient died during the operation.

For the crimes studied in Unit 2, it is enough that you understand the issues surrounding intention and recklessness. All these offences — except wounding or causing grievous bodily harm with intent — can be committed either intentionally or recklessly.

Intention

The meaning of intention is not to be found in any statute but in judicial decisions. It is clear that a person intends a result when it is his or her aim, objective or purpose to bring it about. In *R v Mohan* (1976), Lord Justice James stated: 'an "intention" to my mind connotes a state of affairs which the party intending does more than merely contemplate: it connotes a state of affairs which, on the contrary, he decides so far as in him lies to bring about and which, in point of possibility, he has a reasonable prospect of being able to bring about by his own act.' This might be termed 'dictionary intention'.

Oblique intent

The concept of intention is open to ambiguity. What is the position when someone has clearly caused an illegal result, realising that it would almost certainly occur, although it was not his or her primary intention? There is a well-known hypothetical example of a person placing a bomb in an aircraft with the intention that it will explode when the plane reaches an altitude of 20,000 feet. His specific aim or objective is to obtain the insurance money on the lost aircraft. In these circumstances, he surely knows that when the plane explodes all the passengers and crew will be killed, but does he really intend their deaths? This type of case is one of **oblique intent**.

In the case of *R v Hancock and Shankland* (1986), this issue was at the heart of the case — how the law should deal with the defendant who has created an unlawful result, where it is clear that the outcome was probable, and the defendant may well have foreseen this outcome. The defendants in the case were Welsh coal miners on strike. When one of their fellow miners wanted to return to work, they tried to stop the strike-breaker as he was being driven to another coal mine in a taxi. The route took the miners onto a motorway. When the taxi passed under a bridge, the striking miners threw rocks from the bridge. One of the larger rocks smashed through the windscreen and killed the driver. Clearly, the defendants had killed the taxi driver and if they had been charged with manslaughter, they would have pleaded guilty. However, the charge was murder, which requires there to be intention to kill or commit serious injury. The defendants denied such an intention, admitting only that their intention was to prevent the strike-breaker reaching the coal mine.

Although they were convicted of murder at their trial, the Court of Appeal and the House of Lords both quashed that conviction and substituted a manslaughter conviction, holding that the issue of intention had not been established. Lord Scarman indicated that, in cases like these, juries needed to be told by the judge that 'the greater the probability of a consequence occurring, the more likely it was so foreseen and, if so, the more likely it was intended'. This emphasised the point that foresight of the degree of probability was the only evidence from which intention could be inferred.

In the more recent cases of *R* v *Nedrick* (1986) and *R* v *Woollin* (1998) (see below), a tighter rule was laid down for such cases of oblique intent. This now enables juries to return a verdict of murder only where they find that 'the defendant foresaw death or serious injury as a virtually certain consequence of his or her voluntary actions'. It is worth pointing out that, in both these cases, the original murder conviction was changed on appeal to a manslaughter conviction.

R v Woollin (1998)

This case resulted from the death of a 3-month-old baby. Although initially the defendant gave a number of different explanations, he finally admitted that he 'had lost his cool' when his baby started to choke. He had shaken the baby and then, in a fit of rage or frustration, had thrown him in the direction of his pram, which was standing against the wall some 3 or 4 feet away. He knew that the baby's head had hit something hard but denied intending to throw him against the wall or wanting him to die or to suffer serious injury. The trial judge directed the members of jury that they might infer intention if they were satisfied that, when he threw the baby, the defendant appreciated there was a 'substantial risk' of causing serious harm. In the Court of Appeal, the defendant argued that the judge should have used the words 'virtual certainty', as 'substantial risk' was merely a test of recklessness. The Court of Appeal, although critical of the trial judge, dismissed the appeal, and certified questions for the House of Lords. The House of Lords quashed the defendant's conviction for murder and substituted a conviction for manslaughter.

Lord Steyn gave the main speech, saying that 'a result foreseen as virtually certain is an intended result'. Thus, the phrase 'substantial risk' used by the trial judge blurred the distinction between intention and recklessness, and was too serious a misdirection for the conviction to stand. In *R* v *Matthews and Alleyne* (2003), the vexed issue of whether foresight of virtual consequences did in fact equal intent or was merely evidence of intention was resolved in favour of it being evidential. This means, at least in theory, that a jury could decide the defendant in a murder case had foreseen death or serious injury as virtually certain but still return a verdict of 'not guilty' to murder.

Recklessness

A standard dictionary definition of recklessness is 'unjustified risk-taking'. Following the case of *R* v *G and others* (2003), English law now recognises only **subjective recklessness**.

Cunningham recklessness/subjective recklessness

Here the prosecution must prove that the defendant appreciated that his or her action created an unjustified risk, and then went ahead with the action anyway.

In *R* v *Cunningham* (1957), the defendant ripped a gas meter from a wall to steal the money it contained, causing gas to escape. The gas seeped into a neighbouring building, where it overcame a woman. Cunningham was convicted of a s.23 offence — administering a noxious substance — but he appealed successfully on the ground that the prosecution had failed to prove that he recognised the risk of the gas escape. The question was quite simply whether the defendant *had* foreseen that his act might injure someone, not whether he *ought* to have foreseen this risk.

> **Exam hint**
> In explanatory questions on *mens rea*, what distinguishes a good answer from an average one is the explanation of oblique intent, together with the effective use of cases, such as *Nedrick* or *Woollin*.

Coincidence of *actus reus* and *mens rea*

Mens rea must coincide in point of time with the *actus reus* for an offence to occur. If I happen to kill my neighbour accidentally, I do not become a murderer by thereafter expressing joy over her death, even if a week previously I had planned to kill her but had then changed my mind. *Mens rea* implies an intention to do a present act, not a future one. In most cases, there is no problem in proving the necessary coincidence of *actus reus* and *mens rea*, but there are a few occasions that illustrate the fact that judges can take a more generous view of this issue of coincidence.

One such case is that of *Thabo Meli* v *R* (1954), where the defendants clearly intended to kill their victim. Having attacked him, they threw what they believed to be his dead body over a cliff in order to dispose of it. The victim in fact survived both the murderous attack and the fall, but died subsequently of exposure. On appeal, the Privy Council ruled that it was 'impossible to divide up what was really one series of acts' and that if during that series of acts the necessary *mens rea* was present, that was sufficient coincidence to justify a conviction. This ruling was followed in *R* v *Church* (1966). A more recent case was *R* v *Le Brun* (1992), where again the view was upheld that where there is a series of actions that can be regarded as a linked transaction or continuing act, the coincidence rule is satisfied, provided that at some point during the transaction the required *mens rea* is present.

A final example is that of *Fagan* v *Metropolitan Police Commissioner* (1969). Here the facts were that the defendant had accidentally driven his car onto a police officer's foot when he had been instructed to park his car close to the kerb. When the officer ordered him to move it, Fagan swore and turned off the ignition. When he was later convicted of assaulting a police officer in the execution of his duty, Fagan appealed on the ground that when he drove accidentally onto the officer's foot there was no *mens rea* and when he had *mens rea* (when he swore and turned off the ignition), there was no act but an omission (failure to act), and the *actus reus* of this particular crime required an act. The appeal was dismissed — the court held that Fagan's driving onto the officer's foot and staying there was one single continuous act rather than an act followed by an omission. So long as the defendant had the *mens rea* at some point during that continuous act, he was liable.

Transferred malice

Under the rule of 'transferred malice', if A fires a gun at B, intending to kill B, but misses and in fact kills C, A is guilty of murdering C. The intention (malice) is transferred from B to C. The leading case is that of *R v Latimer* (1886). In this case, the defendant had a quarrel in a public house with another person. He took off his belt and aimed a blow at his intended victim, which struck him lightly. However, the belt then struck a person standing beside the intended victim and wounded her severely. The jury found that the blow was unlawfully aimed at the original victim but that the striking of the second victim was purely accidental. It was held on appeal, however, that the defendant should be convicted of unlawfully and maliciously wounding the second victim.

The other important aspect of this rule is that it is limited to situations where the *actus reus* and the *mens rea* of the same crime coincide. If A shoots at B's dog, intending to kill it, but misses and instead kills B, A is not guilty of B's murder because the *mens rea* of murder is absent. In *R v Pembliton* (1874), the defendant threw a stone at the victim, intending to harm him, but missed and broke a window. The defendant was not guilty of malicious damage, as he lacked the *mens rea* for that offence. (Of course, he could have been convicted of that offence if it could be proved that he had been reckless because he recognised the risk of causing property damage if he missed his intended victim.)

Strict liability offences

Strict liability offences may be defined as those that do not require *mens rea* to be proven — they might also be described as 'no fault' offences. Almost all of them are created by statute law, and many concern road-traffic offences or breaches of health and safety legislation.

A good example of a strict liability offence is the case of *Callow v Tillstone* (1900), where the defendant who was a butcher had asked a vet to examine a carcass to ensure its fitness for human consumption. On receiving the vet's assurance that it was fit, he offered it for sale. The vet had been negligent however, and the meat was in fact contaminated. The defendant was convicted of exposing unsound meat for sale, even though he had exercised due care. Another case that illustrates strict liability offences effectively is *Harrow LBC* v *Shah* (1999), in which a shopkeeper was convicted of the offence of selling a lottery ticket to a minor child, although he thought, reasonably, that the boy was at least 16 years old.

The argument most frequently advanced by the courts for imposing strict liability is that it is necessary to do so in the public's interests. It may be conceded that, in many of the instances where strict liability has been imposed, the public does need protection against negligence and, assuming that the threat of punishment can make the potential harmdoer more careful, there may be a valid ground for imposing liability for negligence as well as where there is *mens rea*. In *Gammon* v *Attorney General of Hong Kong* (1985), Lord Scarman indicated the points that a court should consider to determine whether the presumption in favour of *mens rea* being required could be rebutted:

* That presumption is particularly strong where the offence is 'truly criminal' in character.
* The presumption applies to statutory offences, and can be displaced only if it is clearly or by necessary implication the effect of the statute.
* The only situation in which the presumption can be displaced is where the statute is concerned with an issue of social concern — for instance, road and workplace safety, environmental concerns, consumer protection.
* Even where a statute is concerned with such an issue, the presumption in favour of *mens rea* stands unless it can also be shown that creation of strict liability will be effective in promoting the objects of the statute by encouraging greater vigilance to prevent the commission of the prohibited act.

In *R* v *Blake* (1997), where the defendant was convicted of making broadcasts on a pirate radio station without a licence, the Court of Appeal specifically referred to Lord Scarman's tests when deciding to uphold the conviction. The court concluded that the offence had been created in the interests of public safety since the interference from the unlicensed transmitter could have affected the operation of the emergency services. A further illustrative case is *Alphacell* v *Woodward* (1972), where the House of Lords held that the offence of causing polluted matter to enter a river was a strict liability offence.

It is also argued that the majority of strict liability cases can be described as 'administrative' or 'quasi' crimes. **Quasi crimes** are those offences that are not criminal 'in any real sense', and are merely acts prohibited in the public interest. Parliament makes no such distinction: an act either is, or is not, declared by Parliament to be a crime, but the courts decide whether it is a 'real' or 'quasi' crime on the basis that an offence that, in the public eye, carries little or no stigma and does not involve 'the disgrace of criminality' is only a quasi crime. Then strict liability may be imposed, because 'it does not offend the ordinary man's sense of justice that moral guilt is not of the essence of the offence'.

In *Sweet* v *Parsley* (1970), the defendant's conviction for being concerned in the management of premises used for smoking cannabis was quashed on appeal, as the offence required *mens rea*

This distinction was made in *Sweet* v *Parsley* (1970). Here, Lord Reid acknowledged that strict liability was appropriate for regulatory offences. But, he said, the kind of crime to which a real social stigma is attached should usually require proof of *mens rea*. In this case, the defendant's conviction for being concerned in the management of premises that were being used for the purpose of smoking cannabis was quashed on appeal, on the ground that such an offence was not one of strict liability and did require *mens rea* to be proven.

This argument — that offences which are serious in terms of both potential punishment and social stigma should require proof of *mens rea* — was strengthened by the case of *B* v *DPP* (2000). Here, the defendant, aged 15, was convicted of inciting a child under the age of 14 to commit an act of gross indecency with him, contrary to s.1 of the Indecency with Children Act 1960. He had persistently, but unsuccessfully, asked a 13-year-old girl to perform oral sex on him. When charged, he claimed that he thought she was older, at least 14. The magistrates convicted him, ruling that this was a strict liability offence and therefore even if the defendant had a genuine belief that the girl was over 14, he was still guilty. However, on appeal to the House of Lords, his conviction was quashed because, as in *Sweet* v *Parsley*, it was held that this offence required proof of *mens rea* as to the age of the child — either an intent to incite a child under the age of 14 or recklessness as to whether the child was under 14. The House of Lords argued that in order to rebut the presumption that criminal offences required *mens rea*, the House required a 'compellingly clear implication that Parliament intended the offence to be one of strict liability'.

A further point here is that, in most of these cases, the penalty imposed is a fine and not a community or custodial sentence. However, in *Gammon* v *Attorney-General of Hong Kong* (1985), the Privy Council admitted that the fact that the offence was punishable with a fine of $250,000 and 3 years' imprisonment was not inconsistent with the imposition of strict liability.

Reasons for strict liability offences

The principal reason advanced for the creation of such offences is that they are necessary to protect the public by providing high standards of care. This is most clearly observed in the number of road safety and workplace safety offences: speeding, drink-driving, and many offences under the Health and Safety at Work Act 1974 (e.g. abrasive wheels and power press regulations). The existence of strict liability also acts as a deterrent — factory managers are far more likely to ensure compliance with safety regulations if the consequence of non-compliance is a prosecution followed by a criminal sanction. Such sanctions also result in much improved road safety. An additional argument here is that companies who are responsible for employee safety may think of saving money by cutting corners, and if they do so, they ought to be liable if taking that risk causes harm.

Enforcing strict liability offences is much easier than in more serious offences where *mens rea* has to be proved. In *Gammon*, it was suggested that if the prosecution had to prove *mens rea* in even the smallest regulatory offence, the administration of justice might quickly come to a complete standstill. Finally, given that the penalty for most strict liability offences is a fine, there is little threat to individual liberty, and such offences do not usually create the social stigma of real criminality.

Questions

1 Briefly explain what oblique intention means.

2 What is the meaning of *Cunningham* recklessness?

3 Which rule was created by *Thabo Meli* v *R*?

4 Give another case example for this rule.

5 What is meant by the 'transferred malice' rule?

6 What did the case of *R* v *Pembliton* illustrate?

7 What is the meaning of strict liability?

8 Which case involved selling a lottery ticket to a minor?

9 In which case did Lord Scarman lay down guidance for crimes of strict liability?

10 What was the legal consequence in *Sweet* v *Parsley* in the House of Lords judgement?

Sample exam questions

1 Explain the meaning of *actus reus*. (10 marks)

Five sample answers are provided below, ranging from 'fragment' to 'sound'. Notice what is included in the 'sound' answer to achieve full marks.

> Actus reus *means the physical element of a crime.*

This answer receives 1 mark only — 'fragment'.

> Actus reus *is the physical element of a crime — the 'doing part' — and it has to be a voluntary act. It can also be an omission — a failure to act — such as not wearing a seat belt.*

This answer receives 3–4 marks — 'limited'.

Actus reus is the physical element of a crime, and it has to be a voluntary act — under the control of the defendant. It can also be an omission — a failure to act, where the law imposes a duty to act, as in the case of R v Pittwood, where a level-crossing keeper was convicted of manslaughter because he failed to close the gate to an oncoming train. Another example would be not wearing a seat belt in a car.

This answer receives 5 marks — 'some'.

Actus reus is the physical element of a crime and each crime has its own actus reus, e.g. battery involves inflicting unlawful personal violence, and murder is unlawful killing. It has to be a voluntary act of the defendant — that is, under the defendant's control. If the defendant does something because of duress — the threat of serious injury — this would not be an actus reus.

It can also be an omission — a failure to act where the law imposes a duty to act. This can arise from a contractual duty, as in R v Pittwood, where a railway employee was convicted because he had failed to close a level crossing and a person was killed. Other examples include R v Miller, where a tramp was convicted because, although he had accidentally started a fire, he had then failed to warn neighbours or to take any steps to call the fire brigade.

This answer receives 7 marks — 'clear'.

Actus reus means the physical element of a crime. Each crime has its own different actus reus — battery involves the infliction of unlawful personal violence, theft the appropriation of another's property, murder the unlawful killing of a human being. An actus reus has to be a voluntary act — that is, under the control of the defendant. If the action has been committed under duress (the threat of serious violence or death) it is not an actus reus. Another example was provided in Hill v Baxter, where the judge gave the example of a driver who lost control of his car because he had been stung by bees.

An actus reus can also be an omission — a failure to act where the law imposes a duty to act. In the UK there is no 'Good Samaritan' law requiring people to try to rescue others, but the law recognises the following 'duty' situations. Under contract (as in R v Pittwood, where a railway employee was convicted of manslaughter because he failed to ensure a level crossing gate was closed); where the defendant has created a dangerous situation (as in R v Miller) and has then failed to respond to that situation, for example (by trying to warn others or summon the fire brigade); where the defendant has assumed a responsibility to look after others (as in R v Stone and Dobinson); or where the defendant occupies an official position (as in R v Dytham, where a police officer failed to stop a fight and the victim was killed).

15

Finally, there are circumstance crimes, where the actus reus *is simply the circumstance of the crime, e.g. possession offences (of stolen property, dangerous weapons, illegal drugs).*

This answer receives 10 marks — 'sound'.

2 **Explain with reference to appropriate cases and/or examples what is meant by strict liability in criminal law.** (10 marks)

Task

Read the following sample answer to this question, which has been assessed as 'some'. Rewrite it as both a 'clear' and a 'sound' answer. (Note that the useful cases not mentioned in this answer are *Sweet* v *Parsley* and *Gammon* v *Attorney General of Hong Kong*.)

Strict liability means 'no fault' liability and refers to crimes where there is no mens rea *required. These offences are mostly created by statute for public protection, for example road traffic offences such as speeding or workplace safety regulations. A good case example is* Callow v Tillstone. *These offences are usually punished by fines only because they are called administrative offences.*

Suggested reading

Clarkson, C. M. V. (2005) *Understanding Criminal Law*, Sweet & Maxwell.
Elliott, C. and Quinn, F. (2006) *Criminal Law* (6th edn), Pearson Longman.
Martin, J. (2005) *AQA Law for AS*, Hodder Arnold.
McAlhone, C. and Huxley-Binns, R. (2007) *Criminal Law: The Fundamentals*, Sweet & Maxwell.
Storey, T. and Lidbury, A. (2007) *Criminal Law*, Willan.

Chapter **16**

Non-fatal offences

Now that you have studied the theory in terms of *actus reus* and *mens rea*, you can apply it to actual offences — those grouped together as **non-fatal offences**. There are five of these:

❖ assault
❖ battery
❖ assault occasioning actual bodily harm (ABH)
❖ malicious wounding or inflicting grievous bodily harm (GBH)
❖ wounding or causing grievous bodily harm with intent (to cause GBH)

Assault and battery were two distinct crimes at common law and their separate existence is validated by s.39 of the **Criminal Justice Act 1988**. This was confirmed in *DPP v Little* (1992), where a single charge alleging that the defendant 'did unlawfully assault and batter' the victim was held to be two offences and was therefore unsatisfactory, since different offences have to be charged separately.

The other three more serious offences are defined in the **Offences Against the Person Act 1861**.

Assault

This is any act by which the defendant, intentionally or recklessly, causes the victim to apprehend immediate and unlawful personal violence. In other words, this offence can be described as 'a threat of violence which the victim believes to be a threat'. Accordingly, if any harm is caused, a more serious offence than assault has been committed, although the defendant may also have committed an assault. An example would be if the defendant has shouted at the victim 'I am going to thump you' and has then proceeded to do just that.

16

Actus reus of assault

In a typical case of an assault (as opposed to a battery), the defendant, by some physical movement, causes the victim to believe that he or she is about to be struck. There may even be an assault where the defendant has no intention of committing battery but only to cause the victim to apprehend one. The word 'apprehend' does not require that the victim is actually afraid, merely that the victim is aware that something violent is about to happen.

In fact, it doesn't matter if the victim was not actually in any danger. For example, in *Logdon* v *DPP* (1976), the defendant showed the victim a gun in his desk drawer and said it was loaded, and that he would take her hostage. Although the gun was in fact a fake, this was not obvious from its appearance and the victim was afraid. The defendant was convicted of assault and this conviction was upheld on appeal. However, there cannot be an assault if it was obvious that the defendant could not carry out his threat — for instance, by shouting and gesticulating at passengers on a moving train.

Immediacy

There is a tendency to enlarge the concept of assault by taking a generous view of 'immediacy', to include threats in which the impending impact is more remote. In *Smith* v *Superintendent of Woking Police* (1983), the defendant committed an assault by looking at the victim in her night-clothes through a window, intending to frighten her. Kerr LJ said that it was sufficient that the defendant had instilled in the victim an apprehension of what he might do next. As she was in the house and he was in the garden, he could not have attacked her that very second but, nevertheless, the victim had thought that 'whatever he might be going to do next, and sufficiently immediately for the purposes of the offence, was something of a violent nature'.

It was made clear in *R* v *Ireland* (1998) that an assault may be committed by words alone, or even, as in that case, by silent telephone calls where the caller 'intends by his silence to cause fear and he is so understood'. In *R* v *Constanza* (1997), where the facts were similar to *Ireland*, the Court of Appeal

It was made clear in *R* v *Ireland* (1998) that silent telephone calls could constitute assault where the caller intends to cause fear

expanded the immediacy test slightly. Schiemann LJ held it was sufficient for the Crown to have proved an apprehension of violence 'at some time, not excluding the immediate future'. The Court of Appeal did, however, note that the victim knew the defendant lived nearby and that 'she thought that something could happen at any time'. *Constanza* and *Ireland* also confirmed that words alone could constitute assault. In *Ireland*, Lord Steyn stated 'there is no reason why something said should be incapable of causing an apprehension of immediate personal violence, for example a man accosting a woman in a dark alley saying, "come with me or I will stab you"'. *Constanza* ruled that the words need not necessarily be verbal. Here, the Court of Appeal held that words in letters could amount to an assault. Schiemann LJ pointed out that what was important was that victim apprehended violence. How that apprehension got there was 'wholly irrelevant'.

Note, however, that there may be circumstances where the words used by the defendant could negate the possibility of an assault, as illustrated in the historical case of *Turberville* v *Savage* (1669). In this case, the defendant laid his hand on his sword, saying 'If it were not assize time [when High Court judges were present to try serious cases], I would not take such language'. If the defendant had said nothing, it is clear that the court would have held the act of gripping his sword as evidence of assault.

Mens rea of assault

This can be either intention or subjective recklessness as to causing the victim to apprehend immediate unlawful personal violence.

Battery

Battery is defined as 'any act by which the defendant, intentionally or recklessly, inflicts unlawful personal violence'. Most batteries involve an assault, although this is not a requirement — a blow to the back of the head, completely taking the victim by surprise, is a battery. Examples of battery include a push, a kiss, or throwing water or a projectile which lands on another person's body.

Must there be hostility, anger or aggression for a battery to be committed?

In *Faulkner* v *Talbot* (1981), Lord Lane CJ said that a battery 'need not necessarily be hostile, rude or aggressive', but in *Wilson* v *Pringle* (1987) — a civil case — Croom-Johnson LJ stated that a touching had to be hostile to amount to battery, and in *Brown and others* (1993), the House of Lords approved that ruling when Lord Jauncey described hostility as 'a necessary ingredient'.

Many unwanted touchings are 'technical' batteries: in *Collins v Wilcock* (1984), Goff LJ said: 'It has long been established that any touching of another person, however slight, may amount to a battery, and prosecutors are relied upon to avoid prosecutions of minor incidents. Since the merest touching without consent is a criminal offence, the demands of everyday life require that there is an implied consent to that degree of contact which is necessary or customary in ordinary life. Therefore, nobody can complain of the jostling inevitable in a supermarket or an underground station, nor can a person at a party complain if his hand is grasped in friendship.'

Actus reus of battery

This consists of the infliction of unlawful personal violence by the defendant. The use of the term 'violence' here is misleading — all that is required for a battery is that the defendant touches the victim without consent or other lawful excuse. However, under the **Joint Charging Standard**, in practice, a prosecution is most unlikely unless some injury has been caused. It is generally said that the defendant must have carried out an act, but there can be occasions where mere obstruction can be a battery. There may also be a battery when the defendant inadvertently applies force to the victim and then wrongfully refuses to withdraw it. In *Fagan v Metropolitan Police Commissioner* (1969), where the defendant accidentally drove his car onto a police officer's foot and then intentionally left it there, the court held that there was a continuing act, not a mere omission. It is also settled law that there can be a battery where there has been no direct contact with the victim's body — touching his or her clothing may be enough to constitute this offence, as in *R v Thomas* (1985), where it was stated that touching the woman's skirt was equivalent to touching the woman herself.

Indirect battery

Although most batteries are directly inflicted, there are occasions when the battery is **indirect**. In *R v Martin* (1881), the defendant placed an iron bar across the doorway of a theatre, put out the light and created general panic and confusion, as a result of which some members of the audience were injured. Martin was convicted of inflicting grievous bodily harm, but the court also ruled that he had committed a battery. More recently, in *R v Haystead* (2000) the defendant punched a woman who was holding a small child in her arms. As a result of the blows, she dropped the child on the ground, and the defendant was convicted of battery against the child, even though no physical contact had occurred between the defendant and the child. Another example of indirect battery occurred in *DPP v K (a minor)* (1990), in which the defendant was convicted of battery, after having poured acid into an electric hand-dryer in a toilet which injured another pupil.

Mens rea of battery

The law is settled that either intention or recklessness as to the infliction of unlawful personal violence is sufficient. After a brief period of uncertainty, it is now clear that subjective recklessness — 'the conscious taking of an unjustified risk' — is the relevant test (as confirmed by the cases of *R v Venna*, 1976 and *R v Savage; R v Parmenter*, 1991). The defendant must foresee the risk of causing the application of violence.

Assault occasioning actual bodily harm

Section 47 of the Offences Against the Person Act 1861

For assault occasioning actual bodily harm (ABH), the word 'assault' can mean either assault or battery, but most often it will refer to battery — the infliction of some unlawful violence rather than a threat of violence.

This offence is triable either way and carries a maximum sentence of 5 years' imprisonment, in comparison with the maximum sentence of 6 months for common assault. The conduct element (*actus reus*) is an assault or battery that causes 'actual bodily harm'. This means that this is actually two offences, since the prosecution must be able to prove that an assault or battery took place first, and then that that assault/battery went on to cause injuries consistent with actual bodily harm. This has been given the wide definition of 'any hurt or injury calculated to interfere with the health or comfort of the victim', provided it is not 'merely transient or trifling' (as for example in *R v Miller*, 1954). In *R v Chan-Fook* (1994), the Court of Appeal stated that the injury 'should not be so trivial as to be wholly insignificant'.

One consequence of this definition is that it has been held to cover psychological harm — where the defendant causes the victim to become hysterical or to suffer substantial fear. For instance, in *R v Chan-Fook*, the defendant suspected the victim of theft and manhandled and then locked the victim in an upstairs room. The trial judge directed the jury that it sufficed for ABH that the assault had caused 'a nervous, maybe hysterical, condition'. However, this conviction was quashed on appeal — the court ruled that while the phrase 'actual bodily harm' is capable of including psychiatric injury, 'it does not include mere emotions such as fear or distress or panic nor does it include states of mind that are not themselves evidence of some identifiable clinical condition'. A similar conclusion was reached in *R v Morris*, where the Court of Appeal held that evidence from the victim's doctor (that she suffered from anxiety, fear, tearfulness, sleeplessness and physical tension) was insufficient to establish ABH.

The *mens rea* required for ABH is the same as for battery — intention or recklessness as to the application of some unlawful force to another. This important rule was established in the separate cases of *Savage* and *Parmenter*, where it was held by the House of Lords that the prosecution is not obliged for a s.47 offence to prove that the defendant intended to cause some actual bodily harm or was reckless as to whether such harm would be caused.

In *R* v *Savage* (1991), the defendant admitted throwing the contents of her beer glass over the victim during a bar brawl. The glass slipped out of her hand and broke and a piece of glass cut the victim's wrist. Although the defendant denied intending to cause the injury suffered by the victim, intending only to throw the beer over her, she was convicted of s.47 ABH. This means that a verdict of guilty may be returned upon proof of an assault, together with proof of the fact that actual bodily harm was occasioned by the assault.

Hemera Technologies Inc.

In *Savage*, the defendant was charged with s.47 ABH, even though she had only intended to throw beer over the victim

---

Exam hint

The rule established in *Savage* and *Parmenter* is a key legal point that examiners are looking for. Note that this is one of the most common mistakes made in examination answers. Few marks, if any, are awarded for simply referring to the *mens rea* of s.47 ABH as intention or recklessness, unless there is a clear reference to this rule and these cases.

Note too that 'sound' answers for this offence first require an explanation of the assault/battery offence in terms of *actus reus* and *mens rea*, not just an explanation dealing purely with ABH.

The case of *R* v *Roberts* (1971) confirms that the *mens rea* of s.47 ABH is the same as for assault or battery. As you know from Chapter 15, in this case, the defendant gave a lift in his car to a young woman. During the journey he made unwanted sexual advances, touching the woman's clothes. Frightened that he was going to rape her, she jumped out of the moving car, injuring herself. It was held that the defendant had committed the *actus reus* of s.47 by touching her clothes — sufficient for battery — and this act had caused her to suffer actual bodily harm. The defendant argued that he lacked the *mens rea* of the offence, because he had neither intended to cause her actual bodily harm, nor seen any risk of her suffering it as a result of his advances. This argument was rejected: the court held that the *mens rea* of battery was sufficient in itself, and there was no need for any extra *mens rea* regarding the actual bodily harm.

Malicious wounding or inflicting grievous bodily harm

Section 20 of the Offences Against the Person Act 1861

Section 20 created the offence of unlawfully and maliciously wounding or inflicting grievous bodily harm. The conduct element here is the same as for the more serious offence under s.18 (see below). A **wound** is defined as an injury that breaks both the outer and inner skin. A bruise or a burst blood vessel in the eye would not amount to a wound — see *C (a minor)* v *Eisenhower* (1984), where a pellet fired by the defendant hit his victim in the eye but caused only an internal rupturing of blood vessels not a break in the skin, and therefore there was no wound. Note that a large scratch that only breaks the outer layer of the skin is also not a wound. Grievous bodily harm is simply defined as 'really serious harm' — see *DPP* v *Smith* (1961) — or more simply as 'serious harm', as in *R* v *Saunders* (1985). You should note that, under the Joint Charging Standards, minor cuts would be charged as s.47 actual bodily harm, or even as battery.

> ### Exam hint
> Students often get confused about 'wounding' and 'grievous bodily harm'. For both s.20 and s.18 offences, these are alternative *actus reus* elements. A useful memory aid is that only if bleeding has taken place should wounding be charged. Of course, there could be circumstances where both wounding and GBH could be charged, for example where a major artery has been severed, this would cover both wounding and also GBH (because it has caused serious harm).

Biological GBH

This was established in 2004 in the case of *R* v *Dica*, which involved the conviction of a defendant of s.20 'biological' GBH after infecting two women with HIV. The Court of Appeal, having quashed his conviction and ordered a retrial, confirmed that injury by reckless infection *does* constitute a s.20 offence — and so confirmed that the nineteenth-century case of *R* v *Clarence* (1888) was overruled. This case had concerned a husband who had been prosecuted for infecting his unsuspecting wife with gonorrhoea, but had his conviction quashed by a House of Lords ruling that s.20 required an assault or some form of direct bodily violence.

The more significant part of this judgement appears to relate to the **defence of consent**, as the court ruled that if the other party knew or suspected that his or her partner was so infected, no criminal liability would arise.

Even more importantly, the Court of Appeal has apparently widened the scope of the defence of consent in such cases, distinguishing the case of *R* v *Brown* (1994), where this defence was expressly disallowed by the House of Lords. Here, the court ruled that 'there is a vital difference between consenting to the *deliberate* infliction of harm, and consenting to an activity that you know involves a *risk* of it'. This ruling means that criminal liability does not arise where the other party knows or suspects, and is prepared to take the risk.

In the *New Law Journal* (21 May 2004), J. R. Spencer QC wrote that the court 'condemned it [*Clarence*] as inconsistent with later cases, notably *R* v *Ireland* and *Burstow*, which hold that s.20 covers deliberate harassment leading to psychiatric injury'.

If psychiatric injury can be inflicted without direct or indirect violence or an assault, for the purposes of s.20 physical injury may be similarly inflicted.

Mens rea of s.20

Section 20 requires either intention or recklessness to inflict some harm. This fault element was confirmed in the cases of *R* v *Mowatt* (1968) and *R* v *Grimshaw* (1984), which held that there is no need to prove recklessness as to wounding or grievous bodily harm, as long as the court is satisfied that the defendant was reckless as to *some physical harm* to some person, albeit of a minor character. As in all non-fatal offences where the *mens rea* includes recklessness, this is *Cunningham* or subjective recklessness — the prosecution must prove that the defendant did foresee that some physical harm might be done.

Wounding or causing grievous bodily harm with intent

Section 18 of the Offences Against the Person Act 1861

This is a serious offence that carries a maximum sentence of life imprisonment (in comparison to s.20 with a maximum of 5 years). It comes from s.18 of the Offences Against the Person Act 1861. There are two forms of intent. The first (and most common) is **'with intent to cause grievous bodily harm' (GBH)**. This requires proof that the defendant intended to cause a serious injury — 'specific intent' — as in *R* v *Nedrick* (1986) and *R* v *Woollin* (1998). This can be either **direct intent**, where the defendant's aim or objective was to cause grievous bodily harm, or **oblique intent**, where the jury is satisfied that the defendant foresaw serious injury as virtually certain. In most cases of s.18 GBH, the defendant will have used some form of weapon to inflict injuries on the victim, which makes it easier for the prosecution to prove the necessary intent. Where the prosecution fails to establish intention, the offence will be reduced to the lower s.20 offence, as long as reck-lessness is proved.

Note that there is no offence of wounding with intent to cause wounding. If the defendant were to grab hold of the victim's hand and deliberately stick a pin into a finger through both layers of skin, causing blood to flow, this could only be charged under s.20. Although there is wounding and intent, there was no intent to cause GBH.

The second form of intent available for s.18 relates to circumstances where a lawful arrest is being attempted and the intent is **'to prevent the lawful apprehension of any person'**. The policy behind this element is that attacks on persons engaged in law enforcement are regarded as more serious. Under this, the defendant can be convicted if he or she pushes a police officer to prevent an arrest, and the officer falls and suffers a serious injury. There is no requirement that such serious results should have been foreseen or are even foreseeable. It is, however, a requirement in such cases that the prosecution proves the defendant intended some harm, or was reckless as to whether harm was caused.

Table 16.1 Summary of non-fatal offences

Crime	Actus reus	Mens rea	Cases	Maximum sentence
Assault	Causing the victim to apprehend immediate, unlawful personal violence	Intention or subjective reck-lessness to causing *actus reus*	*Logdon, Ireland, Constanza*	6 months or £5,000 fine
Battery	Infliction of unlawful personal violence	Intention or subjective reck-lessness as to inflicting unlawful personal violence	*Fagan, Thomas*	6 months or £5,000 fine
Section 47 ABH	Assault or battery causing actual bodily harm	Intention or reck-lessness as to the assault or battery	*Miller, Chan-Fook, Savage, Parmeter, Roberts*	5 years
Section 20 GBH/ wounding	Wounding: all layers of skin must be broken; GBH: serious injury	Intention or reck-lessness as to *some* harm	*Eisenhower, Smith, Mowatt, Grimshaw*	5 years
Section 18 GBH with intent	Wounding or GBH as in s.20	Specific intent to cause GBH, or intent to resist lawful arrest	*Nedrick, Woollin*	Life

> ### Exam hint
>
> The issue of *mens rea* for s.20 results in far too many students either stating that the *mens rea* for this offence is intention or recklessness with no reference to the issue of causing 'some harm', or that the *mens rea* is intention or recklessness as to causing GBH. By itself, either of these mistakes means that the answer cannot gain top marks. A further important point is that if the scenario indicates that the victim suffered an injury that could be characterised as GBH and/or wounding, the most appropriate offence will usually be s.20. It is only in circumstances where a weapon such as a knife has been used to inflict the injury that s.18 would be more appropriate. Even then, consideration should be given to the possibility of s.20 if the necessary level of intent for s.18 is not proved.

Joint Charging Standards

The Joint Charging Standards for non-fatal offences are set out in Table 16.2. These are agreed by the police and the Crown Prosecution Service (CPS), and were produced in order to clarify the offences that would normally be charged following different levels of injuries. It is important, however, that you can also identify other potential offences that could be charged — for example, for the loss of a tooth or a cut requiring stitches.

Note that Table 16.2 is a *guide only* and if you refer to these standards you must also use the definitions provided above for each offence. Writing that 'under the Joint Charging Standards, a broken finger will be charged under s.47 ABH' is not good enough. You would also need to note that the *actus reus* of s.47 ABH requires that the defendant committed an assault or battery which then caused ABH, defined in *R* v *Miller* (1954) as 'any hurt or injury calculated to interfere with the health or comfort...'

Table 16.2 Joint Charging Standards for non-fatal offences

Section 39 of the Criminal Justice Act: common assault (battery)	Section 47: assault occasioning ABH	Section 18 or Section 20: GBH or wounding
Grazes or scratches	Loss or breaking of a tooth	Injury causing permanent disability or disfigurement
Abrasions	Temporary loss of consciousness	Broken bones
Minor bruising	Extensive or multiple bruising	Dislocated joints
Swelling	Displaced broken nose	Injuries causing substantial loss of blood
Reddening of the skin	Minor fractures	Injuries resulting in lengthy treatment
Superficial cuts	Minor cuts requiring stitches	
A black eye	Psychiatric injury — more than fear, distress or panic	Severe psychiatric injury — more than fear, distress or panic, and requiring

Sample exam question

> **Richard and his girlfriend, Kate, had a serious argument at the end of which Kate in her rage picked up a kitchen knife and threw it at Richard. It struck him in the shoulder and caused a bad cut and damaged tendons.**
>
> **Explain what the criminal liability of Kate is for the injuries caused to Richard.**
>
> (10 marks)

Task

A suggested answer plan is given below, using the IDEA mnemonic described on p. xiii. Study the plan and write an answer to this question.

❖ **Identify**. The bad cut would constitute wounding, and the damaged tendons grievous bodily harm. Because a weapon (a knife) has been used, the more appropriate offence will be s.18 — malicious wounding and causing GBH with intent.

❖ **Define**. Wounding is defined (in *C (a minor)* v *Eisenhower*, 1984) as a breach to the continuity of the whole skin, and GBH simply means 'serious' or 'really serious' harm — *R* v *Saunders* (1985) or *DPP* v *Smith* (1961). *Mens rea* for s.18 is specific intent to cause GBH.

❖ **Explain and apply**. In this scenario, there is no issue of causation to be considered, as Kate is obviously the factual and legal cause of Richard's injuries — the injuries were caused by the throwing of the kitchen knife. Therefore, the *actus reus* of both wounding and causing GBH is satisfied. As to the *mens rea* for s.18, this requires specific intent to cause GBH. This can be either direct — Kate's aim and purpose — or oblique, which requires the jury to find that Kate, at the time she threw the knife, foresaw serious injury occurring to Richard as virtual certainty (*R* v *Woollin*, 1998; *R* v *Nedrick*, 1986). If the jury failed to find that Kate intended to cause GBH, an alternative charge under s.20 could be brought against Kate. For this, the *actus reus* elements of wounding and GBH are exactly the same as for s.18. The only difference lies in the lower level of *mens rea* required — intention or recklessness as to causing some harm, albeit not serious harm (*R* v *Mowatt*, 1968).

Change the scenario

Consider the position if, when Kate was about to throw the knife at Richard, he ran out of the kitchen and tripped on the mat, falling heavily and breaking his leg.

❖ **Identify**. This is now more likely to be a s.20 GBH offence, although s.18 is still possible. However, a key issue now is that of causation, particularly the escape situation.

❖ **Define**. As above, GBH is 'serious injury' — R v *Saunders* (1985) — and a broken leg is listed in the Joint Charging Standards as GBH. The *mens rea* for s.20 is intention or recklessness as to causing some injury — R v *Mowatt* (1968).

On the issue of causation, the escape does not break the causal chain as it is foreseeable.

❖ **Explain and apply**. Here, Kate is still liable for the *actus reus* of s.20 GBH — as in *R v Roberts* (1971), where it was held that the action of the victim will not break the causal chain if it was a foreseeable response to the threatened attack. Clearly, in the circumstances of the scenario, Richard running away from a knife attack would be regarded as a foreseeable response, similar to the decision in *Roberts* where the victim of a potential sexual assault jumped out of the moving car. In terms of the *mens rea* requirement, it can be argued that Kate's action in threatening to throw the knife was certainly reckless, insofar as she would have foreseen at least some harm being caused to Richard. A possible s.18 GBH charge could also be brought against Kate, although it would be necessary to prove that she had the specific intent to cause GBH when she threatened to throw the knife at Richard.

Suggested reading

Clarkson, C. M. V. (2005) *Understanding Criminal Law*, Sweet & Maxwell.
Elliott, C. and Quinn, F. (2006) *Criminal Law* (6th edn), Pearson Longman.
Martin, J. (2006) *AQA Law for AS*, Hodder Arnold.
McAlhone, C. and Huxley-Binns, R. (2007) *Criminal Law: The Fundamentals*, Sweet & Maxwell.
Storey, T. and Lidbury, A. (2007) *Criminal Law*, Willan.

Chapter **17**

Sentencing

This chapter details the aims of sentencing, the types of sentences available to the courts and the factors that may affect sentencing. Governments have frequently intervened in sentencing policy and the current rules are set out in the **Criminal Justice Act 2003**. Examiners will expect you to be aware of the changes made in this statute and to make appropriate reference to them. All references to sections in this chapter refer to this Act (unless indicated otherwise).

The aims of sentencing

Section 142 defines the purposes of sentencing as:

> ...the punishment of offenders; the reduction of crime (including its reduction by deterrence); the reform and rehabilitation of offenders; the protection of the public; and the making of reparation by offenders to persons affected by their offences.

Punishment or retribution

Lord Denning commented in 1953: 'It is essential that the punishment inflicted for grave crimes should adequately reflect the revulsion felt by the great majority of citizens for them...some crimes are so outrageous that society insists on adequate punishment, because the wrongdoer deserves it.'

Usually, those convicted of very serious crimes are a danger to the public and they may receive long sentences in order to protect the public. The recommendation that the serial killer Harold Shipman should never be released and the 40-year minimum terms given to the those convicted in respect of the failed bombings of 21 July 2005 perhaps also reflect this sense of public revulsion and anger.

Deterrence

Section 142 specifically mentions deterrence as a factor in the reduction of crime. An **individual deterrent sentence** is designed to deter the particular offender from committing a further offence through fear of the punishment. This does not appear to be particularly effective. With regard to prison, 65% of prisoners reoffend within 2 years of release. Research suggests that the best deterrent is the fear of being caught.

A **general deterrent sentence** is one designed to deter other potential offenders. The point here is that in sentencing one offender for a particular offence, it is hoped to deter other potential offenders from committing a like offence through fear of the punishment. So, a general deterrent sentence will be an enhanced sentence — higher than that normally given for the offence in question.

General deterrent sentences are often handed down where a certain type of offence is prevalent (often in a particular locality). A good example is *Attorney General's Reference (Nos 4 and 7 of 2002)*, concerning the theft of mobile phones. Lord Woolf CJ said that the courts must adopt a robust sentencing policy towards people who commit these offences. 'Those who do so must understand that they will be punished severely. Custodial sentences will be the only option available to the courts...unless there are exceptional circumstances.'

Critics point out the essential unfairness of general deterrence sentences, since it involves sentencing an offender to a longer term than is deserved for the specific offence.

Rehabilitation

The aim of rehabilitation is to reform the offender so that he or she will not reoffend. In practice, some sentencing options, such as community sentences, have a more obvious rehabilitative purpose than others (for example, custody or fines). One aspect of community orders is that they can be individualised to the circumstances of the particular offender, and this makes them especially suitable for rehabilitation.

Protecting the public

This is a factor, particularly if someone is convicted of random violent or sexual attacks or gang crime. Custody is the only way in which the safety of the public can be guaranteed, and this is reflected in the fact that people involved in such offences invariably receive long prison sentences. Under s.227, extended sentences are also possible, allowing the imposition of an extra period of custody where a significant risk of serious harm to the public is considered. Up to 8 years could be added for a sexual offence, for example.

Reparation

Increasing attention is being given to the needs and views of victims, and there are already compensation orders that allow for offenders to be forced to make amends to the victim, usually through a financial payment. Clearly this is only practicable where the offender has the necessary financial resources. Reparation could also be given, if appropriate, through an imaginative community order providing for the offender to put right damage done — for instance, by repairing something or painting over graffiti.

Reparation could involve a community order to paint over graffiti

Types of sentences

Custodial sentences

Mandatory sentences are the most severe punishments available. They involve the automatic imposition of custody. Murder has an automatic life sentence and under s.225, an automatic life sentence is imposed if a person is convicted of a second serious violent or sexual offence.

The **Criminal Justice Act 2003** also sets out guidelines on minimum jail terms for people sentenced to life for certain categories of murder. Judges do not like these guidelines. In 2005, the then Lord Chief Justice, Lord Woolf, said he opposed

Parliament passing laws that forced judges to impose particular sentences. The present Lord Chief Justice, Lord Phillips, said in 2007 that it was regrettable that government guidelines on the length of time murderers should spend in prison had the effect of 'ratcheting up' sentences. The government's response was that 'we believe that people should be kept in prison as long as they are judged to be a danger to society'. Juliet Lyon, director of the Prison Reform Trust, said: 'The use of mandatory sentences do not give judges discretion to consider each case that comes before them on an independent basis.'

Discretionary sentences mean that courts have a choice as to whether to imprison somebody. Remember that the courts will have to justify giving a custodial sentence. Section 152 provides that for custody to be imposed, the judge has to be satisfied that the offence is so serious that only custody can be justified.

Under s.144, there is a reduced sentence available of up to a third for those who plead guilty at the first reasonable opportunity. This can be controversial and in 2006, when paedophiles took advantage of it, a review by the Sentencing Guidelines Council was undertaken and the government has suggested that it may give judges discretionary powers to end the one-third discount.

Before the trial judge decides what length of sentence to impose in a particular case, he or she will seek guidance either from a Practice Statement from the Court of Appeal, or by that court's consideration of a suitable tariff for that kind of offence. The **Sentencing Guidelines Council**, which was set up under the 2003 Act, can issue guidance on any aspect of sentencing, including tariffs, and courts are expected to take note of such guidance. The tariff will be the sentence appropriate for an 'average' example of the offence. All offences for which custody can be imposed have maximum sentences. In practice, the maximum is rarely used, but because it is a maximum, it cannot be exceeded however much the judge thinks the offender deserves it.

Suspended sentences

A suspended sentence is a period of custody that is not activated unless the offender commits another offence during a specified period of time, usually 2 years. Under s.118, it can only be imposed in exceptional circumstances. This should mean that it is rarely used.

Community sentences

Before the introduction of the Criminal Justice Act 2003, the courts could use individual community sentences, which they could combine with other sentences. The 2003 Act created one community order under which any requirements can be included that the court considers necessary. They can include all the previous community sentences, such as a community punishment order and community rehabilitation order, together with some new 'requirements'. Each order should have appropriate requirements built in that reflect the seriousness of the offence.

Examples include a curfew requirement, an exclusion requirement, a mental health treatment requirement and an alcohol treatment requirement. There is also a supervision requirement, which puts the offender under the supervision of a probation officer for up to 3 years.

Fines

The Crown Court can impose an unlimited fine. The Magistrates' Court is generally limited to a maximum of £5,000. Where consecutive sentences are passed by magistrates for two or more *separate* either-way offences, their maximum powers are 12 months in aggregate. In the 2003 Act, provision was made for an extension to 1 year's imprisonment, but this power has not yet been implemented. Fines can be combined with other sentences, including custody. One problem is that a fine is only appropriate if the offender is able to pay. Another difficulty is that a fine will have a varying impact depending on the wealth of the offender.

Discharges

Here the defendant is not sentenced as such but, if the discharge is **conditional**, he or she will be sentenced in respect of the original offence if they commit another offence within a specified period, which may not exceed 3 years. An example of a conditional discharge being used is *R* v *Whitehead* (1979), in which the defendant was convicted of shoplifting. She was a lone parent with a disabled child and had no previous convictions.

An **absolute discharge** would be appropriate in cases where the court feels that, although there is technically an offence, a prosecution should not have been brought, perhaps because the offence is too trivial or there are special circumstances affecting the offender.

Exam hint
If the question asks for a suitable sentence to be suggested, deal with this in general terms. For example, if the offence is s.20 GBH, it is likely to be sufficiently serious as to justify a custodial sentence. However, if the conviction was for s.47 ABH, a community sentence could be possible if it was a first offence and the injuries to the victim were not too serious. Do not *specify* an actual sentence — for example, 2 years in prison.

17

Factors that may affect sentencing

Aggravating factors

The **Criminal Justice Act 2003** sets out the kind of **aggravating factors** that the court should take into account and that would make the offence more serious:

❖ Previous convictions for similar offences.
❖ The offence was committed while on bail.
❖ The involvement of racial or religious hostility.
❖ The involvement of hostility on the grounds of disability or sexual orientation.

There are other factors that might aggravate an offence. For instance, the victim might be particularly vulnerable — young, very old or disabled. The offence might have been committed by a group. An attack by a gang, for example, might be treated as more serious than an assault by an individual. Another aggravating factor would be abusing a position of trust, for example a sexual assault by a teacher or doctor. The use of a weapon or a repeated attack would probably aggravate a non-fatal offence and would be likely to lead to a higher sentence. It is also likely that the courts would treat offences committed while under the influence of drugs or alcohol as more serious, though it could be argued that the offender is actually less able to control their behaviour when in this condition and therefore less at fault.

Involvement of racial hostility is considered an aggravating factor for sentencing

Mitigating factors

Mitigating factors will be pleaded on behalf of the defendant and could include the following:

❖ It is the first offence the defendant has committed.
❖ The defendant is very young or very old.
❖ The defendant is a vulnerable offender easily influenced by others.
❖ He or she has expressed remorse and perhaps made an offer to compensate the victim.
❖ The defendant has difficult home circumstances.

A guilty plea will also mitigate. The Sentencing Guidelines Council suggests a reduction of a third for a guilty plea at the first opportunity, but only a reduction of a tenth if the guilty plea is left until the trial starts.

The court will usually wish to refer to a **pre-sentence report** drawn up by the probation service, providing information on the defendant's background. This would be particularly relevant if the court was considering a custodial sentence or a community-based sentence. The court may ask for a medical or psychiatric report where this would be relevant.

Victim impact statements

Finally, victim impact statements may be formally prepared and read to the court, and the court is obliged to pay regard to these when considering sentence.

> ### Exam hint
>
> If the question asks about factors that may be taken into account, check to see if any aggravating or mitigating factors are present in the scenario.
>
> Remember also that the sentencing judge is limited by the maximum custodial sentences allowed for each offence. In the case of non-fatal offences these are:
> ❖ 6 months for assault and battery
> ❖ 5 years for s.47 ABH and s.20 wounding/GBH
> ❖ life for s.18 wounding/GBH with intent
> It is important to stress that these maximum sentences are rarely imposed and in your answer you should not automatically assume that a custodial sentence would be given, even for quite a serious offence. If you do think that prison is appropriate, justify it by referring to the factors that you think aggravate the offence or fail to mitigate it.

Questions

1 What is the main Act that currently regulates sentencing?

2 List the main aims of sentencing.

3 What are the two types of deterrence? What seems to be the most effective kind of deterrent?

4 What is the difference between a mandatory custodial sentence and a discretionary one?

5 Give an example of a mandatory sentence.

6 Why is a suspended custodial sentence likely to be used only rarely?

7 What change in the treatment of community sentences was introduced by the 2003 Act?

8 What is the name of the body set up in 2003 to give guidance on sentencing?

9 What four aggravating factors are mentioned in the 2003 Act?

10 Suggest three other factors that might aggravate an offence.

11 Suggest three factors that might mitigate an offence.

12 What are the guidelines on the amount a sentence should be reduced as a result of a guilty plea?

Sample exam questions

1 Oscar was a member of a group who supported a particular football team. One evening, after their team had lost a match, the group saw Jimmy, who was wearing a football shirt of a rival team. They attacked him, knocked him to the ground and repeatedly kicked him. Oscar was caught, but the other members of the group escaped. Oscar has a number of previous convictions for offences involving violence, but he has learning difficulties and is easily influenced by others.

   Outline the range of sentences available to the court. Taking into account any aggravating or mitigating factors, discuss how the court might treat Oscar. (10 marks)

2 Sylvia had an argument with her boyfriend, Alan. This resulted in Alan hitting her with a cricket bat. Sylvia suffered a badly broken leg that needed surgery. Alan, who has several previous convictions for violence, denies that he was involved.

   Briefly explain the range of sentences available to the criminal courts if Alan were to be convicted of an offence. (5 marks)

3 Briefly discuss the range of factors the court may take into account before he is sentenced. (5 marks)

Most exam questions are likely to ask you about either the range of sentences or the factors taken into account in sentencing. It is a good idea to prepare for such questions by making lists or revision cards and then adding some further comments, or an example. Use the following lists as a starting point:

❖ **Range**: custody; suspended; community; fine; discharge.
❖ **Aggravating factors**: bail; previous convictions; race/sexuality/disability; vulnerable; group; weapon; drugs/alcohol.
❖ **Mitigating factors**: age; vulnerable; home; remorse; guilty plea.

Draw attention to the factors that are most relevant and use them to decide how the courts should treat Oscar and Alan.

Chapter **18**

Introduction to tort

The origin of the word 'tort' (meaning 'wrong'), which came into our legal system after 1066, is Norman French. A useful definition of tort is 'a wrong that entitles the injured party to claim compensation from the wrongdoer'. Another way of putting this is to say that someone is negligent if he or she acts carelessly towards another person, to whom there is a legal obligation to act carefully, and the carelessness causes the other person to suffer some harm or loss.

The **tort of negligence** is an actionable wrong that flows from a breach of duty of care, which causes a victim foreseeable harm or loss. The key elements that the claimant needs to prove are that:

❖ he or she was owed a duty of care by the defendant
❖ the defendant breached that duty
❖ the breach caused the claimant foreseeable harm or loss

This particular tort is by far the most important and most used tort in English law. Winfield writes that 'tortious liability arises from the breach of a duty primarily fixed by law', and it is here that we need to start our study of the tort of negligence. The word 'negligence' is defined by the *Shorter Oxford Dictionary* as 'want of attention to what ought to be done or looked after; lack of proper care in doing something'. In law, negligence is more tightly defined as 'breach of a duty of care that causes foreseeable loss or injury'. To understand its application and importance it is necessary to study in turn each of the following three topics:

❖ duty of care
❖ breach of duty
❖ causation of foreseeable loss or injury

Duty of care

The tort of negligence owes its origins to the tale of a decomposing snail that was found in a ginger beer bottle — *Donoghue* v *Stevenson* (1932). The facts are that the claimant, Mary Donoghue, went with a friend to a café, where her friend bought her a bottle of ginger beer. Donoghue opened it and poured some of the contents into a glass. When she finished the glass, she then poured the remainder of the ginger beer into the glass and at this point the remains of a snail floated to the surface. This caused Donoghue to develop gastroenteritis and nervous shock, and quite naturally in these circumstances she sought compensation from the ginger-beer manufacturer.

The case eventually reached the House of Lords, where Lord Atkin decided the case in her favour with his famous 'neighbour principle'. In summary, this stated that 'you must take reasonable care to avoid acts or omissions which foreseeably could injure your neighbour', who is in turn defined as 'persons who are so closely and directly affected by my act that I ought reasonably to have them in contemplation as being so affected when I am directing my mind to the acts or omissions'. In this case, the ginger-beer manufacturer should reasonably have had the claimant in mind when manufacturing and bottling his ginger beer.

Donoghue v *Stevenson* (1932): 'who is my neighbour?'

This test clearly established that in order for a duty of care to be owed, there must be reasonable foresight of harm to persons who it is reasonable to foresee may be harmed by one's actions or omissions. Such 'duty' examples would obviously include cases involving doctor and patient, solicitor and client, car driver and other road users, employer and employee. However, the problem with this 'neighbour test' is that it has been used to create a duty of care in many less obvious situations, and therefore the courts have had to develop further guidelines to impose some limits on the scope of this principle. The modern approach comes from the case of *Caparo Industries plc* v *Dickman* (1990), which laid down what is called 'the incremental approach'. This asks three questions:

1 Was the damage or loss foreseeable?
2 Is there sufficient proximity (a sufficiently close relationship) between the wrongdoer and the victim?
3 Is it just and reasonable to impose a duty of care?

If the answer to all these questions is 'yes', then a duty of care has been established. This, of course, is only the start — the claimant also needs to establish that the defendant breached that duty of care and finally that the claimant's loss or injury was caused by the breach of duty and that such a loss was reasonably foreseeable (not too remote).

Foreseeability

The issue of foreseeability simply means that a reasonable person would have foreseen some damage or harm to the claimant at the time of the alleged negligence. A doctor's failure to diagnose a common medical problem will foreseeably lead to complications; a car driver's mistake will foreseeably cause a road accident; a mining company that does not observe safety laws will foreseeably have employees injured in accidents, and so on.

The case of *Langley* v *Dray* (1998) provides a clear illustration of this rule. Here, the claimant was a police officer who was injured in a crash while pursuing a defendant driving a stolen car. The Court of Appeal ruled that the defendant knew he was being pursued and therefore, by increasing his speed, he caused the police officer to drive faster and risk being injured. Another helpful case on this issue is *Kent* v *Griffiths* (2000), where a doctor called for an ambulance to take a patient suffering from a severe asthma attack to hospital immediately. The control centre replied 'Okay, doctor', but the ambulance failed to arrive within a reasonable time, and there was no good reason for this delay. The patient suffered a heart attack, which could have been avoided if the ambulance had arrived in time. It was held that it was reasonably foreseeable that the claimant would suffer some harm from the failure of the ambulance to arrive in time.

> ### *Exam hint*
> Remember this is an objective test — the question is whether a reasonable person would foresee the possibility of some harm or loss occurring, not whether the actual defendant foresaw loss or harm. In addition, the test is whether *some* harm or loss is foreseeable — not the particular type of loss or harm that did occur.

Proximity

Proximity means closeness in terms of time, space or relationship, and in many cases the issues of proximity and that of foreseeability will be similar. For instance, in a road traffic accident, the fact that the injured party could foreseeably be harmed will itself be proof of proximity. However, the case of *Bourhill* v *Young* (1943) is an interesting one in this context. The claimant was descending from a tram when she heard a motor accident. She did not actually see it but later saw blood on the road and suffered nervous shock and a miscarriage. Although it was reasonably foreseeable that some people would suffer harm as a result of the defendant's negligent driving, injury to the specific claimant was not foreseeable as she was not in the immediate vicinity of the accident — only hearing but not seeing the accident. Her action therefore failed.

Just and reasonable test

This final test is usually referred to as the **'policy test'**, under which judges are able to limit the extent of this tort. The principal reason for this judicial discretion is the argument that the floodgates would be opened if claims of liability were determined simply by reference to foreseeability. The American judge Cardozo CJ referred to this danger when he warned of 'liability in an indeterminate amount for an indeterminate time to an indeterminate class'.

A good case to illustrate the use by courts of this discretion is *Mulcahy* v *Ministry of Defence* (1996). In this case the defendant was a soldier who had served in the Gulf War, where he had suffered damage to his hearing when a fellow soldier fired a Howitzer shell. The Court of Appeal held that, although both factors of foreseeability and proximity were present, the facts of the case required them to consider this policy issue — effectively to ask whether it was fair, just and reasonable to impose a duty of care on the Ministry of Defence in battlefield situations. Unsurprisingly, it was decided that no such duty of care could be imposed. The application of this test can also be seen in the following types of cases:

❖ **Nervous shock** — *Alcock* v *Chief Constable of South Yorkshire* (1992), where the House of Lords created various 'control tests' to restrict liability to secondary victims in psychiatric injury cases.

❖ **Pure economic loss** — *Hedley Byrne* v *Heller* (1963), where the House of Lords created a new test of 'special relationship' to restrict liability, where the claimant has suffered a direct financial loss.

❖ **Public organisations exercising a statutory duty** — *X* v *Bedfordshire County Council* (1995) where local authorities exercising a statutory power were not held to be liable.

> ### Exam hint
> For a 'sound' answer on explaining duty of care, it is essential to explain this policy test with reference to at least one of the above cases.

Breach of duty

Once the claimant has shown that the defendant owed him or her a duty of care, it is necessary to prove that the defendant breached this duty — in other words, that the defendant acted carelessly. For example, in *Donoghue* v *Stevenson*, the defendant allowed the snail to get into the ginger beer bottle.

The key question that the court asks in order to determine whether this duty has been breached is: 'Did the defendant behave as the reasonable person would have in these circumstances?' This test was described well by Baron Alderson in *Blyth* v

Birmingham Waterworks Co. (1856): 'Negligence [meaning breach of duty] is the omission to do something which a reasonable man...would do, or doing something which a prudent and reasonable man would not do.'

The standard is therefore an objective one. Any personal difficulties or disabilities that might be encountered by the specific defendant cannot be taken into account. This is made clear in the case of *Nettleship* v *Weston* (1971). Here the claimant gave the defendant driving lessons. On the third lesson, the car struck a lamp-post and the claimant was injured. It was decided that the defendant, although a learner driver, would be judged by the standard of the average competent driver: 'The learner driver may be doing his best, but his incompetent best is not good enough. He must drive in as good a manner as a driver of skill, experience and care.'

Tests to determine breach of duty

To assist the court in deciding whether the defendant has breached his or her duty of care, certain straightforward tests have been established. Each test is clearly illustrated by a case, and therefore you need to be familiar with both these tests and the accompanying cases.

Degree of probability that harm will be done

Care must be taken in respect of a risk, where it is reasonably foreseeable that harm or injury may occur. Nearly all human actions or omissions involve the possibility of harm, but not every risky act will be regarded as negligent.

Victoria Bailes

In *Bolton* v *Stone* (1951), the claimant had been injured while standing on the road by a cricket ball struck over the defendant's ground. Evidence showed that a ball had been hit out of the ground on only six occasions in the previous 30 years, and on no previous occasion had anyone been injured. Here, the defendant was found not to have been negligent, as a reasonable person would have been justified in disregarding the risk.

Compare this case with *Haley* v *London Electricity Board* (1964), Here, the defendants left a hammer on the pavement to warn people of excavations. The claimant, who was blind, tripped over it and was injured. It was held that although the warning was sufficient for sighted people, it was not adequate for a blind person. The number of blind people was sufficiently large to make them a group that the defendants ought reasonably to have had in contemplation.

Although leaving a hammer on the pavement was a sufficient warning for sighted people, it was not adequate for a blind person

Magnitude of likely harm

The court considers not only the risk of any harm but how serious the injury could potentially be.

In *Paris* v *Stepney Borough Council* (1951), the claimant, who had one eye, was employed as a mechanic in the defendants' garage, where his job included welding. It was not normal to supply goggles and when a piece of metal flew into the claimant's good eye, he became completely blind. The defendants were held to be liable, although they would not have been liable to a person with normal sight. The greater risk to the claimant meant that greater precautions than normal should have been taken.

Cost and practicality of preventing the risk

Once the court has identified a risk as reasonably foreseeable, the next issue is whether the defendant should have taken precautions against that risk. If the cost of taking precautions to eliminate the risk is completely disproportionate to the extent of the risk itself, the defendant will not be held liable.

In *Latimer* v *AEC Ltd* (1953), a factory was flooded, and the owner used sawdust to reduce the effects of the flooding. However, some areas of the factory floor remained slippery and, as a result, an employee was injured when he fell. The owner was held not to have breached his duty of care because the only way to have avoided that risk was to have closed the factory completely. In the circumstances, this was out of proportion to the level of risk involved.

Note that *Bolton v Stone,* above, also illustrates this test effectively.

Exam hint

These three tests must always be considered when asking if the defendant had behaved as the reasonable person would have done in the circumstances. The trial judge is required to balance on the one hand the probability and magnitude of harm, and on the other, the cost and practicality of taking precautions. In *Bolton v Stone*, the finding of no liability resulted from the fact that there was little probability of harm, and if there were to be an accident, it would not be likely to result in serious injury to anyone. However, the costs of eliminating that (small) risk were so great as to close down the cricket club.

Contrast this case with *Paris v Stepney Borough Council*, where the risks of an accident were high and, given that the claimant had already lost the sight of one eye in a previous welding accident, the size of risk in his case was much higher. The cost of taking precautions in this case was very low — simply the provision of a pair of goggles, together with adequate supervision to ensure the claimant wore them. Therefore, the employers were held to have breached their duty of care.

Potential benefits of the risk

In some cases, the court has to weigh up whether there are some risks that have potential benefits for society. In *Daborn* v *Bath Tramways Motor Co. Ltd* (1946), it was held that: 'If all trains were restricted to a speed of 5 mph, there would be fewer rail accidents, but our national life would be intolerably slowed down. The purpose to be served, if sufficiently important, justifies the assumption of abnormal risk.'

In *Watt* v *Hertfordshire County Council* (1954), the claimant fireman was injured by a heavy jack that had been loaded quickly (but not secured) into the fire engine in order to respond to an emergency call involving a road accident victim. It was held that in these circumstances the risk involved was not so great as to prohibit an attempt to save life.

> **Exam hint**
>
> It cannot be emphasised too strongly that in answering any questions on breach of duty, the 'reasonable person' test is crucial. Too many exam candidates fall into the serious error of listing the risk factors, such as probability of harm, and then mentioning the appropriate cases with no reference at all to the 'reasonable person' test.

Professional persons

Where a particular defendant has a professional skill and the case involves the exercise of that skill, the court will expect the defendant to show that he or she has the degree of competence usually to be expected of an ordinary skilled member of that profession. This means that a general practitioner is only expected to exercise the normal level of skill of a GP, not that of a senior consultant heart surgeon. The leading cases here are both medical — *Bolam* v *Friern Hospital Management Committee* (1957) and *Bolitho* v *City and Hackney Health Authority Committee* (1998).

In *Bolam*, it was held that 'a doctor is not guilty of negligence if he has acted in accordance with a practice accepted as proper by a responsible body of medical opinion skilled in that particular art'. McNair J stated in that case:

> *Where you get a situation which involves the use of some special skill or competence, then the test as to whether there has been negligence or not is not the test of the man on the top of a Clapham omnibus, because he has not got this special skill. The test is the standard of the ordinary skilled man exercising and professing to have that special skill.*

Children

The conduct of a child defendant is assessed by reference to the standard of conduct that can be expected of a reasonable child of the defendant's age. This was decided in the case of *Mullins* v *Richards* (1998), which adopted the reasoning in an earlier Australian case of *McHale* v *Watson* (1966). In *Mullins*, the defendant and the claimant were 15-year-old schoolgirls who were 'fencing' with plastic rulers during the course of a lesson, when one of the rulers snapped and a piece of plastic flew into the claimant's eye, causing blindness. It was held that the proper test to apply was whether an ordinary, careful and reasonable 15-year-old would have foreseen that this game carried a risk of injury. On the facts, the injury was held not to be reasonably foreseeable by such a child — the game was a common one and the girls had never been warned it could be dangerous.

Res ipsa loquitur

This means literally 'the thing speaks for itself' and refers to situations where the judge is entitled to infer that the defendant's negligence caused the event, in the absence of any explanation from the defendant. In *Scott* v *London and St Katherine Docks Co.* (1865), the claimant, a customs officer, was injured by some bags of sugar falling on him while standing near the door of the defendant's warehouse. At the first trial, the judge directed the jury to find for the defendant on the grounds that there no evidence of negligence put by the claimant. However, a re-trial was ordered in which the doctrine of *res ipsa loquitur* was first made:

> *There must be reasonable evidence of negligence. But where the thing is shown to be under the management of the defendant or his servants, and the accident is such as in the ordinary course of things does not happen if those who have the management use proper care, it affords reasonable evidence, in the absence of explanation by the defendant, that the accident arose from want of care.*

In *Lloyde* v *West Midlands Gas Board* (1971), there was an argument that *res ipsa loquitur* was not actually a rule of law but, as per Megaw LJ, a convenient phrase to describe what is in essence no more than a common-sense approach to the assessment of the effect of evidence in certain circumstances. 'It means that a claimant *prima facie* establishes negligence where: (i) it is not possible for him to prove precisely what was the relevant act or omission which set in train the events leading to the accident, but (ii) on the evidence as it stands at the relevant time, it is more likely than not that the effective cause of the accident was some act or omission of the defendant, which act or omission constitutes a failure to take proper care for the claimant's safety.'

Three separate requirements must be satisfied for *res ipsa loquitur* to be accepted:

1 **The doctrine is dependent on the absence of explanation**. This means that if the court finds from the evidence how and why the occurrence took place, the rule will not apply. In *Barkway* v *South Wales Transport Co. Ltd* (1950), the tyre of a bus burst and the bus mounted the pavement and fell down an embankment. *Res ipsa loquitur* did not apply because the court had evidence of the circumstances of the accident and so was satisfied that the system of tyre inspection in the defendant's garage was a negligent one.

2 **The harm must be of such a kind that it does not ordinarily happen if proper care is taken**. The courts have applied this doctrine to things falling from

buildings and to accidents resulting from defective machines, apparatus or vehicles. In *Ratcliffe* v *Plymouth and Torbay Health Authority* (1998), the claimant had gone into hospital for an ankle operation but had sustained a serious neuro-logical condition which it was agreed had been triggered by the injection of a spinal anaesthetic. He argued this was a case of *res ipsa loquitur* because the injection must have been given negligently or it would not have caused this problem. The defendant health authority produced expert evidence that stated that this condition might have been caused by the claimant's susceptibility to spinal cord damage, which could have occurred even if the injection was not administered negligently. The Court of Appeal re-stated the rule above from *Scott* but further stated that that the defendant could prevent the judge from inferring negligence under *res ipsa loquitur* by either showing that he or she took reasonable care, or by supplying another explanation for the events. The court emphasised that nothing in the application of *res ipsa loquitur* changed the rule that the burden of proof was on the claimant. The defendant's alternative expla-nation would have to be plausible, and not merely theoretically possible, but the defendant was not required to prove that it was more likely to be correct than any other. In this case, the defendant had provided such a plausible explanation and it was therefore up to the claimant to prove that negligence, rather than the defendant's explanation had caused his injury, which he could not do.

3 **What caused the accident must be within the exclusive control of the defendant**. If the defendant is not in control, the doctrine does not apply. In *Turner* v *Mansfield Corporation* (1975), the claimant driver of the defendant's dust cart was injured when its back raised itself up when the claimant drove it under a bridge. It was held that since the claimant was in control, it was for him to explain the accident and since he could not provide any evidence from which negligence could be inferred, the action failed. Two railway cases illustrate the degree of control essential for the doctrine to apply. In *Gee* v *Metropolitan Railway Co.* (1873), a few minutes after a local train had started its journey, the claimant leaned against the carriage door which flew open. This was held to be evidence of negligence, whereas in *Easson* v *LNER Co.* (1944), the claimant's action failed because it was held that 'it is impossible to say that the doors of an express train travelling from Edinburgh to London are continuously under the control of the railway company.'

Causation of foreseeable loss or injury/damage

The claimant must be able to prove both that his or her damage or injury was caused by the defendant's breach of duty and that the damage or injury was not too remote, that is, it was reasonably foreseeable.

'But for' question

The first question that needs to be asked is the 'but for' question: but for the defendant's breach of duty, would the damage or injury have occurred? The leading case is *Barnett* v *Chelsea and Kensington Hospital Management Committee* (1968). The claimant's husband attended the defendants' hospital complaining of severe stomach pain and vomiting. The doctor in the Accident & Emergency Department refused to examine him and he was sent home. Five hours later he died from arsenic poisoning. The defendants clearly owed the deceased a duty of care and equally clearly they were in breach by failing to examine him. However, they were not held liable because the facts established that, even if he had been examined, he would have died before diagnosis and treatment could have been carried out. As the deceased would have died regardless of the breach, the hospital's breach of duty of care was not the cause of his death.

Remoteness of damage

Damages may not be awarded even where the claimant has established that the defendant's breach of duty (negligence) factually caused the damage or injury. It must be established that the damage was not too remote.

The present rule of law was laid down in the Privy Council case of *Overseas Tankship (UK) Ltd* v *Morts Dock and Engineering Co.* (1961). This is better known as *The Wagon Mound No. 1* case, after the name of the ship concerned. This case effectively overruled the case of *Re Polemis* (1921), where it had been held that the defendant was liable for all direct consequences of the breach.

Sydney Harbour, location of the oil spill in *The Wagon Mound* (1961)

This test was held to be too wide and in the *Wagon Mound* case the present rule of reasonable foreseeability was laid down. The defendant negligently discharged fuel oil into Sydney Harbour and the oil spread to the claimant's wharf, where welding operations were taking place. The claimants were advised that there was no risk of this heavy oil catching fire on the water and as a result carried on welding. The oil did, however, ignite — sparks from a welder caused a pile of cotton waste floating on the water to catch fire, and this then set fire to the oil. As a result of this fire, damage was caused to two ships and fouling was caused to the wharf by the oil. On appeal, it was held that the defendants were only liable for the fouling to the wharf. The major damage to the ships caused by the ignition of the oil was too remote from the original discharge of the oil. The test for remoteness of damage was whether the kind of damage suffered by the claimant was reasonably foreseeable by the defendants at the time of the breach of duty.

The decision in this case was affirmed in the case of *Doughty* v *Turner Manufacturing Co. Ltd* (1964), which held that the defendant was not liable for the burns suffered by the claimant when an asbestos cover was accidentally dropped into some molten liquid. The resulting eruption of the liquid was too remote.

There are other rules that need to be learnt in addition to these. The first is that, if the kind of damage suffered is reasonably foreseeable, it does not matter that the damage actually occurred in an unforeseeable way. This principle is clearly illustrated by the case of *Hughes* v *Lord Advocate* (1963), where the defendants had erected a tent over a manhole and surrounded the tent with paraffin lamps. The 10-year-old claimant dropped one of these lamps down the hole. Owing to an unusual combination of circumstances, there was an explosion and the claimant was badly burnt. Despite the defendants' argument that the explosion of the lamp was too remote, the House of Lords held they were liable. The question was asked: 'What kind of injury was foreseeable as a result of the breach of duty (leaving the hole unguarded)?' The answer was 'burns'. 'What kind of injury had occurred?' Again the answer was 'burns'. The damage was therefore not too remote.

Another case that can be used to illustrate this rule is that of *Jolley* v *Sutton London Borough Council* (2000). Here the claimant was a 14-year-old boy who had been seriously injured when he had tried to repair an old boat that he had found abandoned in a council park. While it was on a jack, the boat had fallen on him. The defendants admitted that the boat should have been removed from the park but denied liability for the accident, claiming that boys playing on the boat was foreseeable but the attempt to repair it was not. The Court of Appeal agreed with that argument, but the House of Lords reversed the decision — it was foreseeable that children would in some way 'get involved' with the boat. It was not necessary for the defendants to foresee the boy's attempt to repair it, using a jack to lift it.

'Thin skull' test

As you saw in Chapter 15, this test states that when the possibility of damage is foreseeable, defendants must take their victims they find them as regards physical characteristics. This means that the defendant will be liable when the injuries to the claimant are more serious than might have been anticipated because of factors peculiar to the victim.

The leading case that shows how this rule works in practice is *Smith* v *Leech Brain and Co. Ltd* (1961). The claimant's husband was employed by the defendants. His work required him to lower articles into a tank containing molten metal. An accident occurred and Mr Smith was struck on the lip by a piece of molten metal. He later died of cancer that was triggered by the burn. Lord Parker CJ held:

The test is not whether these defendants could reasonably have foreseen that a burn would cause cancer and that Mr Smith would die. The question is whether these defendants could reasonably foresee the type of injury which he suffered, namely the burn. What, in the particular case, is the amount of damage which he suffers as a result of that burn, depends on the characteristics and constitution of the victim.

> **Exam hint**
> Do not confuse 'damage' — causation tests — with 'damages' — the recovery of money compensation. Note also that there are more marks for explaining the legal rules rather than the factual 'but for' rule. Finally, never use cases from criminal law for tort answers (and vice versa).

Damages

The purpose of damages is to put the claimant in the position he or she was in before the tortious act, as far as can be achieved by money. To calculate the award, damages are divided into two kinds — **special damages** and **general damages**.

Special damages

These comprise quantifiable financial losses up to the date of trial and are assessed separately from other awards, because the exact amount to be claimed is known at the time of the trial. The major types of damages are listed below.

Loss of earnings
This is calculated from the date of the tort to the trial.

Tort law decoded
Specific tort problems
Duty of care questions

While most candidates are able to refer to the 'neighbour test' in *Donoghue* v *Stevenson*, there are relatively few answers that give a sound description of this test. A particular problem is that many candidates write of the specific incident in the scenario as having to be reasonably foreseeable, when in fact there just has to be a foreseeability that some harm or property damage could occur. If the incremental approach from *Caparo* v *Dickman* is used, the separate issues of foreseeability, proximity and the policy test are too often simply 'listed', with little explanation of what these tests require. For proximity, some reference to *Bourhill* v *Young* or similar cases is needed for a good answer, and candidates should at least comment on the need to 'prevent floodgates' opening when dealing with the policy test — whether 'it is just, fair and reasonable' to impose a duty of care. Better answers will include some case examples, e.g. *Alcock* v *Chief Constable of South Yorkshire* or *Mulcahy* v *Ministry of Defence* or note that this test has been used to limit liability in nervous shock or pure economic loss cases. A further common problem, even where there has been 'sound' explanation of duty of care, is the weak application of the facts of the scenario to the rules above.

Breach of duty

The most common — and most serious — problem here is the failure to explain the 'reasonable man' test, which is the *only* test which the court will apply. Reference should be made to *Blythe* v *Birmingham Waterworks* and to the objective nature of this test, confirmed by *Nettleship* v *Weston*. The next problem is that too many answers will do little more than list the various risk factors with the accompanying cases: Probability of harm — *Bolton* v *Stone*; cost of taking precautions — *Latimer* v *AEC Ltd* etc. These tests first of all need to be explained in terms of the 'reasonable man' test, for example pointing out that 'the greater the probability of harm or serious harm, the greater care that the reasonable man will take' or that 'the reasonable man is not required to take excessively expensive precautions to prevent foreseeable harm.' If these tests are more fully explained, it then also becomes much easier to apply these to the scenario.

Remoteness of damage

Questions on this particular topic have produced the greatest number of 'no relevant material' comments on exam scripts... What needs to be learnt is that in effect this topic is to tort what causation is to criminal liability. The factual 'but for' rule asks the question: 'but for' the breach of duty of care, would the injury etc. have occurred? The leading case is *Barnett* v *Chelsea and Kensington Hospital Management Committee*. The 'legal' rule is foreseeability of harm — the defendant will not be liable for unforeseeable consequences. Other rules are the 'thin skull 'rule — *Smith* v *Leech Brain* — and the rule derived from *Hughes* v *Lord-Advocate* that provided the injury was foreseeable, the defendant is still liable, even if the way in which the incident occurred was unforeseeable.

Adapted from an article by I. Yule, *A-Level Law Review* (2006), Vol. 1, No. 2, pp. 8–11

Sample exam question

Explain the meaning of 'duty of care', 'breach of duty' and 'damage'.

(10 marks)

Task

Read the following sample answer to this question, which has been assessed as 'some'. Rewrite it as both a 'clear' and a 'sound' answer.

Duty of care

This was created in Donoghue *v* Stevenson *under the neighbour principle, which was based on foreseeability. It was then developed into the incremental approach from* Caparo *v* Dickman *to include proximity (closeness) and policy which asks whether it is 'just, fair and reasonable' to impose a duty of care. A case for proximity is* Bourhill *v* Young.

Breach of duty

*This is based on the 'reasonable man' test — the man or woman on the Clapham omnibus — and it is an objective test. Risk factors are also taken into account, such as probability of harm (*Bolton *v* Stone*), cost of taking precautions (*Latimer *v* AEC Ltd*) and magnitude of harm (*Paris *v* Stepney LBC*).*

Damage

Some harm or property damage must have been caused by the breach of duty. The first test is the 'but for' test which is illustrated by Barnett *v* Chelsea and Kensington Hospital Management Committee, *where a person died of arsenic poison but his widow could not claim, as he would have died whether the doctor had treated him or not. There is another test called 'remoteness of harm' which came from the* Wagon Mound *case.*

Suggested reading

Elliott, C. and Quinn, F. (2007) *Tort Law* (6th edn), Pearson Longman.
Hodge, S. (2004) *Tort Law* (3rd edn), Willan.

Chapter 19

Introduction to contract

A contract can be defined as a **legally binding agreement**. This means that it is an agreement that is recognised as having legal consequences. All of us make agreements every day, but most of these we don't think of as having legal significance, and the law agrees. To be legally binding, an agreement must fulfil certain requirements and, by the end of this chapter, you should have formed an understanding of what are the most important elements of a contract and be able to look at various situations and decide whether a valid contract has been made.

You will also be introduced to the idea of breach of contract, which is where one of the parties to a contract fails to carry out what they have promised. This is where having a legally binding agreement becomes important. When nothing goes wrong it seems hardly to matter whether an agreement is legally binding or not, but, if there is a problem and someone suffers financial loss, they will only be able to recover this if the agreement is legally enforceable.

Formation of contract

To be valid a contract must meet certain conditions and these have to be present when it is **formed**.

There can be several parties to a contract and contracts can be made by individuals, groups or organisations. The same rules apply however complex the arrangements are and regardless of the numbers of people involved, but it is easier to see them operating in simple situation and therefore most examples used will involve just two individuals.

19

Offer and acceptance

This is the most basic and arguably the most important requirement. A valid contract requires one party to make an **offer** and another party to **accept** that offer. This then becomes an agreement. 'Offer' has been defined as an expression of willingness to contract on certain terms, made with the intention that it will become binding on acceptance.

An offer can be specific — made to one person or a group of people, in which case it can only be accepted by that person or group. But an offer can also be general and not limited in who it is directed at. An offer of a reward would be a good example. This could be accepted by anyone who met the conditions.

Invitations to treat

There are situations that look like offers, but they are not. They are an invitation to someone to *make* an offer — an **invitation to treat**.

It is important that you distinguish between an offer and an invitation to treat. The significance of the distinction is that, if an offer is made, all that is required from the other party is an acceptance. However, if there is an invitation to treat, then the other party has to make an offer, which leaves the person who issued the invitation able to decide whether or not to accept the offer. Suppose, for example, that something was advertised at £100, but this was a mistake and it should have been £1,000. If this is an offer and someone accepts it, then it becomes a legally binding agreement, but if the advertisement is an invitation to treat, the person issuing the advertisement has the opportunity to reject any offers made to buy at that price.

Whether something is an offer or an invitation will depend on the circumstances. The following are *not* offers.

Displays of goods in shop windows

As you saw in Chapter 5 in the case of *Fisher* v *Bell* (1961), a prosecution under the Offensive Weapons Act 1959 failed because the offence was to offer for sale prohibited weapons. Although the shopkeeper was displaying a flick knife in his window with a price tag, the court decided that this amounted to an invitation to treat and not an offer for sale.

Goods on display in supermarkets and self-service stores

This principle was established before the appearance of modern supermarkets in the case of *Pharmaceutical Society of Great Britain* v *Boots* (1953). Boots had opened a shop in which the customer selected the products they wanted from displays and paid for them at a cash point. The issue in the case was that the Pharmacy and Poisons Act 1933 required sales to be under the supervision of a registered pharmacist. It was accepted that there was a pharmacist at the cash point, but of course this would not have been sufficient if the contract had already been formed when the customer took the goods from the shelf. The court decided that Boots was not in breach of the Act because the contract was made when the goods were presented at the cash desk and accepted by the cashier and not when they were taken from the shelves. The goods on display were an invitation to treat.

Small advertisements

For small advertisements, such as those in magazines and newspapers, the leading case is *Partridge* v *Crittenden* (1968). An advertisement reading 'Bramblefinch cocks, bramblefinch hens, 25s each' was an invitation not an offer and so a prosecution for offering for sale a wild bird under the Protection of Birds Act 1954 failed. LCJ Parker in his judgement commented that there was 'business sense' in such advertisements being treated as invitations to treat, because if they were offers, the seller may well find that he had contracts with more people than he had goods to supply. However, as we shall see later, there are circumstances in which an advertisement can become an offer.

Price lists, catalogues etc.

The same principle applies to catalogues, circulars, timetables and price lists. Lord Herschell in *Grainger* v *Gough* (1896) commented that:

> ...the transmission of a price list does not amount to an offer to supply an unlimited quantity of the wine described at the price named...if it were so, the merchant might find himself involved in any number of contractual obligations to supply wine of a particular description which he would be quite unable to carry out, his stock of wine of that description being necessarily limited.

Responses to requests for information

In *Harvey* v *Facey* (1893), Harvey telegraphed Facey and asked: 'Will you sell me Bumper Hall Pen? Telegraph lowest cash price.' Facey replied by telegram, 'Lowest cash price for Bumper Hall Pen £900.' Harvey sent a second telegram, 'We agree to buy Bumper Hall Pen at £900 asked by you.' It was held that Facey's telegram was not an offer but merely a statement of the price. The courts have adopted quite a narrow interpretation of what constitutes an offer when information is being supplied. For example, in *Gibson* v *Manchester City Council* (1979), a statement that the Council 'may be prepared to sell the house to you' at a certain price was held to be an invitation to treat, not an offer.

Auction sales

In *British Car Auctions* v *Wright* (1972), a prosecution for offering to sell an unroadworthy car at auction failed because putting goods into an auction is an invitation not an offer for sale. The offer is made by the person making the bid.

Invitations to tender

Normally an invitation to tender for the supply of goods or services is an invitation to treat. This means that the person inviting the tenders is free to accept any of the tenders and not necessarily the cheapest. However, the wording of the invitation is important in that it may restrict the freedom to choose between rival bids. For example, in *Harvela Investments* v *Royal Trust Co. of Canada* (1986), a statement that the highest bid would be accepted was held to be binding.

The following are offers.

Reward posters/advertisements

In some circumstances, reward posters and advertisements can constitute offers. Unlike invitations to treat, offers must be firm, capable of being accepted and clear in requiring certain conditions to be fulfilled. This was established in the celebrated case of *Carlill* v *Carbolic Smoke Ball Co.* (1893).

The Carbolic Smoke Ball Company issued a newspaper advertisement in which it said it would pay £100 to any person who contracted influenza after using one of its smoke balls in a specified manner for a specified period. It also stated that it had deposited £1,000 with a named bank, to show its sincerity in the matter. Mrs Carlill was the customer who held the company to its word. Believing the accuracy of the advertisement, she purchased one of the balls and used it as directed — but contracted influenza nevertheless. She claimed for her £100 and then sued when the company refused to pay her.

The Carbolic Smoke Ball Company's advertisement was an offer rather than an invitation to treat

The Court of Appeal found in favour of Mrs Carlill. Lord Justice Lindley in his judgement drew attention to a number of features in the advertisement that made it an offer rather than an invitation. First, there was an express promise to pay £100 in certain events, expressed in language that was perfectly unmistakeable, and second, the deposit placed with the bank was proof of the intention to pay the £100 in the events that the company had specified.

This is an unusual example of an advertisement that amounted to an offer, but it does show that this is possible if the wording makes it clear that it is intended to be an offer.

Promotional campaigns

A supermarket might encourage customers to buy one product and get another product free, or it might offer two items for the price of one. As with reward posters, all that is required is that certain conditions are fulfilled.

Further rules about offers

Certain

The terms of an offer must be clear and definite, without any ambiguity. For example, in *Guthing* v *Lynn* (1831) a promise to pay an extra £5 'if the horse is lucky' was considered too vague to constitute an offer.

Made by any method

There is no requirement that an offer must be in a particular form. It can be made in writing, verbally or by conduct (e.g. by picking up an item and taking it to the cash desk).

Made to anyone

An offer can be made to an individual, a group, a company or organisation or even, as in *Carlill* v *Carbolic Smoke Ball*, to the whole world.

Lord Justice Lindley commented in *Carlill*:

> *The offer is to anybody who performs the conditions named in the advertisement. Anybody who does perform the conditions accepts the offer. I take it that if you look at this advertisement in point of law, it is an offer to pay £100 to anybody who will perform these conditions, and the performance of these conditions is the acceptance of the offer.*

Must be communicated

A person cannot accept what he or she does not know about. In practice, this is not likely to happen particularly often, but one example might be an offer of a reward for the return of a missing dog. If someone finds the dog and returns it, but that person did not know about the reward, then technically he or she is not entitled to the reward because the offer was never received and therefore cannot be accepted.

Must still be in existence when accepted

A number of problems might arise, for example when no time limit is agreed for acceptance/rejection, or if the person making the offer wants to revoke it — the principle here is that the revocation must be received before the acceptance is made, and this is discussed in the next section.

Termination of offers

An offer can be brought to an end at any point before acceptance and in a number of different ways.

Acceptance/refusal

These are the most obvious and straightforward ways of terminating an offer. Acceptance may be issued in writing, verbally or by conduct. If an offer is refused it is ended, which means that it cannot be accepted later if there is a change of mind.

Counter-offer

In *Hyde* v *Wrench* (1840), Wrench offered to sell his farm to Hyde for £1,000. Hyde offered to pay £950, which Wrench rejected. When Hyde then tried to accept the original offer, it was held that his counter-offer of £950 had ended that offer. This case confirms that all the terms of an offer must be accepted and an attempt to change any of them becomes a counter-offer.

Revocation

Revocation (withdrawal of the offer) must be communicated, although this could be by a third party, as in *Dickinson* v *Dodds* (1876). Dodds offered to sell his house to Dickinson, and the offer was expressed to be 'left open till Friday'. On Thursday afternoon, Dickinson heard from a third party that Dodds had sold the property to someone else. On the Friday morning, Dickinson delivered a formal acceptance to Dodds, then commenced legal proceedings against him. The court held that the offer made to Dickinson had been withdrawn on the Thursday and was no longer capable of being accepted.

The revocation must be received before the acceptance is made. In *Byrne* v *Van Tienhoven* (1880), Van Tienhoven wrote on 1 October, making an offer, but changed his mind and wrote again to Byrne on 8 October, withdrawing his offer. However, Byrne accepted the offer in a telegram on 11 October, before he received the revocation letter, and therefore the acceptance was valid.

Lapse of time

Where no time limit is specified, the offer will remain open for a reasonable time. What is considered reasonable will depend on the circumstances. For example, an offer to sell perishable goods may lapse in a few days, while an offer to sell land would last considerably longer. In *Ramsgate Victoria Hotel* v *Montefiore* (1866), an offer to buy shares in June had lapsed by November. If a time limit is specified, it must be complied with.

Death of person making offer

It has been suggested that the death of either party terminates the offer, as it makes it impossible for the parties to reach agreement. The better view seems to be that as long as the contract does not involve personal services, such as a singer giving a performance, the death of either party should not necessarily end the offer.

> **Box 19.1** *Bilateral and unilateral contracts*
>
> **Bilateral contracts**
> Many contracts involve one party making an offer and another party indicating acceptance either verbally or in writing. These are known as bilateral contracts because both parties promise something. The contract is valid at the moment the promises are exchanged, even though at this stage neither party may have done anything to implement the agreement.
>
> **Unilateral contracts**
> In a situation like the one in *Carlill*, one party is making an offer but acceptance is through the performance of an act rather than through a formal indication. Such contracts are known as unilateral contracts because only one party makes a promise.

Questions

1 Are the following offers?
   ❖ A advertises his car for sale in a local newspaper.
   ❖ A sends details of the car to B who has asked for more information.
   ❖ C puts up a notice saying that he will give a £50 reward to anyone returning his lost cat.
2 Explain in your own words what an invitation to treat is.
3 Give an example of an offer made to the whole world.
4 Briefly explain what the issue was in each of the following cases and indicate whether there was an offer:
   ❖ *Fisher* v *Bell*
   ❖ *Pharmaceutical Society of Great Britain* v *Boots*
   ❖ *Partridge* v *Crittenden*
   ❖ *Harvey* v *Facey*
   ❖ *Carlill* v *Carbolic Smoke Ball Co.*
5 Explain in your own words what these terms mean:
   ❖ counter-offer
   ❖ revocation
6 Explain the difference between a bilateral contract and a unilateral contract.

Acceptance

Acceptance is **unqualified and unconditional** agreement to all the terms of the offer by words or conduct. If conditions or qualifications are added, a counter-offer is created.

Rules on the communication of acceptance

Must be communicated

In *Felthouse* v *Bindley* (1862), the claimant offered to buy a horse from his nephew for £30.15s, adding, 'If I hear no more about him, I shall consider the horse mine at

£30.15s.' In the ensuing action, the court refused to regard the defendant's silence as assent, even though the nephew intended to accept the offer.

Can be inferred from conduct

The principle seems to be that when you start to implement what is in the offer, you have provided acceptance.

If a method of acceptance is specified, it must be complied with

In some circumstances, another, equally good method might suffice. In *Tinn* v *Hoffmann* (1873), acceptance was requested by return of post. Honeyman J said: 'That does not mean exclusively a reply by letter or return of post, but you may reply by telegram or by verbal message or by any other means not later than a letter written by return of post.'

If no method is specified, any method will do as long as it is effective

The person accepting the offer does not have to communicate this directly. It could be communicated through a third party, for example. However, mere rumour of acceptance is not enough.

'Postal rule' applies when ordinary postal system used

The 'postal rule' maintains that acceptance by means of the post is effective as soon as the letter of acceptance is posted, even if the letter is lost in the post. Revocation is valid when received. For instance, in *Household Fire Insurance* v *Grant* (1879), a letter was lost in the post; nevertheless, there was a proper acceptance and a binding contract. In *Henthorn* v *Fraser* (1892), the plaintiff, who lived in Birkenhead, was handed a note at the defendant's office in Liverpool, giving him an option to purchase certain property within 14 days. The next day, the defendant posted a letter withdrawing the offer, which did not reach Birkenhead until 5.00 p.m. Meanwhile, the plaintiff had posted a letter at 3.50 p.m. accepting the offer. That letter was delivered after the defendant's office was closed and was opened the following morning. It was held that a valid contract had been concluded at 3.50 p.m.

Acceptance by post is effective as soon as the letter of acceptance is posted

When instantaneous methods are used

Such methods include phone, fax and e-mail, and acceptance is immediate as long as it is communicated (i.e. it gets through).

In *Entores* v *Miles Far East* (1955), an English company in London was in communication with a Dutch company in Amsterdam by telex. The English company received an offer of goods from the Dutch company and made a counter-offer which the Dutch company accepted — all by telex. For purposes of jurisdiction, it was held that the contract was made in London, where the English company received the acceptance. Denning LJ suggested that the person receiving the acceptance will be bound even if he or she does not read the fax or telex until much later.

In *Brinkibon Ltd* v *Stahag Stahl* (1983), one of the issues was a telex being received when the office was closed. An English company accepted, by telex sent from London to Vienna, the terms of sale offered by an Austrian company. It was held that the contract had been made in Austria, where the telex acceptance was received, but the House of Lords also held that the acceptance could only become effective when the office reopened.

In reality, it is all about reasonableness. In *Brinkibon*, Lord Wilberforce said: 'No universal rule can cover all such cases; they must be resolved by reference to the intentions of the parties, by sound business practice and in some cases by a judgement where the risks should lie.' There have as yet been no cases on e-mails, but there seems no reason why the same rule on electronic transfers should not apply to them.

The postal rule arose when there was no other means of communication. Without the postal rule, contracting parties who posted letters of acceptance would have been unsure whether their acceptances had been successful. In the twenty-first century, a person accepting an offer can easily check whether acceptance has reached the offeror, possibly using an instantaneous method of communication, such as e-mail, telephone or fax.

Some clarification might have been secured through the European Union Electronic Commerce Directive 2000/13. Article 11 stated that when using electronic means of communication the contract is made when the person accepting the offer receives from their service provider (electronically) an acknowledgement that the acceptance has been received. However, this section was not included in the final version of the Directive.

When both parties use their own printed contract forms

If an offer is made by a business using its own standard form but the business receiving the offer alters the terms by sending back its own form, this amounts to a counter-offer. This situation arose in *Butler Machine Tool* v *Ex-Cell-O Corporation* (1979). The claimants offered to sell a machine to the defendants. The terms of the offer included a condition that all orders were accepted only on the sellers' terms, which were to prevail over any terms and conditions in the buyers' order. The defendants replied by ordering the machine but on different terms and conditions.

The Court of Appeal applied the principle that when there is a 'battle of forms', a contract is made when the last of the forms is sent and received without objection. Therefore, judgement was entered in favour of the buyers.

Questions

1 Acceptance must be u........................ and u........................ If it is not, what does it become?

2 Why wasn't there a contract in *Felthouse* v *Bindley*?

3 How would you resolve the following situations and which cases would you rely on?

❖ A posts a letter to B withdrawing the offer at the same time as B posts a letter accepting it.

❖ A telephones B and in the middle of the conversation says that the offer is withdrawn. Unfortunately the line goes dead and B doesn't hear that part of the conversation. B then e-mails accepting the offer.

❖ A sends a fax to B's office withdrawing the offer. It arrives after B has gone home. B then telephones A and leaves a message on her answerphone accepting the offer.

Consideration

Consideration means that each side must promise to give or do something for the other. For instance, if A promises to paint B's house, the promise will only be enforceable as a contract if B has provided consideration. B's consideration in this situation would usually take the form of a payment of money or the promise of a future payment, but it could also consist of some other service (or future service) to which A might agree.

It is possible to have a valid contract even if one party does not provide consideration, for example a promise to make a gift, but only if the contract is made by deed.

Definition

Consideration was defined in *Currie* v *Misa* (1875) as 'some right, interest, profit or benefit accruing to one party, or some forebearance, detriment, loss or responsibility given, suffered or undertaken by the other'. It was defined in *Dunlop* v *Selfridge Ltd* (1915) as 'an act or forebearance of one party, or the promise thereof, is the price for which the promise of the other is bought, and the promise thus given for value is enforceable'.

These definitions seem complicated and unwieldy and the courts have found it difficult to agree on a simple definition. For our purposes, it may be helpful to think of consideration as something of value being offered by each party. As you shall see, sometimes it can be of little value and it certainly does not have to correspond to what something is actually worth.

Types of consideration

What is clear is that consideration can and often does involve a promise by the parties to do something in the future, and this exchange of promises is called **executory consideration**. Either party can sue the other in the event of it not doing what it has promised. In unilateral contracts, however, the party making the offer (e.g. of a reward) is under no obligation until the other party performs (executes) its part of the agreement. This is called **executed consideration**.

The rules of consideration

Something of value must be given by both/all parties

This is the basic principle and it distinguishes a contract from a purely gratuitous agreement (i.e. a promise to make a gift). The law says that consideration must be sufficient. This means that it must be real and tangible and have some actual value. In *White* v *Bluett* (1853), a promise not to complain about the contents of a will in return for the cancelling of a debt was considered to be intangible. It was not offering anything of real value or substance to the bargain.

Does not have to be adequate

Where consideration is recognised by the law as having some value, it is described as 'real' or 'sufficient' consideration. Providing consideration has some value, the courts will not investigate its adequacy, nor will they investigate contracts to see if the parties have got equal value. In *Chappell & Co. Ltd* v *Nestlé Co Ltd* (1960), Nestlé was running a special offer which involved people sending off three wrappers from Nestlé chocolate bars plus some money. It was held that the three wrappers were part of the consideration, even though on receipt the wrappers were thrown away.

Must not be past

This means that any consideration must come after the agreement, rather than being something that has already been done. For example, if A paints B's house and then when the work is finished B promises to pay £100 for the work, this promise is unenforceable because A's consideration is past. In *Re McArdle* (1951), repairs were made to a property and afterwards people who were to inherit the property were asked to sign an agreement that they would reimburse the cost of the repairs. This agreement was not enforceable because the repairs had been done before the agreement was made.

The law recognises, however, that there are situations in which something, such as a service, is provided on the unspoken expectation that ultimately it will be paid for. In the old case of *Lampleigh* v *Braithwaite* (1615), Lampleigh was asked to obtain a King's pardon for Braithwaite, who was accused of killing a man. He incurred considerable expense in doing this and Braithwaite in gratitude promised to pay him £100. It was held that there was a contract because at the time the original request was made both parties would have contemplated a payment. This principle is known as the **rule in *Lampleigh* v *Braithwaite*** and was applied in *Re Casey's Patent* (1892), where the claimant was the manager of a patent for an invention and had worked on it for 2 years. The joint owners of the patent then promised him a one-third share in the invention for his help in developing it. It was held that he could rely on the agreement, because even though his consideration was in the past, it had been performed in a business situation, at the request of joint owners — it was understood by both sides that he would be paid and the subsequent promise to pay merely fixed the amount.

Modern confirmation of this rule was given by Lord Scarman in *Pao On* v *Lau Yiu Long* (1980) when he said that:

> ...*an act done before the giving of a promise to make a payment or to confer some other benefit can sometimes be consideration for the promise. The act must have been done at the promisors' request; the parties must have understood that the act was to be remunerated either by a payment or the conferment of some other benefit; and payment, or the conferment of a benefit, must have been legally enforceable had it been promised in advance.*

Must not be an existing duty

Doing something that you are already bound to do cannot amount to good consideration. The basic rule can be seen operating in *Stilk* v *Myrick* (1809), when 2 out of 11 sailors deserted a ship. The captain promised to pay the remaining crew extra money if they sailed the ship back, but later refused to pay. It was held that as the sailors were already bound by their contract to sail back and to meet such emergencies of the voyage, promising to sail back was not valid consideration. Thus, the captain did not have to pay the extra money. However, in *Hartley* v *Ponsonby* (1857), when 19 out of the 36 crew of a ship deserted, the captain promised to pay the remaining crew extra money to sail back, but later refused to pay saying that they were only doing their normal jobs. In this case, the ship was so seriously under-staffed that the rest of the journey had become extremely hazardous. It was held that sailing the ship back in such dangerous conditions was over and above their normal duties. This change in circumstances discharged the sailors from their existing contract and left them free to enter into a new contract for the rest of the voyage. They were therefore entitled to the money.

The modern example of *Williams* v *Roffey* (1991) seems to indicate that in business contracts the courts will try to find consideration in circumstances where on the face of it the consideration appears to be part of an existing duty. Roffey had a contract to refurbish a block of flats and had subcontracted the carpentry work to Williams. After the work had begun, it became apparent that Williams had underestimated the cost of the work and was in financial difficulties. Roffey, concerned that the work would not be completed on time and as a result would incur a financial penalty under his contract with the owner, agreed to pay Williams an extra payment per flat. Williams completed the work on more flats but did not receive full payment. He stopped work and brought an action for damages.

Roffey had a contract to refurbish a block of flats and had subcontracted the carpentry work to Williams

It was held by the Court of Appeal that where a party to an existing contract later agrees to pay an extra 'bonus' in order to ensure that the other party performs his obligations under the contract, then that agreement is binding if the party agreeing to pay the bonus has thereby obtained some new practical advantage or avoided a disadvantage. In the present case there were benefits to Roffey, including (a) making sure Williams continued his work, (b) avoiding payment under a damages clause of the main contract if Williams was late, and (c) avoiding the expense and trouble of hiring someone else. Therefore, Williams was entitled to payment.

Third parties and consideration

Some contracts involve an agreement to benefit someone other than the parties to the agreement. For example, in *Tweddle* v *Atkinson* (1861), an agreement was made between William Guy and John Tweddle that each would give a sum of money to William Tweddle, who had married William Guy's daughter. Unfortunately, William Guy died before making the payment and William Tweddle sued Guy's estate for the money. His claim failed. One of the judges based his decision on the fact that he had offered no consideration, arguing that 'consideration must move from the promise' (i.e. the person to whom the promise is made). But this case also raises the principle of **privity of contract**, which is the idea that only people who are a party to a contract can enforce it, even though it might intend to benefit third parties. The modern law as set out in the Contracts (Rights of Third Parties) Act 1999 has altered the position of third parties significantly, allowing them to enforce agreements where they are expressly identified as beneficiaries, and it is likely that cases like *Tweddle* v *Atkinson* would be decided differently now.

Questions

1 Give a definition of consideration.

2 What do we mean when we say that consideration does not have to be adequate? Give an example.

3 What is meant by 'past consideration'?

4 Why were *Stilk* v *Myrick* and *Hartley* v *Ponsonby* decided differently?

5 Why was there no contract in *Tweddle* v *Atkinson*? Why might this case be decided differently today?

Intention to create legal relations

In practice, it is quite easy for agreements to be made which contain offer and acceptance and in which both parties provide consideration. However, the law recognises that often the parties do not intend to create a legally binding contract. This is particularly so within families and between friends. The law therefore says that there must be an intention to create legal relations and makes a distinction between social and domestic agreements (where the assumption is that there is no intention to create legal relations) and commercial and business agreements (where the law assumes that the parties intend the agreement to be legally binding).

Social and domestic agreements

The cases suggest that agreements within families will generally be treated as not legally binding. For example, in *Jones* v *Padavatton* (1969), Mrs Jones offered a monthly allowance to her daughter if she would give up her job in the USA and come to England and study to become a barrister. Because of accommodation problems Mrs Jones bought a house in London, where the daughter lived and received rents from other tenants. They later quarrelled and the mother sought repossession of the house. The court decided that there was no intention to create legal relations and that all the arrangements were just part of ordinary family life. Therefore, the mother was not liable on the maintenance agreement and could also claim the house.

In *Balfour* v *Balfour* (1919), the issue was the promise made by a husband to pay his wife an allowance while he was abroad. He failed to keep up the payments when the marriage broke down. The wife sued but it was held that arrangements between husbands and wives are not contracts because the parties do not intend them to be legally binding. The court also decided that she had given no consideration for the husband's promise.

In contrast, in the case of *Merritt* v *Merritt* (1970), the husband had already left his wife and they met to make arrangements for the future. The husband agreed to pay £40 per month maintenance, out of which the wife would pay the mortgage. When the mortgage was paid off he would transfer the house from joint names to the wife's name. He wrote this down and signed the paper, but later refused to transfer the house.

The court held that when the agreement was made, the husband and wife were no longer living together, therefore they must have intended the agreement to be binding and their intention to base their future actions on the agreement was evidenced by the writing. The husband had to transfer the house to the wife.

It is easy to see that the circumstances are significantly different between these two cases and why the court was able to conclude on the facts that the presumption should not apply.

The courts have also had to consider cases that do not just involve members of the same family, and here the principle they apply is that the presumption that the arrangement is a purely social one will be rebutted if money has changed hands. For instance, in *Simpkins* v *Pays* (1955), a lodger and two members of a household entered a competition in the lodger's name and paid equal shares. It was held that the presence of the outsider rebutted the presumption that it was a family agreement and not intended to be binding. The mutual arrangement was a joint enterprise, to which cash was contributed on the understanding that any prize would be shared.

In *Parker* v *Clarke* (1960), a young couple, the Parkers, were persuaded by an older couple to sell their house and move in with them. They would share the bills and the younger couple would inherit the house. Details of expenses were agreed and confirmation of the agreement was put in writing. The Parkers sold their house and moved in, and Mr Clarke changed his will accordingly, leaving the house to the Parkers. Later, the couples fell out and the Parkers were asked to leave. They claimed damages for breach of contract. It was held that the actions of the parties showed that they were serious and the agreement was intended to be legally binding. Therefore, the Parkers were entitled to damages.

Commercial and business agreements

An agreement made in a business context is presumed to be legally binding unless a different intent can be shown. In *Rose* v *Crompton Bros* (1925), paper manufacturers had entered into an agreement with the claimant to act as sole agents for the sale of the defendant's paper in the USA. The written agreement contained a clause that it was not entered into as a formal or legal agreement and would not be subject to legal jurisdiction in the courts, but was a record of the purpose and intention of the parties to which they honourably pledged themselves. It was held that the sole agency agreement was not binding owing to the inclusion of the **'honourable pledge clause'**.

Football pools are a specific exception to the rule that agreements of a commercial nature are presumed to be legally binding. In *Jones* v *Vernon Pools* (1938) and in *Appleson* v *Littlewoods* (1939), the courts ruled that the statement on the coupon that the transaction was 'binding in honour only' meant that it was not legally binding.

The same principle applies to 'letters of comfort'. In *Kleinwort Benson* v *Malaysia Mining Corp.* (1989), a bank agreed to lend money to a subsidiary of the defendant company. As part of the arrangement, the company gave a letter of comfort, which stated that it was the company's policy to ensure that the business of its subsidiary is at all times in a position to meet its liabilities. Unfortunately, the subsidiary went into liquidation and it was held that the letters of comfort were statements of the company's present policy, and not contractual promises as to future conduct. They were not intended to create legal relations, and gave rise to no more than a moral responsibility on the part of the defendants to meet the subsidiary's debt. The court concluded that if the bank wanted a legally binding guarantee, it should have insisted on one.

On the other hand, situations where free gifts or prizes are promised are deemed to be legally binding, because the purpose is generally to promote the commercial interests of the body offering the gift or prize. In *McGowan* v *Radio Buxton* (2001), a prize in a radio competition was stated to be a Renault Clio car. However, when the prize was awarded it was a model car rather than a real one. The radio company claimed that there was no legally binding contract because it was not a commercial arrangement, but the court held that there was an intention to create legal relations and also that, looking at the transcript of the broadcast, entrants to the competition would expect the prize to be a real car.

Motoring Picture Library/Alamy

In *McGowan* v *Radio Buxton* (2001), the court held that there was an intention to create legal relations

In *Edwards* v *Skyways* (1964), an airline pilot was made redundant and was informed by his pilots' association that he would be given an *ex gratia* payment (i.e. a gift) by the airline. The airline failed to pay and argued that the use of the words '*ex gratia*' showed that there was no intention to create legal relations. It was held that this agreement related to business matters and was presumed to be binding. The court stated that the words 'ex *gratia*' or 'without admission of liability' are used simply to indicate that the party agreeing to pay does not admit any pre-existing liability. It cannot preclude the legal enforceability of the settlement itself by describing the payment as '*ex gratia*'.

Questions

1 What general distinction does the law make when considering whether there is an intention to create legal relations?

2 Why were *Balfour* v *Balfour* and *Merrit* v *Merrit* decided differently?

3 Why was it decided that there was an intention to create legal relations in (a) *Simpkins* v *Pays* and (b) *Parker* v *Clarke*?

4 What was the decision in (a) *Rose* v *Crompton Bros* and (b) *Jones* v *Vernon Pools*?

5 Why was there a contract in *McGowan* v *Radio Buxton*?

Breach of contract

When a party fails to perform an obligation under a contract, it is said to be in breach of contract. An **actual breach** is when there is a failure to fulfil an obligation under the contract, or not fulfilling it to the required standard.

An **anticipatory breach** occurs when one party shows by express words or by implications from his or her conduct at some time before performance is due that he or she does not intend to observe his or her obligations under the contract. The rights of the injured party depend on the nature of the term broken.

Breach of warranty

A **breach of warranty** is a breach of a minor term that does not go to the root of the contract and only gives rise to a claim for damages.

Breach of condition

This is a breach of an important term, giving the right to terminate the agreement and repudiate (cancel) the contract. What this means in practice is that the injured party is prevented from using a minor breach of contract as an excuse for cancelling the whole contract. If, for example, a new car is delivered that has a faulty interior

light, it is reasonable to expect the supplier to put it right at his or her expense (damages), but not reasonable to allow the purchaser to cancel the contract and demand his or her money back. However, if there was a series of technical failures, which were not easy to put right and which resulted in the car breaking down, you can see that these relate to the very purpose of the contract and understand why the law in this situation might allow the purchaser to cancel the contract and buy a different car somewhere else.

Anticipatory breach

In cases of anticipatory breach, the injured party is not under any obligation to wait until the date fixed for performance before commencing his or her action, but may immediately treat the contract as at an end and sue for damages. This principle was established in *Hochester* v *De La Tour* (1853), where an employer told his employee (a travelling courier) before the time for performance arrived that he would not require his services. The courier sued for damages at once. The court held that he was entitled to do so.

The injured party in an anticipatory breach of contract also has the option of waiting for the performance date to pass and then suing for breach. This is what happened in *Avery* v *Bowden* (1855), a case involving an agreement to supply a cargo for a ship at a port in Russia. The claimant was advised that the cargo would not be supplied. At this stage, he could have sued successfully for anticipatory breach. Instead, he waited the 45 days until the date the cargo was due to be supplied and then sued. Meanwhile, the Crimean War had broken out and performance of the contract became illegal and therefore unenforceable because Britain was at war with Russia.

One issue in cases of anticipatory breach is to ascertain whether, once repudiation has been communicated to the injured party, that party accepts the repudiation or not. The question of whether silence or inaction can amount to acceptance of repudiation was considered in *Vitol SA* v *Norelf Ltd* (1996), in which the repudiating party notified the other that they considered the contract at an end. However, no action was taken by the injured party, either to act on the repudiation or to affirm the contract, on receipt of this information. The House of Lords held that silence or inaction can amount to acceptance of a wrongful repudiation of a contract.

Where the injured party elects to repudiate for a breach of condition, the general effect is to terminate the contract from the date of the election. Thus, all obligations accruing before that date remain to be performed but all those accruing after the election are avoided. So, in an appropriate case, the injured party who elects to repudiate may sue for damages for non-performance of those obligations that remain to be performed.

The injured party may elect to affirm the contract and, if this is done, the contract remains in force and the injured party may sue for damages. If the election to affirm takes the form of a clear and unequivocal statement by the injured party to the party in breach that he or she wishes to continue with the contract, then this may amount to a **waiver** of repudiation and the right to repudiate will be lost. If, however, the injured party is merely pressing for performance, he will not be barred from electing to repudiate if it becomes clear at a later date that satisfactory performance will not be forthcoming.

Mitigation of loss rule

The injured party may not always be able to insist on affirming the contract, because under the principle of **mitigation of loss**, the injured party usually has a general duty to take reasonable steps to mitigate his or her loss.

In *White and Carter (Councils) Ltd* v *McGregor* (1962), there was an agreement for advertising display plates for a garage company to be affixed to council litter bins for a period of 3 years, the idea being that the advertising revenue would pay for the council's bins. The defendant garage company repudiated the contract on the same day that it was made and before the advertising plates were even ordered. The plaintiffs elected to affirm the contract, prepared the plates and affixed them to the litter bins. In other words, they continued with the contract and sued the defendant. The court held that even though the contract had been repudiated at such an early stage, the plaintiffs were entitled to refuse to accept the repudiation, perform their side of the bargain and sue for the payment as a debt.

It might have been thought that the plaintiffs should have mitigated their loss by attempting to re-let the advertising. But the burden of proving that they could indeed have done this was on the defendant and it seems that the defendant could not prove so.

Questions

1 What is meant by 'anticipatory breach'?

2 What is the difference between a condition and a warranty?

3 What is the mitigation of loss rule? How did this work out in *White and Carter (Councils) Ltd* v *McGregor*?

Remedies for breach of contract

Repudiation of the contract

As you have seen, this remedy is available only when there has been a breach of condition. It is a far-reaching and drastic remedy and will result in any goods supplied or money paid under the contract being returned.

Damages

This remedy is available for all kinds of breach of contract, and may be appropriate even in cases where the contract has been rescinded. The principle as stated in *Robinson* v *Harman* (1848) is that 'when a party sustains loss by reason of a breach of contract he is, so far as money can do it, to be placed in the same situation with respect to damages as if the contract had been performed'.

Liquidated damages

Sometimes the parties may agree in advance what would be reasonable compensation in the event of a breach, and this is referred to as liquidated damages.

Unliquidated damages

These are damages that have not been agreed to in advance and they will be determined by the court.

Substantial damages

These are damages designed to compensate for actual losses suffered.

Nominal damages

This is where the court awards a small amount — indicating that although technically the party has a claim, the court does not feel that actual compensation is appropriate.

Exemplary damages

The court also has the power to award a much larger sum that would be needed to compensate the injured party. This would demonstrate the court's disapproval of the party at fault.

Causation

There must be a causal link between the breach of contract and the damage suffered. This is a question of fact in each case. If the loss arises partly from the breach and partly as a result of intervening events, the party in breach may still be liable, providing the chain of causation has not been broken. For example, in *Stansbie* v *Troman* (1948), a decorator failed to lock the premises he had been working in and a thief entered and stole property. He was liable for the loss because it was the result of his failure to comply with his contractual duty to secure the premises on leaving.

In *Smith, Hogg & Co.* v *Black Sea Insurance Co.* (1940), a shipowner was held liable to a charterer in damages for loss of a cargo, which had been caused by a combination of perils of the sea and the unseaworthiness of the ship. But in *The Monarch SS Co. Case* (1949), a shipowner was not liable to a charterer when, as a result of delay, the ship ran into a typhoon, because such an event could have occurred anywhere at any time.

❖ Outline two situations that would not be offers. Refer to two cases.
❖ Explain the situation concerning reward posters. Refer to a case.
❖ Mention two other rules about offers. Refer to a case.
❖ Mention two ways in which offers are terminated. Refer to a case.

Acceptance
❖ Write a one-sentence definition.
❖ Explain the general rule on communication. Refer to a case.
❖ Explain the rule if a method of acceptance is specified. Refer to a case.
❖ Explain the postal rule. Refer to a case.
❖ Add a comment on 'modern electronic' methods. Refer to a case.

> **2 Gary offers to sell his car to Sandeep for £2,000. Sandeep offers
> £1,500 and Gary says that he will accept nothing less than £2,000.
> Sandeep goes away to think about it. She returns the following
> week to say that she will pay £2,000. Meanwhile Gary has sold the
> car to someone else.**
>
> **Applying the rules on offer and acceptance, advise Sandeep of her
> rights**   (10 marks)

Here is how you might apply the IDEA mnemonic to question 2:
❖ **Identify**. This question focuses on the rules on offer and acceptance, in particular
  the rules on termination of offers.
❖ **Define**. An offer is an expression of willingness to contract on certain terms and
  an acceptance is unqualified and unconditional agreement to all of those terms.
  An offer will come to an end if it is rejected, if there is a counter-offer, if there is
  revocation or sometimes if there is lapse of time.
❖ **Explain and apply**. In this scenario, an offer has been made by Gary, who makes
  it clear by his words that he is willing to sell his car for £2,000 and intends to enter
  a binding agreement. There is no question of this being an invitation to treat.
  However, the issue is whether the offer is open for Sandeep to accept. There are a
  number of rules on when an offer comes to an end.

You should be able to apply this structure to a range of problem-solving questions.
Note how the sample answer given below links the rules to facts and refers to the
cases that seem to be most relevant.

> *Sandeep's initial response is to offer £1,500 and this would be treated by the law as
> a counter-offer, which has the effect of ending the original offer (Hyde v Wrench).
> Gary then appears to repeat the offer, by saying that he would accept nothing less
> than £2,000. It could be argued that because he had already offered to sell to her at*

this price, he would expect his words to be understood as meaning that the offer was still open. This is quite different to the situation in Gibson v Manchester City Council, *where the council said that they 'may be prepared to sell'.*

Assuming that Gary intends his words as an offer, Sandeep now clearly communicates her acceptance of this offer. This will become a binding contract regardless of the fact that Gary has sold the car to someone else.

Applying the rules on termination of offers, there seems to be no evidence that Gary has revoked his offer. In Dickinson v Dodds, *contact was made through a third party and in* Byrne v Van Tienhoven *the offer was withdrawn by a letter. Gary does not seem to have made any effort to contact Sandeep. Sometimes offers may end because of lapse of time, but* Ramsgate Victoria Hotel v Montefiore *suggests that several weeks would be required rather than the 1 week mentioned here.*

3 **Tariq agrees to help Karl move house and he spends a whole day moving heavy furniture. A few days later Karl unexpectedly puts his car up for sale and Tariq agrees to buy it. He suggests that the price be reduced to take account of the work that he did to help Karl when he moved house. Karl initially agrees, but later changes his mind and says that Tariq has to pay the full price.**

Advise Tariq on whether there is a valid contract to buy the car at the reduced price. (10 marks)

Task

Write an answer to this question using the IDEA approach. With every problem-solving question, you need to identify the issues that are relevant. You then need to define the important rules in that area of law, explain them in more detail and apply them to the facts.

Sometimes the exam question will identify the broad area of law for you. This question does not. You will need to identify the fact that the issue here is one of consideration and in particular the problem of past consideration.

4 **Farm Products Ltd agrees to supply animal feed to Gordon for £10,000. However, before they can deliver it, the wholesale price dramatically increases and Farm Products Ltd says that Gordon will now have to pay £12,000. Gordon refuses to pay and sues for breach of contract. All suppliers of similar feed are now charging £12,000. Gordon has the opportunity to buy replacement feed from another supplier at £10,000 but does not do so, because he says that it is not**

organic and that if he feeds it to his animals he will not make as much money when he sells them. Farm Products Ltd claims that Gordon said nothing to them about wanting organic feed.

(a) Briefly explain the meaning of breach of contract and discuss whether Farm Products Ltd is in breach of contract with Gordon. (10 marks)

(b) Assuming the company is in breach of contract, outline how the court would calculate an award of damages to Gordon. (10 marks)

Tasks

1 Answer part (a). Your answer should define breach of contract, conditions and warranties, actual breach and anticipatory breach, and the various options open to the injured party. You then need to apply these rules to the facts.

2 Answer part (b). Your answer should outline the purpose of damages, the rule in *Hadley* v *Baxendale* and the idea of remoteness, and the rules on mitigation of loss. You then need to apply these rules to the facts.

5 Umar wanted to buy a large quantity of mobile phones for his shop. He phoned Mobiles plc, who agreed to supply him with a quantity of phones for £60,000. Mobiles plc immediately realised they had been using an old price list and tried to contact Umar on the phone, but failed to do so. Mobiles plc therefore posted a new one to Umar, which he received on the next day. Mobiles plc refused to supply the phones at £60,000 and Umar refused to pay the revised price of £70,000. Mobiles plc's new prices were the same as other suppliers of the phones.

(a) A valid contract requires an offer to be accepted.
  (i) Explain, using examples, the meaning of the term 'offer'. (8 marks)
  (ii) Explain, using examples, the meaning of the term 'acceptance'. (7 marks)

(b) Using the explanations given in your answer to (a), discuss whether Umar has made a valid contract with Mobiles plc. (10 marks)

19

(c) Assuming there is a valid contract between Umar and Mobiles plc, Mobiles plc may be in breach of that contract. Briefly explain the meaning of breach of contract and discuss whether Mobiles plc is in breach of its contract with Umar. (8 marks)

(d) Assuming Umar claimed for breach of contract:
  (i) Identify which court would hear the case and outline the procedure that would be followed before a trial. (5 marks)
  (ii) Outline how the court would calculate an award of damages to Umar in the situation given. (7 marks)

Suggested reading

Blood, P. (2007) 'Contract law: bilateral and unilateral contracts', *A-Level Law Review*, Vol. 2, No. 3, pp. 6–7.

Smith, D. (2008) 'Acceptance in the formation of contracts', *A-Level Law Review*, Vol. 3, No. 3, pp. 22–25.

Chapter **20**

Criminal and civil courts

This chapter focuses on proceedings in the criminal and civil courts. For the criminal courts, it revisits the classification of offences (summary, either-way, indictable) and examines the burden of proof and standard of proof required. It also summarises the procedure to trial — bail, plea and sending for trial — and proceedings in the criminal courts.

For the civil courts, the chapter discusses the procedure to trial — claim form, three tracks, case management — and revisits alternative dispute resolution (ADR).

Criminal courts

Classification of offences

Criminal offences fall under three different classes:

* **Summary offences** — these are less serious crimes that can only be tried by magistrates. Examples include most road traffic offences (e.g. speeding).
* **Either-way offences** — these comprise offences which, as the name suggests, can be tried either by magistrates or in a Crown Court before a judge and jury. Such offences include theft, burglary and assault occasioning actual bodily harm (e.g. s.47 of the Offences Against the Person Act 1861). If a defendant is charged with an either-way offence, he or she will appear before the Magistrates' Court in a 'plea before venue' hearing, which decides which court will try the case.
* **Indictable offences** — these are the more serious offences, such as murder, manslaughter, rape, causing grievous bodily harm with intent (e.g. s.18 of the Offences Against the Person Act 1861), which must be tried by a judge and jury in the Crown Court. The indictment is a formal document setting out the alleged offences against the defendant, which is read out at the beginning of the trial by the court clerk.

Speeding is a summary offence

Burden of proof and standard of proof

The most fundamental rule of English criminal law is that the defendant is presumed to be innocent until proven guilty. It is up to the prosecution to prove that guilt — not for the defendant to prove his or her innocence. This important principle was underlined in the case of *Woolmington* v *DPP* (1935), where Viscount Sankey stated: 'Throughout the web of English Criminal Law one golden thread is always to be seen, that it is the duty of the prosecution to prove the prisoner's guilt.'

Because of the serious consequences of a guilty verdict, including loss of freedom, the standard of proof is high — 'beyond reasonable doubt'. The judge in a Crown Court trial will direct the jury to convict the defendant only if they are sure that he or she is guilty. The benefit of any doubt is given to the defendant and must result in an acquittal.

The function of the Magistrates' Court

Magistrates' Courts hear applications for bail under the Bail Act 1976. If granted, this means that the defendant is released from custody until the trial date. Under the Act there is a presumption in favour of bail being granted because of the principle that the defendant is innocent until proved guilty. Nonetheless, bail may be disallowed on the following grounds:

❖ The **seriousness of the offence** — bail is rarely granted in a murder case.
❖ The possibility that the defendant may **abscond** (fail to turn up for trial).
❖ The fear that the defendant may **interfere with witnesses**.
❖ The possibility that the defendant will **re-offend**.

claim. When the claimant has received that payment, he or she will then notify the court that the matter is settled.

Allocation of tracks

Any other response from the defendant in a civil claim will result in the case being allocated to the appropriate 'track' under the Civil Procedure Rules. The different tracks are:

* **Small claims track**, for virtually all claims under £5,000 (except claims for personal injury, where the limit is £1,000).
* **Fast track**, for claims worth between £5,000 and £15,000, where there is an expectation that the trial will only last 1 day and involve no more than two expert witnesses. Fast track cases are heard in the County Court by either a district or circuit judge.
* **Multi-track** — this is the default track for all claims that do not fit into either the small claims or fast track, and is therefore the most complex track for claims. Most claims for between £15,000 and £50,000 will be heard in the County Court, whereas claims for more than £50,000 will normally go to the High Court.

Small Claims Court

The procedure in the Small Claims Court is different from all other types of civil litigation as it is designed to be as informal as possible. The hearing takes place not in a court room, but in an informal room like a committee room and it is usually held before a district judge without a court clerk present. The claimant will be invited to state his or her case and to call any witnesses. Evidence is not given on oath and the judge will make brief notes of the proceedings. The defendant can then question the claimant and any witnesses, and then the claimant will explain his or her case and also call witnesses. The claimant then has the opportunity to question the defendant. The district judge will summarise the evidence he or she has heard and then give his or her judgement.

Fast track — County Court

Before the hearing itself, the parties will be required to comply with a timetable laid down by the judge concerning the exchange of documents (referred to as 'discovery'), and the number of expert witnesses to be called. The judge may impose a limit of one expert witness for each party, or even decide to have only one court-appointed expert witness. The timetable will have a trial date set within 30 weeks of the claim being formally made to court. To speed up proceedings even more, an indexed bundle of documents must be lodged within the court, not less than 3 days but no more than 7 days before the trial itself. The trial takes place within the County Court before a district judge, recorder or circuit judge.

Multi-track — County Court or High Court

The location of the hearing depends on the value of the claim or its legal complexity. There will often be a **case management conference** before the procedural judge to lay down a timetable for discovery of documents and to discuss the likely length of the trial. This judge will effectively be a case manager — directing and controlling the legal work conducted by both the parties and monitoring the procedures adopted. There are no standard or automatic directions and the judge has a wide discretion in managing the case. Where it is felt necessary, a trial of preliminary issues may be ordered.

Appeal procedure

It is always open to the 'loser' in a civil case to try to appeal the decision of the trial judge to a higher court, but leave to appeal must be obtained from the trial judge. In most appeal cases, the grounds for appeal relate to legal issues rather than arguments about the facts of the case. If the appellant is successful in his or her appeal, the decision of the trial judge may be overturned, or damages may be reduced. In the case of *Sutcliffe* v *Pressdram* (1991), when the wife of the Yorkshire Ripper was originally awarded £600,000 in damages against *Private Eye*, the magazine appealed against the award of damages and they were reduced to £60,000 in the Court of Appeal.

The routes for appeal are:

❖ from Small Claims Court to a single circuit judge in the County Court
❖ from fast-track cases in the County Court to a single High Court judge
❖ from multi-track cases in the County Court to the Court of Appeal (Civil Division), presided over by two Lord Justices of Appeal
❖ from the High Court to the Court of Appeal (Civil Division), presided over by three Lord Justices of Appeal
❖ from the Court of Appeal to the House of Lords, provided leave to appeal has been given, either by the Court of Appeal itself or after application to the House of Lords; such leave will only be given if the case raises issues of 'general public importance'

Alternative dispute resolution

Under the Civil Procedure Rules, introduced following the publication of the Woolf review of the civil justice system (*Access to Justice*), there is now a clear duty on the courts 'actively to manage cases justly'. This includes encouraging the parties to use an **alternative dispute resolution (ADR)** procedure if the court considers that appropriate and then facilitating the use of ADR.

If one of the parties unreasonably refuses to consider this option, the court has the power to disallow legal costs in the subsequent court case. This was the result in

Dunnett v *Railtrack* (2002). In this case, having lost her case in the High Court, Susan Dunnett appealed to the Court of Appeal, which recommended that the parties try to deal with the issue by ADR. Railtrack refused and duly won the appeal. However, because of its unreasonable refusal to consider the possibility of ADR, the court did not award Railtrack its legal costs. Since the value of the claim was only £9,000 and the legal costs of going to the Court of Appeal exceeded £100,000, this was a serious error on Railtrack's part.

This decision was criticised, as it could be interpreted as giving courts the power to impose ADR on the parties. Indeed, in *Shirayama Shokusan Co. Ltd* v *Danovo Ltd* (2003), Mr Justice Blackburn decided the High Court did have the jurisdiction to oblige one or more unwilling parties to go to mediation. This controversy was finally resolved in 2004 by the cases of *Halsey* v *Milton Keynes General NHS Trust* and *Steel* v *Joy and Halliday*. In both these cases, the defendants refused to consider ADR because they believed that the respective claims had no reasonable prospect of success, and the courts in both cases refused to disallow the award of costs. In *Halsey*, the Court of Appeal laid down guidelines for courts to follow in personal injury claims:

❖ The court does not have the power to order reluctant litigants to mediate and to do so would be a breach of Article 6 rights — the right to a fair trial before an independent tribunal.
❖ The court's role is limited to encouraging the parties to enter ADR.
❖ Where a party reasonably believes that their case is 'watertight', they may be justified in refusing mediation.
❖ All those involved in litigation should routinely consider with their clients whether their disputes are suitable for ADR.
❖ While most cases are suitable for ADR, there should not be a presumption in favour of it.

This decision was followed in *Daniels* v *Commissioner of Police for the Metropolis* (2005). The claimant, who was a serving police officer, claimed for compensation in relation to injuries she had suffered on a training course. The defendants refused to consider a negotiated settlement and the case was dismissed by the trial judge. The claimant was ordered to pay the costs involved of £50,000. The Court of Appeal was asked to dismiss part or all of the costs order but, having reviewed the decision in *Halsey*, the court ruled that it was entirely reasonable for a public body such as the police to take the view that it would contest what it reasonably considered to be an unfounded claim in order to deter other similarly unfounded claims.

Box 20.1 *Summary of civil court procedure*

❖ The claimant writes to the defendant indicating the basis for the claim.

❖ If there is no response, or a denial of liability by the defendant, the claimant makes a claim to the County Court (if the claim is for less than £50,000), or to the High Court (if for more than £50,000). The claim form stipulates the particulars of the claim, the defendant's name and address, the value of the claim and a statement of truth.

❖ The case will then be allocated to the Small Claims Court, the fast track or the multi-track, depending on value of the claim and the level of legal complexity.

❖ In the Small Claims Court, there will be an informal hearing before a district judge.

❖ In a fast-track hearing, there will be a timetable laid down by the judge for the discovery of documents and a trial date set, which should not be more than 30 weeks from the date of the action started.

❖ In a multi-track hearing, there could be a case management conference to deal with procedural issues or even a trial could be ordered to deal with preliminary issues.

❖ For all tracks, the judge will try to encourage the parties to consider settling their dispute using ADR.

❖ If a case does go to trial, the losing party could appeal against either the decision of the trial judge or the award of damages.

Suggested reading

Gillespie, A. (2007) *The English Legal System*, Oxford University Press.

Turner, C. (2007) 'Criminal appeal routes', *A-Level Law Review*, Vol. 2, No. 2, pp. 30–31.

Price, N. (2005) 'Investigating civil procedure: the civil courts and ADR', *A-Level Law Review*, Vol.1, No. 1, pp. 10–13.

Price, N. (2006) 'Procedure in the criminal courts', *A-Level Law Review*, Vol. 2, No. 1, pp. 14–16.

Index of cases

Case citations are printed in blue type.

A

Index of statutes

General index